D0409099

Knife Creek

Center Point
Large Print

Also by Paul Doiron and available from Center Point Large Print:

The Bone Orchard
The Precipice
Widowmaker

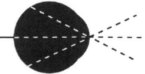

**This Large Print Book carries the
Seal of Approval of N.A.V.H.**

Knife Creek

Paul Doiron

CENTER POINT LARGE PRINT
THORNDIKE, MAINE

MIAMI-DADE
PUBLIC LIBRARY

This Center Point Large Print edition
is published in the year 2017 by arrangement with
St. Martin's Press.

Copyright © 2017 by Paul Doiron.

All rights reserved.

This is a work of fiction.
All of the characters, organizations, and events
portrayed in this novel are either products of
the author's imagination or are used fictitiously.

The text of this Large Print edition is unabridged.
In other aspects, this book may vary
from the original edition.
Printed in the United States of America
on permanent paper.
Set in 16-point Times New Roman type.

ISBN: 978-1-68324-466-0

Library of Congress Cataloging-in-Publication Data

Names: Doiron, Paul, author.
Title: Knife Creek / Paul Doiron.
Description: Center Point Large Print edition. | Thorndike, Maine : Center Point
Large Print, 2017. | Series: Mike Bowditch mysteries ; 8
Identifiers: LCCN 2017021747 | ISBN 9781683244660 (hardcover : alk. paper)
Subjects: LCSH: Game wardens—Fiction. | Wilderness areas—Maine—Fiction.
| Cold cases (Criminal investigation)—Fiction. | Large type books. | BISAC:
FICTION / Mystery & Detective / General. | GSAFD: Suspense fiction. | Mys-
tery fiction.
Classification: LCC PS3604.O37 K58 2017b | DDC 813/.6—dc23
LC record available at https://lccn.loc.gov/2017021747

For Kristen. Always.

Into this wild abyss,
The womb of Nature and perhaps her grave.
—JOHN MILTON, *Paradise Lost*

1

The pigs were coming. I could hear the sows grunting and the piglets squealing as they moved toward us through the underbrush. I listened for the raspy-throated growl of the boar that might be with them. My friend Billy Cronk, who had hunted razorbacks in the Texas scrub when he was stationed at Fort Hood, had given me some advice before my hog hunt. Dispatch the male first, he'd said. Otherwise, I might find myself knocked to the dirt by a two-hundred-pound killing machine. Trampled, disemboweled, or slashed to ribbons: there were plenty of ways a man could die at the tusks of a blood-mad boar.

I was lying on my stomach on the forest floor with my rifle barrel resting on the root of an ancient yellow birch. Somewhere below me, hidden in the bushes beneath the bluff, was my girlfriend, Stacey, also armed. It worried me that I couldn't see her in all her camouflage.

The first week of July had brought ninety-degree temperatures to the low hills and river floodplains of western Maine. The tree canopy overhead filtered the summer sun and filled the clearing with an emerald-tinted light, but the saw-toothed leaves did nothing to soften the heat. The incessant whine of mosquitoes in my ears was its own form of torture. Dripping with sweat, I felt a brief urge to strip naked and roll like a pig in the puddled mud below me.

The oppressive humidity, the tormenting bugs, the absurdity of the assignment itself—the whole scenario had the surreal quality of a drugged-out dream. Feral hogs didn't belong in Maine. But they had been multiplying by the millions down south and been pushing steadily northward for decades, and now their vanguard had finally crossed the state border from New Hampshire. I was a Maine game warden, and my assignment today was to stop the outriders in their tracks.

As the sun had risen behind me, streaks of light shafted through the trunks, and I could see yellow motes of pollen suspended in the dead air. The birds had started up their morning chorus: red-eyed vireos with their nonstop burble; a white-throated sparrow belting out his signature tune; and a single great-crested flycatcher that had alighted at the top of my birch and let out a shrieking whistle that made me jump inside my skin.

I glanced again to my right, but still couldn't see Stacey. The woman had a talent for melting into the forest that brought to mind the ghost stories Puritan settlers used to tell of Wampanoag warriors appearing and disappearing into the trees like woodland spirits; as if the Native Americans' superior bush craft were evidence

10

of their allegiance with the devil. I used to think that I was a skilled hunter, but my remarkable girlfriend had forced me to admit otherwise. At age twenty-nine, I was finally man enough to admit a lot of unpleasant truths about myself.

Neither of us had ever shot a wild boar before, though. So in this respect, at least, we were at an equal disadvantage.

Stacey and I had been dating for two years, and living together for five months, and recently I'd begun thinking about engagement rings. Her parents, Charley and Ora Stevens, who had been like family to me even before I first set eyes on their younger daughter, had given me their implicit blessing. But how would Stacey respond when I actually got down on one knee with a jewelry box held out in my supplicant hands? She'd been engaged before, and it hadn't ended well.

But my worries about her ran deeper than whether or not she would accept my marriage proposal.

For one thing, she was having problems at work. Stacey was a biologist for the Department of Inland Fisheries and Wildlife, the same state agency where I was employed. She was IF&W's resident moose expert and increasingly frustrated by know-nothing officials who placed politics above science, usually at the expense of the defenseless animals she had devoted

11

her life to studying. It was well-known in the commissioner's office that my girlfriend was not one to suffer fools.

She was also still haunted by the deaths of three coworkers in a helicopter crash over the winter. She wasn't sleeping more than five hours a night, and it showed in the dusky half-moons beneath her eyes. Before I asked her to marry me, I wanted to feel that she was back on the path to well-being.

Complicating our lives further was uncertainty around my own job. I'd just applied for a promotion to the rank of warden investigator—our version of a detective—and endured a battery of interviews. Everything seemed to have gone well, but some senior officers in the service still carried grudges against me for my youthful rebellions.

I was so lost in thought that I didn't even hear the pigs until they were almost upon us.

I clicked off the safety on my rifle. Then I peered around the birch, feeling the rough strips of paper on my cheek, and watched the shrub leaves begin to thrash. A sow appeared. She was cocoa brown and ridge backed with gray patches on her chin—utterly unlike any domestic pig I'd seen—and I estimated her weight at approximately one hundred pounds. She froze as she came out into the open and flared her floppy ears.

Pigs have an uncanny sense of smell, but I'd

read that their eyesight is poor. I had no idea how good their hearing might be.

A moment later, the piglets bumbled out. I counted six of them, adorable little things. They had fawn-colored snouts but were otherwise striped with black and brown streaks that extended down the lengths of their bodies to their wispy tails.

For whatever reason, it hadn't occurred to me that I would have to kill the little squeakers, too. If I didn't, they would grow up to be forest-destroying, disease-carrying adults. The only baby mammal I had ever executed was a fawn whose back had been broken by a car. That had been an act of mercy. This, however, felt different. Borderline murderous.

A second sow, bigger than the first, pushed into the clearing behind the other pigs. Her prehensile nose twitched, and she turned her head into a patch of cinnamon ferns growing beside the wallow. She grunted excitedly as she began digging in the soft dirt. Who knew what pungent delicacy she had detected there.

I had read that feral hogs often traveled this way, in groups made up of females with their young. Sounders, these families were called. Mature boars tended to be solitary. So maybe there was no point waiting for a male that might not even be in the vicinity.

Better to wait a minute and be sure, I thought.

13

Stacey must not have shared my sense of caution. Before I could even aim down the aperture sight of my AR-15, two shots rang out and both sows dropped dead. The piglets scattered willy-nilly into the ferns. I despaired of having to chase after them.

The sulfurous smell of gunpowder hung in the air. Stacey arose from her place of ambush and glanced up at me. She rolled down her neck gaiter. "I wasn't sure you had a shot from your angle," she said by way of apology.

When hunting multiple animals, it is considered bad form not to give your partner an opportunity to shoot. Taking both sows was unlike the woman I knew. But as I said, Stacey hadn't been herself lately.

She took a step into the shallow, shit-brown water to examine the smaller of the dead sows. I could still hear the fading squeals of the piglets as they retreated into the broadleaf forest across the Knife Creek Trail. I grabbed a birch root and swung my legs over the edge of the bluff, intending to lower myself down into the hollowed-out space at the edge of the mud bath.

Suddenly there was a loud crack—as of a dried-out log being snapped in two.

A moment later, a huge dark shape came charging out of the bushes across the clearing. Sunlight flashed from the boar's tusks as it lowered its massive head. Stacey was still crouched near the smaller sow, and her center of gravity was low. It was the only thing that saved her from being bowled over. Her reflexes allowed her to swing her whole body aside, almost in the manner of a matador dodging a bull. But the awkwardness of the movement upset her balance, and down she went in the mire.

I let go of the root and began sliding down the incline.

As I did, the boar gave a guttural roar and thrashed his head at Stacey's kicking legs.

Still sliding, I brought the barrel of the AR-15 up in the crook of my right arm and fired. The bullet must have struck the boar in the ham because he pinwheeled around, searching for his invisible attacker.

I felt my legs slip out from under me when I hit the bottom. And I splashed, ass-first, into the mud.

Stacey couldn't bring her rifle up into a firing position, let alone chamber a round, so she kicked at the boar instead.

The giant pig slashed with his tusks again. This time, Stacey cried out.

There was no time to aim. From my seat in the mud, I pointed the barrel and squeezed the trigger.

The 5.56 mm round passed cleanly through the boar's enormous heart.

Stacey scrambled away, crablike, in the dirty water. "God damn it! Son of a bitch!"

"Stace?" I threw my weight forward and began crawling toward her. "Are you all right?"

"I'm not sure." Her filthy hand went to her injured calf. The blood made it look as if her fingers were bejeweled with rubies.

"How bad is it? Did he nick an artery?"

"I don't think so." She pulled the neck gaiter over her head and clutched the leaf-patterned fabric against the wound.

The dead boar lay at her feet. I couldn't get over how enormous he was, his head especially, or how the muscles bulged beneath his bristly coat. Many of the black bears I'd seen in the Maine woods were smaller than this monster hog.

"I'll go get the first-aid kit," I said.

I gathered up my rifle, switched on the safety, and slung it over my shoulder. My water-filled boots sloshed as I ran down the path. I heard Stacey call from behind me, "Please don't call an ambulance!"

In her mind she was already humiliated by her uncharacteristic carelessness. It had been bad enough that I'd witnessed her almost getting killed.

It took me five minutes to return with the med kit. We'd recently been issued Combat Application Tourniquets—an ancient medical technology improved during the recent wars in Iraq and Afghanistan—and taught how to use them, primarily to save ourselves during a gunfight. Better to lose a limb than a life, we'd been told. I hoped to God I wouldn't need to use one on my girlfriend.

I found Stacey standing on the harder ground beside the wallow. She was leaning on her Winchester, using the bolt-action rifle as a cane for support. She'd lost her cap in the scuffle, and her long brown hair was dreadlocked with mud.

I was about to tell her she needed to stay off her bleeding leg when she let out a gasp. She straightened up as if she'd received a fierce electric shock. "Mike?"

"Yeah?"

"What is this?"

The second sow had torn up the ferns and hobblebushes to get at something buried in the soft ground. I saw fragile bones, some with shreds of flesh still on them: the broken skeleton of some unknown creature. The small skull had been crushed, either by the pig or by something else. What the heck was it?

I lowered myself onto one knee to inspect the mystery carcass. I reached out my gloved hand to brush aside the recently turned earth.

Suddenly Stacey hissed, "Don't touch it!"

That was when I glimpsed the grimy pink cloth beneath the bones.

"Mike," she said in a terrified voice I'd never before heard. "I think it's a baby."

2

A few weeks earlier, wardens in my district had gotten a memo to be on the lookout for feral swine. There had been recent sightings across the border, in the White Mountains of New Hampshire. A plague seemed to be imminent.

Dutifully, I had posted signs at all of my trailheads, alerting hikers and mountain bikers to the possible presence of dangerous hogs in the area and providing a number to call if any were spotted. The poster showed a photograph of a wild boar looking appropriately ferocious: a creature you definitely didn't want to piss off.

Then, two days ago, a frightened hiker had reported hearing pigs on his way down the Knife Creek Trail in Birnam. I'd returned at dusk to search for signs. The path paralleled a burbling brook with a self-explanatory name: it appeared to have been cleaved from the glacial till with a blade.

Not a hundred yards from the parking lot and maybe fifty yards from the trail itself, I'd stumbled upon the first pool of mud. It had been dug out of a parcel of cattails where water seeped up from the earth and drained into Knife Creek. It was the kind of weedy depression where kids normally caught leopard frogs, only the pigs had eaten all the frogs, just as they had trampled all the cattails. The thicker muck along the edges was stamped with their delicate hoof marks, not unlike those of deer, except that the tracks were more rounded and splayed differently. The pigs had also rubbed the dried mud from their sides against a blighted beech tree. They had worn the bark smooth and left behind bristles that belonged to no mammal native to these woods.

Here was the definitive proof: wild boars had come to Maine at last.

"Technically, they're not wild," Stacey had said when I'd returned home with news of my discovery. "They're feral."

"What's the difference?"

"A feral animal is an animal living in the wild that's descended from a domesticated species."

Our house that night had felt as suffocating as if it had been boarded up for a decade. I pressed a bottle of cold beer to my forehead. "I thought our invaders were descended from Russian boars that got loose from a hunting preserve in New Hampshire."

"Yeah, but they've bred with domestic pigs since then," Stacey said. "Most of the feral swine in the country are descended from barnyard animals. There are something like five million of them, according to the U.S. Department of Agriculture."

"Why does the word *swine* make me think of movies about Nazis?"

Stacey's eyes were jade green but uncharacteristically bloodshot from her recent bout of insomnia. "Because your imagination is sick and twisted, Mike Bowditch."

Yours would be, too, I'd thought, *if you'd seen everything I'd seen.* I was in a mood to have fun with her. "George Orwell cast pigs as villains in *Animal Farm.* He must have known something."

"Feral swine aren't villains, but what they do to the environment is incredibly destructive. They'll tear up whole forests and fields rooting around for food. They pollute streams by digging up wallows and shitting in them. They cause one and a half billion dollars in crop damage each year. Not to mention the cost of the diseases they're carrying."

I suspected disease (or the fear of it) was the real reason the U.S. Department of Agriculture had granted me and my fellow wardens a license to kill any porcine invaders we came across. The language in the memo to us had verged on the hysterical: "Feral swine have been known to carry several diseases and parasites, including hog cholera (classic swine fever), pseudorabies, brucellosis, tuberculosis, salmonellosis, anthrax, ticks, fleas, lice, and various worms. Feral swine are highly mobile, making it easy for them to spread disease quickly in Maine's wildlife and domestic livestock populations. Feral swine carry several diseases that can infect humans, including brucellosis, balantidiasis, leptospirosis, salmonellosis, toxoplasmosis, trichinosis, trichostrongylosis, sarcoptic mange, tuberculosis, tularemia, anthrax, rabies, and bubonic plague." I'd had to look up half of these arcane diseases, but I had been a history major at Colby College, and I knew that anytime you see a contemporary reference to the Black Death, you should run for the hills.

I had planned on hunting these pigs myself, but Stacey had invited herself along, playing hooky from departmental meetings back in the state capital that I'd understood to be important and where her presence had been mandated.

When we'd arrived at the trailhead, I noticed that some wise guy had vandalized my poster. He'd written *I smell bacon* in permanent marker across the laminated notice. The predawn air was already warm and asphyxiating, like a plastic bag pulled down over your head, and it was easy to imagine that we were headed off into a tropical jungle and not one of Robert Frost's quaint New England woods.

We couldn't possibly have imagined what lay buried ahead of us, waiting for the pigs to nose its bones to the surface.

Neither of us had sensitive stomachs—we'd seen too much gore in our jobs. But this was different. This was the stuff of nightmares.

Stacey staggered to the nearest fallen tree and sat down hard on it, having already forgotten her wounded leg. Her face took on a grayish cast. "I'm going to be sick."

I turned aside to give her the dignity of privacy while I studied the tiny, rotting corpse. Now that I recognized the skeleton as human, I could see it clearly, the way a jigsaw puzzle comes together when you find the missing piece. I was no forensic anthropologist, but it seemed to me that infant couldn't have been more than a couple of weeks old when she was put here. Rightly or wrongly, the pink cloth made me assume it was a girl.

Behind me, Stacey strained to speak. "Who would—? How could someone—?"

I couldn't even bring myself to reply. My mind was caught up in a whirlwind of questions.

Had the baby been alive when it was abandoned here?

No, this seemed to be some sort of halfhearted ceremonial burial. The pink swaddling sheet said as much.

A homicide then? Shaken to death by an angry parent? Or dropped on its head during an alcoholic binge?

Those were all solid possibilities.

Maybe it had been an innocent crib death, and the parents just freaked out because they were afraid of going to the authorities because they were felons or drug addicts or suffered from mental defects.

That kind of thing happened all too often.

Or it might have been a stillbirth and the distraught mother hadn't known what to do.

I'd read of women who had hidden their pregnancies and then, in unthinking panic, abandoned their newborns in trash cans. And still other women who didn't even realize they were pregnant until they'd doubled over in pain with amniotic fluid leaking from between their legs.

"Mike?" Stacey said. "We need to call someone."

I blinked my eyes until the tears cleared. Then I reached into my jacket pocket for my cell phone. I hit the autodial for the dispatcher.

"Twenty-one thirty-two," I said, giving my call numbers. My voice sounded as if my throat were stuffed with cotton balls.

"Go ahead, twenty-one thirty-two."

The dispatcher's first name was Sue, but even though we spoke nearly every day, I didn't know her last name; didn't know what she looked like or how old she was; whether she was married or had kids.

"I've got a possible homicide. It's a dead infant in a shallow grave. Location's about a hundred yards from the Knife Creek trailhead off the Saco Road. Requesting a medical examiner and state police crime-scene investigators. Tell them I'll

23

meet them at the parking lot and can lead them to the death scene."

I decided to leave the hogs unmentioned for the time being.

"Anything else?" The tremor in Sue's voice told me she was not unaffected by my report.

I glanced at Stacey, hand clasped to her red calf, a look of agony on her face that had more to do with what we'd found than her injured leg. She had forbidden me from asking for a paramedic. She didn't appear to be in shock or in danger of passing out from blood loss. Reluctantly I acquiesced to her wishes.

"I think that should do it."

"I'll call you back with an ETA," the dispatcher said.

Stacey rested a heavy hand on my shoulder as I cleaned and bandaged the slash on her leg. The bleeding had already begun to slow. But as a man with more scars than Frankenstein's monster, I recognized she was going to need stitches.

"Why here?" she said, the question a mere whisper in my ear.

I raised my head and we locked eyes again. "What did you say?"

"Why bury a baby here of all places?"

I glanced around at the leafy green woods. From an investigative standpoint, the clearing was an absolute disaster. Three dead hogs. Pig tracks everywhere. Ferns and saplings trampled.

Swarms of flies laying eggs in the stinking piles of manure. I had never witnessed a crime scene more contaminated than this. Aside from the cadaver itself, the state police techs would be lucky to find a single piece of evidence that might prove useful at a trial.

"It's near the trailhead," I said. "Close enough to the parking lot but far enough from the path so that it wouldn't be stumbled over."

"You told me you found the wallow two days ago. You said it looked like the pigs had just been here."

"Yeah. So?"

Her fingers dug into my trapezius muscle. "Think about it, Mike."

Of course, I realized. The baby couldn't have been here three days earlier or the feral pigs would have sniffed it out immediately. Which meant the dead infant had been buried sometime in the past forty-eight hours.

"There's no way they chose this spot by accident," Stacey said. "They had to have known about the pigs."

The awfulness of the revelation unfolded itself before me. "They left it here to be eaten."

She clenched her jaw as if to keep from vomiting again. "This is officially the worst thing I have ever seen."

I had stopped keeping my own list of moral obscenities years ago. It had gotten too long.

I rose to my feet, wrapped my arms around her shoulders, and pressed her muddy head to my stomach. I couldn't think of a single thing to say that might console her.

After a minute, she pulled away. "Now what do we do?"

"I told Dispatch I'd meet the first responders at the trailhead."

"Can I go instead? The idea of waiting here alone—"

"Yeah, of course."

I watched her limp painfully off, using her rifle to steady herself, through the alders and bracken in the direction of the road. She knew enough about preserving evidence at a crime scene to use the same path we'd made coming into the clearing.

To Stacey, what we had found seemed inconceivable. But I had ceased putting limits on my imagination. As a law enforcement officer, I had seen and heard about atrocities that I would never have believed if I'd read about them in a thriller.

For example, a serial killer in British Columbia had fed his female victims to his pigs. Robert Pickton had a farm outside Vancouver called (and I am not making this up) the Piggy Palace Good Times Society. He may have slaughtered as many as twenty-seven women and fed their bodies to his hogs. Some he may have ground up and mixed with pork to sell at farm markets. Certified organic. The BC health authority was forced to issue a warning against eating ground pork or sausage that might have come from the area, but there had probably already been plenty of unwitting cannibals in Greater Vancouver.

The Canadian tabloids called him the Pig Farmer Killer.

The Pigheaded Killer.

Pork Chop Rob.

As if there were anything funny about his abominable acts.

The murders Pickton committed had been enabled by incompetent investigators and negligent prosecutors. Good men, charged with protecting the public from harm, had been unable to bring themselves to believe that monsters walk among us in human form. They discounted their own intuitions and so allowed a rapist and a murderer to go about his grisly business, unmolested. The moral of the story, as I understood it, was that the persistence of evil in the world is often made possible by failures of imagination. As a rookie fresh out of the criminal justice academy, I had suffered from the affliction myself.

But I would be damned before I let it happen again.

I removed my sopping cap and used my shirt-sleeve to wipe my skull. I'd shaved my buzz cut down nearly to the scalp for the summer. Then I scanned again the pool of mud and the flattened ferns and bushes that surrounded it.

Blowflies were already seeking out the open mouths and glazed eye sockets of the pigs. The insects were going to have plenty of time to lay their eggs in my dead hogs. The state police were unlikely to give me permission to remove them until they had thoroughly searched every square inch of this messed-up clearing.

I followed my own footsteps back to the dead infant. I took a breath and steeled myself to study the remains again.

"Why here?" Stacey had asked.

In some ways the choice made sense. The nearby trail was infrequently used. Its parking lot was mostly hidden from the main road by pines and oaks. Whoever had buried this child would have assumed the evidence would be eliminated within days if not hours. The gravedigger had to have been someone local. The chances that a stranger to the area had blundered down the path and happened on this oh-so-convenient pig wallow were so slim as to be negligible.

Birnam was a hamlet of fifteen hundred people—so rural it lacked even a village center. The slow-flowing Saco River looped in oxbows along the eastern edge of town. Thousands of hard-partying rafters and canoeists rode the river each summer and camped on its sandy banks.

Most of them put in upstream, in Fryeburg, and floated south in the bathtub-warm water. South of Birnam the Saco entered a bog so expansive and pathless it was more like a watery maze. Already this summer, I had been called in twice to help boaters find their way out of the labyrinth.

The Burnt Meadows highland was on the opposite side of town from the river. The name came from the wildfires of 1947 when 87 percent of Birnam was burned to ashes—a sign of natural disasters to come if one listened to climatologists. The paths up the granite hills led through scrub oak barrens and stands of rare pitch pine, but they were seldom used. Hikers seemed to prefer the far more spectacular trails of the White Mountains across the state line in New Hampshire. Knife Creek dropped in a series of steps down from the top of the mountain.

Until the previous month, the town hadn't even been part of my territory. But then the warden who had been assigned to District Six had quit the service, and my sergeant had said that I would be doing double duty, patrolling an area twice the size of Washington, D.C., for the foreseeable future.

The river and the hills—that was pretty much all I knew about Birnam.

And now I'd stumbled on a dead baby. I already understood that this was a morning I would spend the rest of my life trying and failing to forget.

I heard voices in the woods behind me and turned to see who was approaching. Stacey's camouflage outfit made her hard to pick out, but the other person with her, a short woman in a blue uniform and a wide-brimmed hat, clashed so dramatically with the forest backdrop that I knew at once she was a state trooper. Then she stepped into a circle of sun as bright as a stage spotlight and I saw her all-too-familiar face. My heart sagged inside my rib cage.

For weeks, I had been dreading this inevitable encounter, but there was no avoiding it now.

I waited as Stacey led the short blond officer to the edge of the clearing.

"I should have known it would be you," said former Maine game warden and current Maine state trooper Danielle "Dani" Tate.

3

Dani Tate had been the warden who'd taken over my old district on the midcoast after the first of my several transfers. At the time, she'd been a raw rookie, just out of warden school, with a chip on her shoulder the size of Mount Rushmore.

Her attitude was partly a result of certain innate physical traits. At five feet four inches tall, she had been the shortest warden in the service— probably the shortest warden ever. She was also one of only 4 females in a force of 120 men. The Maine Warden Service might have served as the original inspiration for the term *old boy network*.

To establish herself, she had felt compelled to deemphasize her gender by strapping down her breasts, speaking in an artificially deepened voice that cracked just often enough you knew it was a put-on, and concealing her natural prettiness behind a permanent scowl. That she held a black belt in Brazilian jujitsu and could outrun, outshoot, and outdrive her fellow cadets had spared her the usual hazing. But her classmates didn't go out of their way to include her in their reindeer games, either.

Our relationship had been fraught from the beginning. She'd heard I had been a reckless, headstrong screwup in my early years as a warden. (The truth, in other words.) My reputation for insubordination had offended everything she believed in as a law enforcement officer, and when we'd first met, she did absolutely nothing to hide her contempt.

In time, she came to see that I wasn't the disgrace my enemies had said I was. While many other wardens wrote tickets resulting in fines, I arrested genuine bad guys, who ended up in jail. My methods might have been unorthodox, but they yielded results.

But with this revelation came something even worse. Danielle Tate had developed an infatuation with me. Just as I'd begun dating Stacey, everyone clearly saw the crush that Tate couldn't hide. Stacey, being her confident self, thought it was cute, but I had found it mortifying.

Tate hadn't reacted well to being rebuffed. It must have embarrassed her to admit that she had feelings for me and then have me publicly dating the hot wildlife biologist in the department.

For that reason, I was relieved when I'd heard that Tate had transferred out of the Warden Service over the winter and had taken a job as a trooper with the state police. The news had startled me because I'd thought Dani would be a warden for life, and I asked our mutual friend Kathy Frost, a retired warden, what had happened.

Kathy had answered evasively, "You need to ask her yourself. I tried to talk her out of it, but she's as stubborn as you, which is hard to believe. I don't feel like I should be sharing her secrets."

Which only piqued my curiosity even more. But I'd resolved to let Tate keep her secrets and make a fresh start. Besides, we might not even cross paths again. Maine is the largest state in New England—almost as big as Hungary in total square miles—and the state police are spread thin. I figured she'd be assigned to some distant barracks near the New Brunswick border or in the heart of the central farmland—far from me, in any case.

Then I'd gotten word that she'd joined Troop B, headquartered in the nearby town of Gray, and I realized her patrol would take her through my district each and every day. Tate and I would be seeing each other at traffic stops and bail enforcement checks and the dozens of other occasions that bring emergency responders into contact with each other.

And sure enough now, here she was: the first officer to arrive at the death scene.

"Bowditch," she said.

"Tate." My tongue seemed pasted to the top of my mouth. "I'd heard you'd joined the state police."

"It wasn't exactly an official secret."

Tate had flat features and flint-colored eyes.

She had shoulder-length blond hair, which she wore tucked under her campaign hat. Her body had always appeared solid and square to me, but I'd only seen her in civilian clothes on several occasions—not wearing a uniform cut for a male body—and so I doubted that I had any clue how she truly looked under that masculine, armored costume.

Stacey was watching us with a barely suppressed smile. "Small world, you being assigned to Troop B."

"I didn't request it," Tate said as she set a black backpack on the ground.

"So who else is coming?" I asked.

"Pomerleau and the CSI guys. The sheriff will be sending a couple of his people. Grant is the ME on call. I'm not sure if he's bringing an anthropologist. I'm supposed to cordon off the area until the sergeant arrives. You're going to have to show me how you walked in and out of here so we can preserve as much of the evidence as possible." Tate moved her gaze to the flyblown corpses of the pigs in the mud. "Nice shooting. Did you get any of the squeakers?"

Of course, Tate had noticed the smaller hoof-prints in the mud. She'd always been an expert tracker.

"Afraid not," I said. "I'm going to have to come back here later to hunt them."

"That'll have to wait until the scene is mapped."

The three of us stood there without speaking. The sound of an eighteen-wheeler grinding its gears carried up from the road.

"Do you want to see it?" I asked, meaning the corpse.

"Only after the evidence techs bag it."

"You're not curious?"

"Not enough to further contaminate the scene. I know you've always considered regulations to be suggestions, Bowditch. But the state police isn't as forgiving as the Warden Service when it comes to making your own rules."

Same old Tate.

"I'm going to sit down if you two don't mind," Staccy said, returning to her log and touching her bandage. No blood had seeped through at least.

Tate hitched her thumbs under her gun belt. "So he got you pretty good in that leg?"

"I think my swimsuit-modeling career is over."

"Ha ha," the trooper said without smiling. She turned away from us, snapped on a pair of blue gloves, and removed crime-scene tape from her bag to begin stringing a cordon.

"What can I do?" I asked.

"Stay out of the way."

The white-throated sparrow sang again from his place of hiding—a beautiful lonesome song.

"That woman is seriously steamed at you," Stacey whispered. "You are such a heartbreaker, Bowditch."

"She's right about one thing, though. We shouldn't be making jokes here."

Suddenly, Stacey leaned forward and put her forearms on her knees so that her dirty hair hid her face. She made no sound that I could hear, but from the way her head and shoulders were shaking I could tell that she was sobbing.

I put my hand on her shoulder. "Baby, I wasn't criticizing you."

"It's just that it's so horrible." Her throat sounded raw. "I don't even know what I'm saying. My brain is just . . ."

"No one can predict how they'll react to things like this."

"There's just been so much death lately. It's everywhere I look. It's the only thing I see. I feel like I'm losing my fucking mind."

When she finally glanced up, the tears had run rivulets through the dried dirt on her face. "I'm not a heartless person!"

"I know that, Stacey. Your problem is—I'm not even sure it's a problem. You have too much heart."

I squeezed her shoulder again and felt how unyielding her muscles were to my touch. "Let's go wait in the truck for the detectives," I said. "I've donated enough blood to the mosquitoes of Birnam Wood."

At that moment, Tate shouted from across the clearing, "Bowditch, did you see this?"

She was pointing at the trunk of an ancient beech. It had the craterlike scars of the blight that was devastating so many of the forest giants. Leaving Stacey, I made my way around the fence of yellow tape to where Tate was standing. It was the nearest tree to where the baby had been buried.

Four feet off the ground, facing away from the grave, letters had been carved into the bark. They were too faint to have been made by a knife or some other metal or plastic instrument. A sharp piece of wood might have made them, but my first impression was that someone had scrawled the initials using his or her fingernail.

KC

"It looks recent," Tate said in her fake-gruff voice. "Like someone just scratched it here. Do you think it's a headstone marker? The baby's initials or something?"

I had no idea. The one thing of which I was certain was that I had shone my flashlight on that very same beech when I'd scouted the wallow two evenings earlier. I knew for sure because it was the tree the pigs had been using to rub the dried mud from their hides. And the letters had not been there at the time.

4

An hour later I stood beside my truck in a parking lot filled with law-enforcement vehicles and watched the death examiner carry out in his own arms a small black bag containing the remains of the half-buried infant. He was young for the job but already balding, dressed in a sweat-stained oxford shirt and flat-assed chinos, and I knew at once that he must be a parent himself because the agony in his face could only have belonged to a man imagining his own child wrapped in that airless plastic bundle.

In Maine, all homicides, outside of those committed in the larger cities, are investigated by the state police. The detective assigned to this case was a fortyish woman named Ellen Pomerleau, who worked Major Crimes out of the same barracks as Tate. Pomerleau emerged from the woods behind the coroner, her white blouse and slacks spattered with mud and pig shit. She had a pinkish complexion, pale eyes, and tangled hair that was so blond it was the color of piano ivory. She had applied white zinc to her lips to keep them from burning.

She and I watched the medical examiner and his assistant drive off in their black van, headed for the autopsy lab in Augusta.

"What kind of evidence did your guys find?" I asked.

"Aside from those initials on the tree?"

"Aside from those."

"You know that pink cloth you thought was a baby blanket? Get this. It was a pink T-shirt, pretty well shredded. There was a tag inside the collar—said it was an official souvenir of Major League Baseball—so maybe that will lead us somewhere. The crime lab will do a DNA test, but even then . . ."

She didn't need to say anything more. Every person who is involved with the investigation of homicides knows how films and, especially, television have misled the public about the wonders of forensic science. Juries now expected all sorts of wizardry from the prosecution based on myths they'd learned from Hollywood. To show up in a DNA database, the mother or father of the buried baby would've had to have been convicted of a violent sex crime.

On the other hand, I had also heard that human DNA had been successfully extracted from maggots four months after they'd fed on a corpse. So who could say what the techs might discover?

"How are you going to investigate this?" I asked.

"We'll do some knock-and-talks to start. Canvass the houses along the road. Ask the neighbors if they've seen anything suspicious."

"What do you say to people? 'Excuse me, did you happen to see a person parked here carrying a dead baby and a shovel?' "

"Something like that. The higher-ups will probably want to do a press conference. Get the word out. Maybe a hiker or mountain biker saw something. I wouldn't put money on it, but you never know."

I glanced around the parking lot. "How about hiding a few game cameras somewhere? Record the plate numbers of whoever parks here?"

Pomerleau gave me a wry smile. "Because the criminal always returns to the scene of the crime?"

The detective was teasing me, but she knew as well as I did that the old saying has roots in reality. Not all criminals return to the scene, but many do. Arsonists, for example, frequently show up in the crowds outside the buildings they set afire. Burglars, having successfully robbed a house, might try their luck again if they suspect the owners have subsequently replaced their valuables. And I had read that certain notorious serial murderers had made a habit of revisiting the locations of their crimes—the abductions, the killings—as a way to relive the thrill of the experience.

"I don't mind putting a camera up for you," I said. "I've got plenty of them."

"Thanks, but we've got this, Bowditch."

"I was surprised your techs don't want to take the sow that was feeding on the cadaver."

"Maybe if the pig had eaten more. It sounds like she'd just started chowing down when you shot her. The ME should be able to get what he needs from the corpse itself. He'll probably have to call in the forensic anthropologist, though. To determine how old that little girl was."

"Well, just so you know, I'm going to need to go back in there. Either at dusk tonight or at first light tomorrow."

Pomerleau cocked a white eyebrow—and waited.

"To shoot the piglets."

She put her hands on her narrow hips, above the belt with her gun and badge. "I sometimes forget what crazy jobs you wardens have."

I shrugged. What was there to say?

Stacey had retreated inside my pickup and had been turning on the ignition periodically to run the air-conditioning. I thought that she was just making it harder on herself. A few minutes of coolness made the day that much hotter. But I knew that starting up the engine was also a not-so-subtle signal that she was eager to start removing pigs. I'd already called my butcher to tell him that we would soon be arriving with three hogs. After a brief pit stop at the emergency room, that was, so Stacey could have her wound attended to.

"One thing I've been wondering," I said. "Assuming the best-case scenario—"

"And what would the 'best-case scenario' be?"

"I don't know. Say it was a teenage mom and the baby was stillborn. What's the exact crime here?"

"Deciding questions like that is what district attorneys are for," Pomerleau said. "But I can tell you one thing for certain."

"What's that?"

"Never assume it's the best-case scenario. You and your girlfriend can remove your pigs now. Have fun and good luck shooting your piglets."

With that, Pomerleau departed, along with everyone else on the scene who might have lent us a hand.

Not that I could blame them.

It was dirty work dragging the pigs out of the woods. Dead bodies are awkward, unhelpful items to move. The pigs didn't smell as bad as I had thought they would and certainly didn't reek as deer do with their foul tarsal glands. But I couldn't say I enjoyed getting up close and personal with those pigs.

Both sows weighed almost as much as Stacey, and the boar must have run close to 250 pounds. I had brought a polyethylene sled that I used for deer and moose hunting, but the heavy carcasses still had to be wrestled into it, and we could only move one hog out at a time—which meant three trips back and forth during the hottest hour of the day.

I ran out of drinking water between the second and third hog.

Both Stacey and I had put on work gloves for the job, but I had trouble getting a good grip on the boar's cartoonishly thin legs and ended up using my bare hands, and then the sled had to be hauled out of the low-lying wallow, through the underbrush, and down the trail. I tried pulling with the tow rope over my shoulder, and that worked fine until we reached the downslope. The weighted sled picked up speed and slammed into the backs of my legs so hard I nearly fell back into it. I had a brief vision of sliding down the hill (just me and the boar sharing a toboggan) before I regained my footing.

A swarm of carrion flies—eager to lay their eggs—joined the mosquitoes and deerflies accompanying our little cavalcade of death. Between trips, we paused at the truck to apply fresh coatings of bug repellent to our skin, rubbing it in hard behind our ears, knowing that it would drip off anyway, as sweaty as we were.

Neither of us was in a mood to make conversation.

I kept thinking of an article I had read about scientists who were genetically modifying pigs to serve as organ donors for humans. Our two species, it seems, are remarkably similar under the skin. I tried to imagine what it would be like walking around knowing that you had a pig heart beating in your chest—whether it would make you feel like some sort of mutant monster.

I had no idea what similarly odd thoughts might be churning inside Stacey's head. She kept her sunglasses on until her body heat fogged them up for the umpteenth time. Eventually we manhandled the last sow into the pickup bed. She ran her forearm across her bug-bitten forehead and blinked to refocus her vision.

I brushed my bare hand against the side mirror and managed to give myself a second-degree burn. "Where have you been, Stace?"

"What do you mean?"

"What have you been thinking?"

"That I will never eat bacon again as long as I live."

I smiled at the joke until I realized her deadpan expression wasn't an act.

She kept quiet as we set off to the nearest hospital, where she could have her leg cleaned and stitched.

"I don't see why I need stitches. My leg is barely bleeding."

"What if it gets infected? Have you ever seen gangrene in real life? Have you ever smelled it?"

"As a matter of fact, I have. I've seen lots of

horrible things I haven't told you about, Mike."

The words were meant to chasten me, and they did. I changed the subject. "The last time I visited the Bridgton Hospital was for stitches, too. Remember? Of course I had only been stabbed by a deranged woman and not gored by a boar."

She picked at the black dirt beneath her fingernails. "When's Carrie Michaud's trial, anyway?"

"Who knows. Her lawyer's dragging it out. They're hoping I might resign or die in a car crash—anything that means me not testifying."

"I still say you should have shot the bitch. That's what I would have done."

Once, I would have agreed with her. But that was before I knew what it was like to kill another human being. In my career I had been directly responsible for the deaths of at least three people, all of whom had arguably deserved it. But that didn't lighten the weight of the beam I carried across my shoulders.

One of the key differences between Stacey and me was that I knew what it meant to take a life.

We'd both had difficult childhoods and troubled young adulthoods. My parents had divorced when I was nine years old, and I had been estranged from my emotionally abusive father up until his death. Stacey's parents were two of the kindest, sanest people I knew, but at the center of their marriage was one horrible day when her father, Charley, had tried to teach her mother, Ora, to

45

fly a small plane. He had been the longtime chief pilot of the Maine Warden Service and more at home in the air than a peregrine falcon. He had wanted to share his love of all things aerial with his earthbound wife, but something had gone wrong during one of their lessons, and they had plummeted to the ground. The crash had left Stacey's mother with a broken spine, paralyzed from the waist down. And it had left Stacey's father with a sense of guilt so painful you could see it in the looks he gave his wife.

It had taken years of my knowing Stacey for me to begin to understand the effect the accident had had on her. I had come to believe that she had two warring halves to her personality: the natural optimist and the nurtured pessimist. As a result, she couldn't enjoy a moment of happiness without anticipating its imminent end. In my experience, people who always expect the worst usually have a way of making it come to pass. So it was with my girlfriend.

"I've been thinking what would have happened if I hadn't been there with you today," she said.

"What do you mean?"

"Whether you would have found that baby on your own or whether the pigs would have finished it off without anyone ever knowing the truth."

"I'd say it was a good thing you were with me. It's always a good thing when you're with me."

"I suppose so. But I can't help feeling like I just opened Pandora's box."

I didn't want to say it out loud when she was already feeling so shaken, but I thought she might be right.

5

M y "butcher" was a seventeen-year-old high-school dropout named Ricky Elwell.

Ricky was the son of the late Richard "Dick" Elwell, who had been a backwoods legend in his time, having disassembled thousands of deer, moose, and bear for hunters across the state of Maine. Dick had been a small man with a caved-in chest and a caved-in face who looked twenty years older than he was. He was an unrepentant chain-smoker who used to sip from a pint of Allen's coffee-flavored brandy while he ran his bone saws. By the time the cigarettes finally choked the life out of him, he had been down to seven fingers and half a thumb.

I therefore shouldn't have been surprised by the sight of Ricky as he emerged from the darkness of the barn where he continued his father's trade. He had put on an apron that still bore blood-stains from the previous fall's hunting season. When he waved hello, I saw that he had lost his left ring finger since I'd last seen him.

"Jesus, Rick," I said, "what happened to your hand?"

He was a skinny, black-haired kid with a head that belonged on a person twice his size. His hair was cut in a heavy bang that fell like a crow's wing over one dark, mischievous eye. He examined the intact digits of his right hand with a puzzled expression.

"Your left hand," I said.

"You mean this finger?" He wiggled the stub at me.

"How did you lose it?"

"Didn't lose it. I cut it off deliberate."

Stacey didn't know Ricky, but she should have realized that Dick's boy would have inherited his old man's desert-dry wit. "What? Why?" she asked.

"My girl wanted to put a ring on it. I figured cutting it off was the only way to shut her up about us getting hitched."

"Did it work?" Stacey grinned, finally catching on.

"You bet it did. Next thing I knew, she'd gotten herself knocked up by Chip Emmons. His dad owns the autobody at Six Corners. I could've warned the poor bastard about Brittney if only he'd asked me." Ricky pasted a cigarette to his lower lip and lit the end with his old man's Zippo. "So let's have a look at these cob rollers of yours."

Ricky was too petite to peer over the side of the Sierra, so I was forced to open the bed for him. As he hopped up, I noticed he was wearing basketball shorts under his apron and flip-flops with white athletic socks. He poked and prodded the dead hogs as if he were a doctor performing a yearly physical on them.

"Well?" I said.

"They're pigs all right."

"We appreciate the confirmation."

"I always figured wild boars would've looked wilder somehow. But I guess these are hairier than normal hogs. And the boar's teeth are longer than average. How about you let me keep those? My mom makes wicked cool jewelry out of teeth and bones. She never worked with wild boar before, as far as I know. And her birthday's coming up."

"I think we can make a deal," I said. "So this means you can butcher them for us, I take it?"

"Oh, sure. I been sawing up pigs since I was a kid."

"That long, huh?" Stacey said.

The family farmhouse was connected by an ell to an enormous barn. I backed the pickup into the gaping-mouthed structure, while Ricky waved me on with the ember of his cigarette glowing orange in the darkness. He'd turned on just a single light inside, maybe because he thought it would be cooler.

Chains and hooks hung from the rafters. Before he passed, Dick Elwell had replaced the old dirt floor with hard concrete, and he had installed drains so he could spray down the inevitable blood. There were wooden butcher blocks and stainless steel tables attached to deep sinks. Half a dozen freezers and refrigerators hummed in the shadows. In the fall and the winter, those appliances would be jam-packed with wrapped packages of ground moose meat, bear sausages, and venison backstraps, but this time of year, I wasn't sure what they contained or why Ricky kept them running.

My predecessor in the district had warned me that Dick Elwell had been known to do butchering jobs for poachers. Allegedly, he'd charged three times his usual rate, if not more, for illicit work. That was the local gossip, anyway. But I'd never found any illegal deer meat inside those freezers when I'd asked the butcher to open them for me. My bet was that Dick had another one somewhere—down cellar, under the house itself—where he kept his frozen contraband.

Had Ricky picked up that part of his father's business? I wondered. The black-market meat market?

It was a question for another day. At the moment I had enough to worry about.

"Do you need help?" Stacey asked him.

"Heck, no, ma'am. I'm a licensed professional. But you're welcome to stand back and watch me work. You can even applaud if you feel like it."

Stacey shook her head at me, smiling. I was glad to see her good humor returning.

Ricky winched the boar out of the truck first.

The chain was fastened to an overhead pulley system that would have made Rube Goldberg's eyes pop out of his head. The butcher boy flicked his switch to lift the pig free of the vehicle, then swung the heavy carcass clear of the pickup. He put on a pair of gloves that went all the way to his armpits and selected a gutting knife from his collection of blades.

"I ain't used to having to do the field dressing," he said. "Is the state gonna pay me extra for it?"

"I'll talk to the governor about it," I said.

"Give him my regards when you do."

This kid had learned more than butchering at his father's knee.

"You sure you don't need a hand?" Stacey asked.

"Well, I suppose you can wrap your arms around him while I cut—hug him like he's your lucky boyfriend here."

Ricky began by grabbing the boar's hairy penis in his left hand, then began making shallow cuts around its tiny testicles. I felt a sympathetic pang in my groin as he pulled the genitals up and away from the body so he could knot off the urethra with a slip tie.

His knife was as sharp as a scalpel as he made an upward incision along the length of the belly. He was careful not to nick any of the internal organs, especially the bladder and the colon, both of which were crawling with bacteria. I could see the coiled intestines, like links of blue sausages; the brown slab of liver; the twin flaps of lungs; and finally—once he'd cracked open the rib cage—the big, muscular heart.

While he worked, his younger siblings, eager to see Maine's first wild boars up close, formed a semicircle behind us. One of them must have called or texted a friend, because more kids, and even a few shiftless adults, began to appear at the barn door. Ricky was like a doctor performing an anatomy lesson in a nineteenth-century surgical theater. This was what passed for entertainment on a July afternoon in Steep Falls, Maine.

"You might want to watch your boots, Warden," Ricky said, reaching both gloved arms inside the cavity.

The next thing I knew he was tugging the viscera loose from inside the bisected boar. The guts fell with a gross splash onto the concrete. When the smell of them hit my nose, I nearly gagged. No wonder Dick and Ricky were chain-smokers.

"Gross!" shrieked a girl behind me.

"Awesome!" said one of the boys.

Cigarette clenched between his lips, Ricky bent over the glistening pile of guts. He seemed to be searching for something. After a moment, he found it. The misshapen bullet that had pierced the boar's heart ventricles.

"You want this for a souvenir?"

"No thanks."

"I do! I do!" said a red-haired boy who'd walked his bike into the barn.

Ricky tossed it to him, but it bounced hard on the floor, prompting a mad scramble by the little kids, like baseball fans chasing a foul ball under the seats.

Stacey backed away from the hanging boar. She looked even more tired and somber than she had before. A dead animal, especially one that has been disemboweled, is a thing without dignity. I enjoyed hunting, but this was always the moment—watching a once-living creature, possessed of its own mind and unique experience on earth, turned into bloody cuts of meat—when I felt guilt.

"Can you fetch that cooler for me, Warden?" Ricky gestured at an enormous plastic Igloo.

"I got it," said Stacey.

It made a sloshing sound as she dragged it across the floor. "What's in this?"

"Saltwater slurry," Ricky said. "It'll cool the meat down quicker than ice."

The next step was to turn the boar upside down. Ricky lowered the carcass to the floor and loosened the steel noose. He fastened two cables on the rear legs, then ran the motor again to lift the dead hog back into the air. He made deep cuts along the insides of the legs and the back flanks and worked the knife between the skin and the muscle. Then he started to pull at the hide. It came off in big, hairy strips to reveal white-marbled muscles: the meat itself.

The skin hung down around the boar's head, hiding it from view, as he began removing the shoulders and tenderloins. Next came the ribs and loins. Snapping the ribs apart required a tree pruner. The hams were next, followed by the feet.

"Hold on a minute," Stacey said. "We're going to need the head."

The U.S. Department of Agriculture agent had asked us to send the brain to the state university where it would be dissected and tested for disease.

Ricky knocked some ashes loose and reached for a hose to wash out the empty cavity. "As long as I can keep those tusks. So what do you want meatwise? I can do chops, tenderloins, sausages. I got a new smoker to make some bacon."

"I'm not keeping it," I said. "I'm donating the meat to the poor."

"If you're giving it away, can I take some?" a man, who was missing his front teeth, said. "I'm as poor as a church mouse."

"You are not!" a bearded man said, and laughed. "What about that scratch ticket you won last month? Compared to me, you're Scrooge McDuck."

At least these jokers hadn't heard about

the dead baby yet, or they would have been peppering me with questions about the gruesome discovery.

"Sorry, guys, it's going to the food pantry." I turned to Ricky, who was lighting yet another Old Gold. "Give me a call when I can come pick it up."

"Remember, I only take cash."

"You're going to have to settle for a check from the State of Maine."

"It better not bounce is all I can say. I ain't paying any of those bank fees. I've been burned by too many deadbeats."

"The State of Maine is good for it," I said with confidence.

Stacey's bitter laugh told me she was of a different opinion.

"So you'll owe me for three pigs."

"Two pigs." Stacey pointed at the truck. "That one and that one. Don't bother butchering the big sow. No one's going to eat her."

It was the hog that had dug up and begun to feed on the infant's corpse.

Ricky scowled. "What for? What's wrong with her?"

"Never mind," I said. "Just do as Stacey says, please."

"Well, what am I supposed to do with a whole pig?"

"Burn it in that oil drum you got out front."

"I don't like wasting meat. What if I feed it to my dogs?"

"Absolutely not," said Stacey. "In fact, I think we should take her with us, Mike, to dispose of ourselves."

"Don't you trust me, ma'am?" Ricky said.

"Not even a little." She turned on her heel and made her way through the peanut gallery out into the antiseptic sunlight.

"Damn, Warden. Anyone ever tell you your girlfriend is a regular badass?"

No one had ever needed to.

6

When we finally got home, I took a shovel from the garage and dragged the sow by myself to the back of the property, through a thicket of scratchy barberry and Japanese knotweed, which many people mistake for bamboo because of its hard, hollow stalks. Both were invasive plants—imported by clueless gardeners—and just about unkillable.

Beyond the bushes was an old cellar hole, maybe five feet deep and walled with fire-blackened fieldstones: the remnant of a long-forgotten homestead. Farther down the hill was a mound from which random woodland plants sprouted: Indian cucumber, Canada mayflower, goldthread. It had been the garbage dump of the original settlers, now covered with humus and matted oak leaves. More than once I had come out here with a spade to play amateur archaeologist. I'd found rusted bedsprings and copper lanterns; I'd unearthed intact medicine bottles in a variety of bright colors that made me imagine that someone in that vanished dwelling had been addicted to laudanum.

I had decided to bury the sow there, deep in that earthen pile of trash. Despite the thirsty deerflies, I peeled off my shirt and undershirt. It was too damned hot to care about anything but finishing the job at hand.

It wasn't lost on me that I was giving the sow a more dignified burial than someone had that baby.

When I returned to the house, I found Stacey waiting for me. Her white robe was open, and she wasn't wearing anything but her cotton bra and panties underneath. "Took you long enough," she said.

"You didn't have to wait for me."

"What else was I going to do? Return messages from Barstow?"

Barstow was her boss in Augusta, the director of Fish and Wildlife Resource Management. "How pissed was he that you took the day off to go pig hunting?"

"He was pretty pissed, but what's he going to do? I'm Maine's moose whisperer, remember?" A reporter had given her the nickname in a newspaper article about her crusade to rescue moose from the winter-tick epidemic.

"I hope you're not pushing your luck, baby."

"I don't want to talk about it. I don't want to think or talk about anything." She slipped the robe loose of her strong shoulders. "Take off your pants."

The living-room curtains were open. "Here?"

"Why not?"

"But I'm filthy."

"So am I."

When I was a teenager, before I'd lost my virginity, I'd had ideas of sex that were downright courtly, by which I mean that I envisioned the carnal act as something to be done by candlelight on canopy beds, and always with gentleness and courtesy, out of respect for the delicate nature of my imagined future partner. It would never have occurred to my naïve fifteen-year-old self that I might one day be aroused by a woman's sweaty, smelly body; that I might find it more arousing than one adorned with perfume and negligee; that I might prefer a fraying couch to a feather bed; that I might find the roughness of our passion—the hair pulling and lip biting, the obscene whispers in each other's ears—more intimate than anything "romantic."

Sex was how Stacey and I chose to deal with the horrors of what we had seen that day. By the time we finished in the shower, we were not only clean. We were spent.

We toweled off in silence. She didn't bother wrapping her long hair in a terry-cloth turban but let the dark tendrils trail down her back as she walked barefoot through the living room. "Do you want a beer?" she called.

"I can't. I have to go to work again."

A moment later, she returned to the bathroom door, clutching her towel above her breasts

60

to keep it from slipping off. "Can't it wait till morning?"

"I want to finish it tonight."

She nodded, imagining what I was setting off to do, understanding my urgency. "I don't think I can go with you."

"I'm not asking you to."

"Those poor piglets."

My first serious girlfriend, who had grown up in the Connecticut suburbs, a train ride from New York, would have implored me to spare the orphaned animals. She would have asked why I couldn't livetrap them to be relocated elsewhere or maybe even re-domesticated somehow.

Wouldn't it be possible, she might have asked, *for you to capture them to give to a farmer to grow up alongside his barnyard pigs?*

I would have had to remind her that pigs are not bred on farms to live comfortably until death takes them in old age. Even before they are born, they have an appointment with the slaughterhouse.

Stacey didn't need to be reminded. She had grown up with chickens destined for the chopping block and with cows fated for the abattoir. Like me, she was a lifelong hunter and fisher. Not a drop of sentimentality was in her Stevens blood. But that didn't mean she couldn't feel sympathy and sorrow for God's creatures.

She sat in her robe on the bed, sipping from a

bottle of beer, while I got dressed in a fresh set of camouflage clothes.

"What are you going to do for the rest of the afternoon?" I asked.

"I wouldn't mind taking a nap, but I need to get some groceries. We've got a lot of people coming on the Fourth. Has Kathy said if she can make it yet?"

"She said she's coming—and she's bringing the puppy."

Stacey sat up with a grin. "That's awesome! She's a Belgian Malinois, right? How old again?"

"Twelve weeks."

"Our first house party. Should be interesting."

"As long as no one calls the cops."

"A bunch of wardens get together—you never know what could happen."

I noticed that Stacey still hadn't mentioned calling her boss to explain her absence from the important meeting that morning.

"Aren't you going to eat anything before you go?" she asked.

"I'll get a sandwich on the road. Unless I get lucky and find them right off, I'll probably be back after dark."

"Can you do me one favor?"

"Sure."

"Don't bring them back here. Bury them some-where else."

I took her head in my hands and raised her

suntanned face to mine. We kept eye contact the entire time we kissed. There were tears in hers.

I arrived back in Birnam in late afternoon. I drove up and down the road near the trailhead, slowing before each house to make my own inspection. Pomerleau and Tate would have knocked on every door by now—not only to ask whether the occupants had seen anything suspicious, but in case the person who had buried the newborn might actually reside within. By and large the homes were sad, poorly maintained places, separated from each other by hundreds of yards of mixed woods, far enough from their neighbors to make keeping to oneself a way of life.

The woods of Maine also contained many abandoned farmhouses and cabins: old homesteads whose owners had died without heirs, or who had so thoroughly let their ancestral dwellings fall into disrepair that later generations had found them uninhabitable, not to mention unsalable. From a distance it was hard to tell which buildings were occupied and which had been left to the deer mice.

After two unproductive turns up and down the road, I pulled into the Knife Creek Trail parking lot. The air had been still all day, as breathless as the inside of a killing jar. But a faint breeze now ruffled the oak and beech leaves overhead.

To the west, thunderheads had begun to form over the mountains, as they always seemed to do on sweltering afternoons like this. The clouds didn't always result in storms, but these looked particularly ominous, as dark as the smoke from an angry volcano.

I pulled up the weather radar on my phone and saw a red-and-yellow blob advancing across the map of New Hampshire. Unlike modern humans, many of whom are remarkably oblivious of weather, almost willfully oblivious in certain cases, animals can sense when the barometric pressure is falling. Most species seem to react to approaching electrical storms by taking cover and hunkering down. Unless I literally stumbled over my piglets, I was unlikely to find them until the lightning storm had passed on to the east.

Judging by the radar, it looked as if I might have half an hour before the skies opened and Zeus started hurling thunderbolts. I had driven all the way out here. I decided I might at least have a quick look.

I removed my rifle from its hard plastic case. It was the same government-issued Windham carbine I had used earlier to kill the boar. Based on the M16 rifle, first used in combat in Vietnam, the AR-15 was a weapon of war designed solely for executing other men. As fun as it was to shoot, I never let myself forget the black gun's origins.

I slung the rifle over my shoulder and locked the truck. The lot was crosshatched with so many tire treads I could have told you this had been the site of a police emergency even without having been present for it. The U.S. Border Patrol calls the art of tracking humans and vehicles "cutting sign," and their agents consider themselves to be the best in the business. I liked to think that Maine game wardens could give the feds a run for their money.

For instance, I could pick out my own prints from among those of the many boots and shoes that had scuffed the dirt. Stacey's, too. I wished now that I had paid more attention that morning as we had hiked in to the wallow. If I had shone a flashlight on the trail back then, might I have seen the telltale tracks of whoever buried the infant in the mud?

Even before I reached the crime scene I saw yellow ribbons of police tape flapping. Certain officers had been given the task of cleaning up the site after the forensics team had finished its work, but they must have been careless or in a hurry to escape the claustrophobic woods. I made a sweep of the clearing, picking up litter. In addition to the scraps of tape, I found a Big Red gum wrapper, caught in the upper fronds of a fern, as well as a dropped ballpoint pen, the kind used by state troopers to write tickets. I pocketed the trash to dispose of later.

I squatted down beside the old beech tree to look again at the initials carved into the bark. Who or what was KC? Something about the letters struck me as furtive, as if whoever had scratched them had done so quickly so as not to be noticed.

A hard gust rattled the treetops. It sounded as if a flock of birds had come to roost in the branches and were rustling about up there among the leaves, invisible to the naked eye. The temperature began to drop. I knew that I should return to the parking lot to wait out the storm in the comfort and safety of my rubber-wheeled truck. But just as I was turning to go, I heard a squeal in the undergrowth up the hillside. Then another and another.

I removed the rifle from my shoulder and clicked off the safety.

7

When I had finished, I returned to my truck and hauled out the polyethylene sled and trudged back into the woods while the first drops of rain began to fall and the treetops continued to shake. There had been eight of them, not six, and I placed each gently into the sled, the way you might set down a sleeping child.

The first crack of thunder—ten miles to the west—sounded to me like the angry outburst of a disapproving god. Even though I had done what had needed doing, I felt deserving of being judged.

Leafy twigs dropped to the ground, and the now-chilly air swirled between the trunks of the trees. I pulled hard on the rope to outrace the coming downpour. Loaded as it was, the sled still weighed less than it had when I'd hauled out the boar. I was able to deadlift the whole thing off the ground and slide it into the bed.

For reasons I couldn't explain, I drew a blue tarp over them. They wouldn't feel the water, but somehow it seemed the right thing to do.

The skies opened seconds after I'd slid behind the steering wheel. The volume of water that fell in those first minutes was astounding. The windshield became utterly opaque from the gushing flood. When I tried the wipers, they did nothing to clear the glass. The weight of the raindrops seemed capable of crushing the steel roof on my head. I was stuck here in the lot, not going anywhere, a prisoner of the storm.

Then the lightning started. I saw the first bolt leap across the sky and then an almost simultaneous boom in the direction of the Saco River. I thought of the rafters, float-tubers, and canoeists—most of them liquored to the gills—out on the water. Many of them didn't know enough to realize what prime targets they were for electrification.

Just as foolish were those taking shelter beneath the huge oaks and pines along the sandbanks. Clustering together under a tall tree was about as safe in a lightning storm as joining hands around a metal flagpole.

I turned up the police radio while I waited for the worst of the weather to pass, fearing I might soon receive a summons to pull charred bodies out of the water.

After a while, my mind drifted back to the morning's horrors. Where had she come from, that broken little girl? The Saco Road was heavily traveled, but the Knife Creek Trail was little used. You didn't have to live across the street from the parking lot to know the hillside above was a tangle of hiding places.

I regretted now that I hadn't taken the time

to explore Burnt Meadows when I'd first been assigned to cover the district. Maybe if I knew the trail better—and more important, who used it—I would have had some insights into the thoughts of whoever had chosen the spot to conceal a corpse.

With the rain pouring down, I reached for the battered *Maine Atlas and Gazetteer* I kept under my driver's seat and turned to the quadrangle for the southernmost corner of Oxford County. The page showed the trailhead with a dotted line leading up the eastern ridge of the hill toward the low, tree-covered summit. Unfortunately, the scale of the map was too small to reveal any topographical details that might've helped me visualize the landscape.

To an outside observer, my truck might have appeared to be an unredeemed mess, cluttered as it was with raincoats, tools, firearm cases, and discarded coffee cups. But I knew each and every item that I carried with me on patrol and where it resided within the vehicle. I knew, for instance, that the aluminum fly-rod tube behind the seat didn't hold an actual L.L. Bean fishing rod, but instead contained a roll of antique topographical maps prepared by the U.S. Geological Survey. I unscrewed the metal cap, and the compressed sheets of yellowed paper curled open across my passenger seat.

The map I had for this region was dated 1941. The names of the roads were mostly unfamiliar, having been replaced with route numbers in the subsequent decades.

But it wasn't the highways that interested me. The detailed 1941 map showed the trail Stacey and I had hiked that morning. The path had been in continual use for decades. But the map also showed other, fainter trails, including what looked like an old logging road that ascended into the highlands from the north and intersected the Knife Creek Trail less than a quarter mile from the pig wallow.

Pomerleau was assuming—as I had—that whoever had buried the baby had parked at the Knife Creek trailhead and hiked up from the Saco Road, but what if the person had come from another direction?

The lightning passed. The downpour ended as abruptly as it had begun. The moon appeared.

There was no harm in having a look, I decided.

The road around the back side of the mountain was named the Rankin Road on the map, and it had never been paved. The town had laid down a bed of gravel sometime in the distant past, but the pebbles had been washed away and plowed aside, leaving a sand surface that was soaked with water from the just-passed storm. I could hear the grit splashing against my truck's undercarriage as I swerved to avoid water-filled potholes of uncertain depths.

The first inhabited house I passed had white shingles and the ridged metal roof common to these Maine foothills. The usual pickups and SUVs were out front, along with a flame-colored Pontiac Firebird with a FOR SALE sign behind its rain-smeared windshield.

The next cluster of buildings advertised itself as an alpaca farm, although I saw none of those graceful animals in the moonlit fields.

I had no idea if the state police had canvassed these residences, or if Pomerleau had erroneously deemed them to be too far from the trailhead, since no one else, as far as I knew, had any knowledge of the old logging road. The ancient path might no longer even exist.

When I reached the place where I suspected the old trail might have intersected the Rankin Road, I slowed to a crawl and opened the driver's window so I would have an unobstructed view into the dark, dripping undergrowth.

I never expected to see another pig wallow at the side of the road.

The mud bath wasn't as big as the one near Knife Creek. Probably the hogs had gotten scared into the woods by passing vehicles before they could fully excavate it. But the trampled weeds and deep puddles left no doubt my sounder had come through here regularly.

I stopped the truck but left the headlights on and the engine idling as I got out to inspect the pit. I focused the beam of my SureFire on the far side. Hard to tell if the tote road began there or not. I ducked my head under a fan of wet sumac leaves and followed a path of broken weeds up the hill, through a stand of red cedars. Past the wall of foliage that had grown up along the drainage ditch, I could finally discern the remnants of the abandoned tote road.

The wet branches of the sumacs slapped my face and rained water down my shoulders as I made my way back to my truck. Which way to go? There were no tracks to guide me. No houses were visible in either direction.

But as I was getting back into my truck, a glow appeared in the trees, coming from the main road. High beams that shifted down to regular headlights when they touched the reflectors on the tail of my truck. I waited until a pickup came bumping along into view. It was one of those old Chevy C/Ks, a relic of the past century, about ten thousand miles away from ending up as scrap metal in a junkyard, judging by the sputtering of its engine.

I crossed the road so I could talk with the driver. He dutifully stopped and rolled down his window, a man in his fifties with a gray mop of hair. His pale face was long, his nose was narrow except for flaring nostrils, and his lips were so thin they might as well not have been there.

"Evening, Warden," he said in a breath that

72

smelled slightly of beer and more strongly of cigarettes. "What's doing?"

"Oh, you know. Just poking around. How about you?"

"Going home. Just got out of work."

"You live along this road?"

"Naw. I live down in Brownfield. I like to drive home different ways to look for deer and such." He ran his hand through his wild gray hair. "So what's the story with that dead baby you guys found over at Knife Creek? It was all the buzz over at the store today."

"The store?"

"You know Fales Variety, out on the Saco Road? I'm Eddie Fales. I own the place. Everyone at the store was saying it was the hard-ass new warden in town who found the baby. I'm guessing it must have been you."

I extended my hand. "I'm Mike Bowditch."

"I've heard of you." His lopsided smile suggested he possessed some secret knowledge of my dossier. "You should stop in some morning. Coffee's always free at my place for first responders. How come you've never come by before?"

"I'm just covering this district until the department rehires the position. If you own the corner store, you must know everyone who lives along this road."

"Everyone who smokes cigarettes, buys scratch

tickets, and drinks beer." He had a scratchy laugh. "In other words, yeah. I know everyone who lives along this road."

"I passed a few houses coming in from the main drag. Anyone live farther along?"

"You mean between here and the fork? There's Lockman's hunting cabin, but that bastard is only here in the fall. And there's one of the Nasons' shitty rentals, but no one's living there, last I heard. Naw. There's nothing but woods."

"One more question."

He inhaled deeply and then rubbed his stubbly chin. "The answer is yeah, I cracked a beer before I left. I always have one when I am closing out the register. But just one."

I wasn't sure if I believed Fales about the single beer, but he wasn't visibly intoxicated, and I had other interests tonight. "How about pigs?"

"You mean like those wild boars in the news? Naw, I've never seen one. But that's why I've been driving home this way—hoping I do. It's legal to shoot a feral pig if I see it, right?"

"Afraid not." I handed him one of my business cards with my cell phone number on the back. "Give me a call if you spot one, and maybe I'll give you some of the meat."

He let out another of his parched laughs. "Yeah! I'm sure you will. Have a good night, Warden, and remember what I said about the free coffee."

I watched his hunk of junk putter down the

road until the brake lights were swallowed up by the darkness.

From what he'd said, there was no point in my driving farther into the woods. I was prepared to turn around and go home when it occurred to me that Fales hadn't followed up his question about the dead baby. He'd said it was the topic of conversation all day at his store—and then he'd changed the subject at the soonest opportunity. Clearly, the man was intelligent and curious. It was odd he hadn't tried to pry any inside information out of me.

I decided to keep driving and have a look for myself.

I crawled along at ten miles an hour searching with my high beams for anything that would give me a reason to stop.

I found it in a piece of litter. It was just a speck of red on the shoulder.

I climbed out of the truck and bent over for a look. It was an empty pack of Big Red chewing gum. The same brand I'd found at the first wallow. Earlier, I'd presumed the wrapper had been dropped by one of the careless cops at the scene. But what if it had been there before, but outside the cordon? What if it had been blown in as the storm had swept through the forest?

On an impulse, I returned to my patrol truck and turned off the engine. I was blind as a mole when the headlights went out. I waited for my eyes to adjust to the dark. Slowly my night vision returned.

The road curved around a stand of red pines that grew straight as ship masts from the sandy soil. The tall trees were devoid of lower branches, so I could see between the scaly trunks, around the bend, and deep into the woods beyond.

I might have missed the house otherwise.

It was set back at the end of a long, unpaved drive that looked more like a disused Jeep trail, with no mailbox or house number to mark its entrance. The unlit building was a blocky shadow that was only visible because of its unnaturally square outline against the grainy light between the pines.

This must have been the rental house Fales had mentioned, I realized. He'd said that the building was unoccupied. But it sure didn't look that way to me.

Tire marks went into and out of the drive. Someone had tried to brush them away with a pine branch, but they had been in a rush and done a poor job with their improvised broom. The gesture at concealment had taken effort, though. And unusual determination. Someone was hiding from the world behind those dark windows, and I was intrigued to know why.

8

I didn't bother with a flashlight. The moon was nearly full, and I could see well enough now that my pupils had expanded.

My plan was to approach the house cautiously and to make a quick inspection under the cover of shadows. If it seemed unoccupied, I would move on down the road. But if someone seemed to be in residence, I would bring my truck in with the high beams on to give the occupant warning of my arrival. In woods as deep as these, knocking at the door of a strange house after dark is an effective way to get yourself shot in the chest.

As I drew closer to the building, it began to take shape. I had assumed it was a crumbling old manse, but I couldn't have been further from the truth. In fact, the structure looked middle-aged. The three-story, cedar-shingled building was taller than it was wide, with a cinder-block foundation and a drive-in garage. It had a pitched roof to let the snow—so heavy here in the winter—slide off easily. Curiously, the only windows facing the road were on the third floor. The second floor turned a blank face to the drive.

I made a circle around the perimeter, pushing my way through the abundant ferns. I saw three propane tanks against one wall. They were the kind that people use to heat a small trailer or cabin, not a house of this size. With minimal help a single man could muscle these tall white cylinders in and out of position.

The back of the structure was newly shingled, the cedar shakes noticeably paler than the older wood around them.

A set of steps led up along the edge of the house to a door that looked to open on a kitchen or mudroom. A small window in the door was covered by a blind—with a tracing of light along its edges.

My gut had been right. Someone looked to be home.

I retreated back to my patrol truck and got on the phone with Ellen Pomerleau.

"It's Bowditch. So I'm back over in Birnam—"

"What?"

"I had unfinished business. Remember?"

"That's right. The piglets. Should I ask how it went?"

My nonanswer was my answer.

"Anyway, I have a question for you. Did you or your troopers canvass the Rankin Road this afternoon?"

"I figured it was too far from the trail to be worth the effort. But it was on our list if we ran into a brick wall with our initial interviews."

"Did you run into a brick wall?"

"What are you getting at? Should I have a bad feeling about this phone call?"

"Rankin Road isn't far at all from the Knife Creek trailhead as the crow flies. Not even half a mile. There's an old cutoff path. It's not on the modern topo maps, but I found it on a 1941 U.S. Geological Survey."

She paused to absorb this information. "You consulted a map from the 1940s?"

"It's a good map. Anyway, I am parked outside a house on Rankin. I don't know the address because there's no mailbox or house number. I can give you the GPS coordinates, though. The town will have records whose it is."

She paused again, like a mother waiting to hear her teenage son get up the courage to admit he's crashed the family car. "And what makes this particular residence so noteworthy?"

"The pig tracks led over this way. Also, I found a crushed pack of gum—Big Red—that matched a wrapper I found earlier this evening at the Knife Creek wallow."

"Pig tracks and gum wrappers?"

"I'm a game warden. Sometimes those are the only kinds of clues we find."

Pomerleau paused. "I understand you want to help, Bowditch. Your reputation isn't exactly a well-kept secret among our Major Crimes units. But you need to listen to me and back off here. You do your work, and we'll do ours."

"This is my work. I need to know if they've seen other pigs in the area."

"Oh, please. You're coming up with a bullshit excuse to meddle in our investigation. It's not your job to interrogate the locals about that dead baby you found. And for the life of me I can't understand why you're calling now. Is it to ask my permission? You have to know what I am going to say."

The truth was that I had an unsettled feeling about the house, and I wanted the state police to know where I was in the event that something bad happened. But Pomerleau was mostly right about my real motivations.

She exhaled heavily into her cell's microphone. "How about this? Tomorrow, I'll send over a trooper to do a knock-and-talk at your mystery house. Once she's spoken to the residents, I'll give you the all's clear, and you can go back to quiz them about your feral swine."

I noticed she used a female pronoun when she mentioned the trooper. Pomerleau must have been referring to Tate.

"Bowditch?" Pomerleau summoned me back to the conversation.

"Yeah?"

"Do we have a deal?"

"I'll wait for your call." I said, then hung up.

How long would it take Pomerleau to realize that I hadn't promised *not* to knock on the door of the hidden house? Not long. And she would be steamed about it. But at least by then I would have advanced the ball a few yards.

I flashed my pursuit lights silently for a full minute, filling the trees with pulses of blue. For all I knew, the person or persons inside were asleep—it was late enough—but I wanted to do my best to announce my presence as a law enforcement officer before I knocked. I didn't want to give some elderly shut-in a heart attack.

Ready or not, I turned into the driveway and followed the thin, bumping lane until my headlights were shining brightly against the garage door. I climbed out of the vehicle and backed away a few paces until I could see the whole of the building. Sure enough, a light had come on in the third-floor window.

I made my way up the side steps to a little concrete landing. There was no doorbell or welcome mat. A brighter light snapped on behind the blind in the window.

I knocked politely on the storm door.

The blind went up, and I found myself looking at the face of a gaunt, hard-faced woman— probably in her thirties—with hair so red it was almost crimson.

At first glance, she didn't look like a new mother.

At first glance, she looked as if she was more likely to eat a child than give birth to one.

I pulled open the storm door, expecting her to open the heavier one, but she continued to glare at me through the panel of glass. Her eyes were a dark brown and prematurely wrinkled at the corners. Her lips were chapped and ragged, as if she chewed them. She had one of the pointier chins I had seen in my life, almost perfectly triangular.

"What do you want?" she shouted.

"Maine game warden. Can you open the door please?"

"Why?"

"I need to ask you some questions."

"About what?"

"Wild pigs that came through your property."

"Show me your badge!"

I removed the billfold from my pocket and snapped it open. I held the badge up to the window for her to inspect. While she studied my shield, I took the opportunity to peer past her into the kitchen. The drab room was utterly devoid of decoration. The appliances and cabinets all had a second-rate vibe, were of the kind a builder buys on a single shopping trip to a home-and-garden superstore.

This sure looks like a rental house, said a voice in my head. Strange that Fales—who seemed to fancy himself the town crier—didn't know this woman was living here.

After a moment, I put the billfold away. The

woman gnawed at her lower lip but made no move to unlock the door. Her complexion was mostly pale, but she had the sun-spotted look of someone who had once spent entire summers working on her tan.

"Satisfied?" I said finally.

I heard the lock click and the bolt slide back. Then the door opened.

She was a woman of medium height—five-seven or so—and as bony in body as her face was skeletal. Her crimson hair was cut in a straight bang across the front and straight again at shoulder length in the back. At first glance I had taken her for a chain-smoker, but no smell of tobacco came off her skin or from the room. The house had a distinctive odor, however: cinnamon. Whether it came from scented candles or a spray, it was so strong as to be cloying.

"What do you want?" She had a faint accent I didn't recognize. New York City maybe? Long Island?

"I'm Mike Bowditch with the Maine Warden Service."

"Yeah, I saw your name on your ID."

"What's your name?"

"Becky."

"Last name?"

She placed her fists on her narrow hips and tilted her chin at me. "Why do you want to know?"

I didn't have any legal authority to push. "Do you live here alone, Becky?"

"Why do you want to know?"

Some people—you can tell instantly that no amount of friendly chitchat or even vague threats will get them to open up. Most hardened criminals fall into that category. They know their rights better than average citizens, who can be so clueless you almost feel sorry for them. I once arrested a drunk driver, a dentist with a spotless record, who kept telling me, "I trust you, Officer" and "I will do everything you say," as if my first priority weren't making a case against him that would almost certainly ruin his life.

"I don't suppose you've seen the signs I posted about feral pigs in the area."

The irises of her eyes were more bronze than brown, an unusual color that didn't match her crimson hair in the slightest. "No."

"So you haven't seen any?"

"Pigs or signs?"

She knew what I meant. "I saw the prints of feral swine down at the edge of your driveway. It looked to me like they crossed your land here. I figured you might have seen them." It was a white lie—but close enough.

"I haven't seen any pigs. Is that it?"

Suddenly, another, younger woman appeared in the kitchen. She had the exact same crimson hair.

84

Even the same cut. But she was more voluptuous, even a little heavy. And her expression wasn't hostile so much as confused, tired looking, maybe drugged. She had big eyes and big lips, a dark mole on her cheek.

I've seen her before, I thought.

But before I could make the connection, Becky noticed that I was looking past her. She swung around, saw the other woman, and snapped, "I told you to go to bed!"

The younger woman took several steps back without turning.

Then Becky began to close the door.

I thrust my boot between the door and the frame to stop her. "Who is that?"

"My sister. What's it to you?"

The other one had disappeared into the next room. "What's your sister's name?"

"She didn't see any pigs either, if that's what you want to know. Try the llama farm up the road." Becky glared up at me with those fierce eyes of hers. "Do you want to move your foot?"

"One more question. Have you seen anyone suspicious around in the past few days?"

"What do you mean—suspicious?"

"A vehicle you didn't recognize parked at the side of the road. Maybe some young people who didn't look like hikers searching for a path up the backside of the mountain."

Her ragged lips pulled back from her teeth.

"Do you want to move your fucking foot now? Or do you want me to amputate your toes?"

As soon as I slid my boot back, Becky slammed the door. We spent five seconds trying to outstare each other through the window before she yanked the blind down.

I backed away from the house and raised my head so I could see the upper floor. The silhouette of a woman was outlined in the window above the stoop. I couldn't make out her features, but from her shape, I recognized her as Becky's sister. What struck me was that she had both palms pressed against the window. Adults rarely did that, I realized. Unlike children, they were careful to avoid leaving smudge marks on the glass.

Then I saw her turn as if summoned away by her sister, and the light in the window went out.

I wasted no time returning to my truck. I felt that I should call Pomerleau to report what I had seen, but it hadn't been fifteen minutes since the detective had made me promise not to overstep my bounds.

What to do?

I turned on my cell phone and stared into the glowing screen. Then I hit the icon for the contacts app. I scrolled with my finger until I came to Danielle Tate's name. I wasn't sure how she would receive a phone call or text from me at this late hour. But the State of Maine uses a standard system for employee e-mail addresses. I started a new message and commenced to type:

Tate:
Pomerleau told me you'll be doing knock-and-talks tomorrow morning along Rankin Road. There's a suspicious house you should check first. I found it while I was following pig tracks. Two strange women were there tonight. Not sure if there's a connection to the dead infant, but something weird—drugs?—is going on in this place. Call me in the morning, and I'll show it to you.
Bowditch

As soon as I'd hit send, I realized that I had deliberately withheld identifying the house. I didn't have to plumb the depths of my psyche to know why: I wanted an excuse to come back. Now Tate would have no choice but to include me in her interview.

It still blew my mind that she, of all the wardens I knew, had chosen to leave the service to take a job with the state police. Usually you saw people move in the opposite direction: troopers who were tired of a life on the highway who gave up their better salary and benefits to take a position working as "off-road cops."

Tate was smart enough to know why I had withheld the location of the house and what it was about the women that had triggered my suspicions, beyond the older one's surliness and the younger one's blankness.

Start with the fact that they had both been wearing identical crimson wigs.

Suspicious? I would say that qualified.

9

Stacey was asleep when I got home. Given her problems with insomnia, I was surprised and relieved to see her stretched out across the bed. Our house had no air-conditioning, and she'd kicked the covers down around her ankles. She was wearing only her underwear.

I went downstairs to my so-called study, which was less of a den or an office than a random room where I stored unwelcome reminders of the past. After my mother had passed away, my stepfather had kindly "suggested" that I clear out my possessions from the attic of his suburban McMansion. Sometime before she fell ill, my mom had gathered up all my mementos—toys, report cards, God only knew what—and packed them into cardboard boxes.

"You'll want these someday, Michael," my stepfather, Neil, had said. "You should be able to get at them without having to call me first."

He'd explained everything with such calm rationality that it hadn't occurred to me until later that he was systematically redecorating the house to remove all traces of my mother. My mom and he had met long ago, after her divorce from my father, when she was temping at his law office in

Portland. I wondered if Neil had recently found himself a new secretary.

Not that I could blame him for moving on. My mother had been dead four years now. My visits to the house where I had spent my teenage years had become fewer and fewer. My stepfather was a good man who had loved my mother and endured her tantrums with patience and good cheer. He had treated me, his unadopted son, as well as I had deserved. But I had found that I didn't miss him at all. These days, when one of my patrols took me past his cul-de-sac in Scarborough, I just kept going without a thought, as if the home belonged to any other stranger.

I plugged in my laptop, pulled up the home page for the town of Birnam, and opened the tab for the property records. A searchable map allowed busybodies to see who owned each parcel of land. It took a while, but eventually I identified the house of the crimson-wigged ladies. The owner was a limited liability corporation—Pequawket Properties—which meant that my guess about the home's being a rental had been on the money.

Next, I checked my e-mail. Gary Pulsifer, a warden I knew up in the ski mountains bordering Canada, had sent me a message earlier that I hadn't bothered opening. The title of the note was "A Woman Set Up a Night Camera in the Woods and You Won't Believe What Happened Next." Pulsifer was such a joker I'd assumed it was one of his usual dumb links. But when I actually opened the message I found the following:

Thought you might be interested in these photos Jill Beveridge took near her camp in Chain of Ponds. Recognize a familiar face? Looks like your boy's found a lady friend.

Attached were four pictures taken with a night-vision camera, the kind we often use to record the comings and goings of poachers at illegal deer stands.

I didn't know this Jill Beveridge, but she must have had a permit to put out a bait pile for predators. People sometimes set a camera with motion sensors over a road-killed deer carcass, hoping to catch images of skittish animals. Pulsifer had sent me four of these photos. Each was black-and-white with a time and date stamp at the bottom.

The first had been taken around dusk—I could tell from the fuzziness of the light—and showed a golden eagle plucking at the rotting deer flesh. Golden eagles are not often glimpsed in Maine. This was a rare photo indeed. *Very cool,* I thought.

The second and third pictures knocked the breath out of me.

At first glance I assumed they were of a large,

dark-furred coyote. But in the third photo the canine had raised his big head, and his retinas were shining like the eyes of a four-legged phantom straight into the camera lens.

This animal was no coyote. This animal was a wolf.

This animal was Shadow.

Five months earlier, I had lost a wolf dog in my care in the high timber roughly twelve miles south of Chain of Ponds. I had previously confiscated the canine from some drug dealers and been searching for a home for him when I'd found myself in a firefight and been forced to let him loose so he wouldn't take a bullet for my carelessness. I'd worried that Shadow, who had been raised, as far as I knew, among people, might have trouble surviving in the wild, but here he was, as healthy and magnificent as ever. If anything, he looked even bigger.

The date stamp showed that the picture had been taken a few days earlier. It cheered me to think that Shadow was still out there roaming the impenetrable no-man's-land along the Quebec border. A fleeting thought went through my head that I should drive up to Chain of Ponds and meet this Jill Beveridge and have her show me where she'd set up her camera. I'd only known Shadow for a few days, but I'd felt he had taken a liking to me and had considered adopting him myself. Maybe I could coax him out of the wild.

And then what? I doubted that I could convince Stacey that we should open our home to a nearly purebred 140-pound wolf.

I scrolled down to the fourth and final photo.

By then, I'd forgotten Pulsifer's cryptic remark: "Looks like your boy's found a lady friend." Now I understood his meaning.

In the fourth picture Shadow was joined by a second canine, not quite as large, with a lighter, almost whitish coat. It was another wolf, and knowing how aggressive males tended to be with one another, I had to assume, as Pulsifer had, that this one was a female. Where had she come from? Wolves had been native to the state at the time of its colonization by European settlers, but had been wiped out over subsequent decades. Today, both the U.S. Fish and Wildlife Service and the Maine Department of Inland Fisheries and Wildlife categorized eastern wolves as "extirpated." The nearest breeding population was in the mountains north of the St. Lawrence River in Canada. Still, occasional credible reports—and even forensic evidence—came of isolated individuals in Maine. Whether these animals had been released from captivity or were intrepid wanderers that had somehow found their way south through the enemy territory of Quebec remained an open question.

Yet Shadow had met up with one. Too bad for his new friend—and for the environmentalists pushing to bring a breeding population of wolves back to Maine—that my former wolf dog had been neutered.

I looked forward to showing Stacey these pictures in the morning. As a young girl, she had believed in the cursed project to reintroduce woodland caribou to the slopes of Mount Katahdin, and we'd argued more than once whether mountain lions—also officially extirpated—had established a new redoubt in the state. Nothing would make her happier than seeing that Chain of Ponds was now the home of a nascent, if inevitably doomed, wolf pack.

I wandered back out into the living room, thinking of her. She'd always been erratic, even worse than me at my lowest moments, but I'd seen myself as a stabilizing influence in her life until last winter, when a helicopter carrying three of her biologist friends had crashed, with no survivors, way up north, near the Allagash Wilderness Waterway. She'd skipped an important meeting with her boss to go hog hunting with me, and there would be consequences. Was she intent on being fired?

In the half dark of the house I studied the big leather sofa in front of the fireplace. I was afraid of waking her. Maybe if I slept downstairs tonight? It was hot enough that I needed no blanket.

I stripped down to my T-shirt and underwear

and stretched out across the soft, cool animal hide. What did it say about me that I slipped so easily into a dreamless sleep? That I was bone-tired or that I had finally reached the place I had long feared—where repeated exposure to humanity's worst sins had permanently removed my capacity to be shocked?

The cardinal woke me. We had a pair of them, as one always does, a male and a female, and he was whistling in a crab apple outside the living-room window.

It was five o'clock sharp.

Punctual bird, I thought.

I found my phone and checked my e-mail again. Tate was also up before the sun.

> It would be nice if I didn't need a Magic 8 Ball to figure out your secret messages. But whatever. I'll call you at 6:30.

I gathered up my dirty hunting clothes—I hadn't realized how much they reeked—and softly padded upstairs to the bedroom.

In the night Stacey had flopped over onto her stomach. She lay with her arms at her sides in the same posture a drowned woman might assume floating beneath the surface of the lake that had claimed her life. It seemed too early to wake her, given the extent of her sleep debt. So

I gathered up the same field uniform I'd worn the day before. I shaved in the guest bathroom downstairs. My deep suntan had made my blue eyes all that much brighter, and since Stacey had moved in and I'd cut down on my beer and whiskey consumption, I had managed to push middle age even further into the future.

My last ritual, after dressing in my uniform in the morning, was to put on my dead father's dog tags. He had worn them from basic training at Fort Benning, through Ranger school, on two tours of duty in Vietnam, and nearly every day of his life afterward, believing them to be some sort of amulet that protected him against death. Recently, I had begun wearing them myself, maybe for the same superstitious reason, despite my long estrangement from the man.

Stacey was still out cold when I stepped into the darkened bedroom. I couldn't sneak off without waking her, I realized. She needed to get up, needed to go back to work and face the music. Before we'd started dating, I'd heard the words some of her male coworkers had used to describe her: "difficult," "arrogant," "crazy," "bitch." It always amazed me to contemplate the double standard that strong-willed women had to endure in the workplace.

I sat down on the bed beside her so that the springs swayed. "Stace?"

No response.

"Stacey?" Gently I touched the middle of her back.

One eye fluttered open. "What time is it?" she mumbled.

"Five-thirty, but I've got to get going."

She rolled onto her side. The sheet was damp beneath where she'd been sleeping. "The piglets?"

"I took care of them." What an obnoxious euphemism that was.

"Did you—?"

I reached out to take her hand. "I buried them on my way home last night, on the public land near the Wire Bridge."

She yawned against the back of her hand and looked about the dim room, her mind slowly returning to wakefulness. "You didn't sleep here."

"I slept on the couch. You were sacked out, and I didn't want to wake you."

"So where are you going now?"

"Rankin Road. I followed the pig tracks and met a couple of strange women at a rental house. Something isn't right there. I'm meeting Tate in a little bit so she can interview them."

Stacey sat up at last. "Say that again?"

I settled down on the corner of the warm bed and told the story of the night before, this time in detail.

"What do you mean the women were strange?" she asked.

"They were wearing matching crimson wigs."

Her eyes opened wide. "I'll be curious to hear how your conversation goes."

"Are you going in to work?"

"Of course. My dad always says that when trouble's brewing, it's best to confront it right away."

So her supervisor really had been angry with her, despite her denials. "How much trouble are you in for missing that meeting?"

She waved a hand. "I've been in worse."

Plenty of times in the early days of my own career I'd seemingly been dead set on pushing my superiors to fire me. But every time, I had pulled back from the abyss. Stacey, on the other hand, seemed to be throttling up the closer she drove to the cliff's edge.

"I almost forgot," I said. "Shadow's turned up. A woman up in Chain of Ponds got a picture of him at a bait pile with a night-vision camera. He was with a female wolf."

"No shit?" She reached a hand around the back of her slender neck to massage the muscles under her long hair. "I thought he was neutered."

"It doesn't seem to be cramping his style."

"You know he's going to get shot by a coyote hunter eventually? Either that or be hit by an eighteen-wheeler on Route 27."

I released my grip on her hand. "That's a cold thing to say."

"I'm sorry, but you know it's the truth. You have a weird fixation on that animal, Mike. The way you talk about him—"

"What do you mean?"

"Like he's some supernatural being or something."

I stood up from the bed. "I feel responsible for him is all."

"It seems that there's more to it than that." She drew her knees up to her chest, revealing the bandage on her wounded leg.

"And I think you're trying to distract me from worrying about you, Stacey."

"Is it working?" She tried to suppress a smile.

"Not in the least."

She crouched, gathered the rumpled covers from the floor, and heaped them onto the mattress. "Don't say I didn't try."

10

Instead of making coffee at home as usual, I decided to take Eddie Fales up on his offer and visit his store at the intersection of the Saco and Rankin Roads for some free joe.

I drove without stopping all the way to Birnam. The drive gave me an opportunity to reflect on our brief conversation the night before. It wasn't always easy for me to distinguish between people who were cagey because they had something to hide and people whose senses of humor inclined toward the eccentric. Fales's seeming lack of interest in the dead infant might have been a red flag. Or it might just have been that he'd spent all day gabbing about the subject and was tired of talking. I could have taken his statement that he didn't know those two women were living in that hidden house as his attempting to conceal something from me. Or Becky and her so-called sister might just have rented the place recently.

In any case, I found his rusted Chevy parked out front—small business owners often worked longer hours than game wardens—but a sign in the window said the doors opened at six o'clock, and I wanted to play it cool.

Fales Variety was aptly named. Failure seemed just around the corner for this corner store. It was small and old and dirty looking with a couple of ancient gas pumps out front. All it would take to put it out of business would be for some modern convenicnce-store chain to open a shiny new station down the road, and all the regulars who'd been coming here for ages would abandon Fales in a heartbeat for cheaper gas and make-your-own milk shakes.

It should have been a peaceful wait; I should have been able to listen to the birds and smell the pines. But commuters were roaring past on their way into Portland. All I heard was engines. All I smelled were fumes.

It was just past sunup, and I was already sweating through my uniform. In the summer the Warden Service allows us to wear short sleeves, but it's small comfort, since we are required to wear a Type III ballistic vest at all times. The vest is made of Kevlar covered by an olive-colored fabric to match our field uniform, and it will stop most bullets, except those fired from high-caliber guns at short range. It will not stop shrapnel. Nor will it stop a piercing or slashing weapon such as a knife. I'd learned that lesson the hard way five months earlier. The brush with death had left me with a curious star-shaped bruise on my back—burst blood vessels that never healed—and a scar, like a red worm, on my forearm.

Ever since the stabbing, I had found myself taking protective measures I would never have considered before. I had started carrying a Benchmade dagger in my boot that I could use if an assailant took me to the ground. I had sewed a pocket *inside* the pocket of my pants to stash a second, hidden handcuff key in case my manacles were used against me. I had begun wearing additional trauma plates that inserted into concealed pockets on the vest: two in the front and one in the center of the back. These plates were made of unbreakable ceramic and added fifteen pounds to the already significant weight of the vest. Factor in my duty belt—which supported my SIG .357 sidearm, two magazines, two sets of handcuffs, a flashlight, a multitool, and a canister of pepper spray—and I was loaded up with close to fifty pounds of gear, over and above my uniform and boots. No wonder I was perspiring like a racehorse.

At six sharp I saw a hand appear in the door, flipping the sign from CLOSED to OPEN.

An electronic bell chimed when I stepped inside the door, and Fales glanced up from behind the register. His thick gray hair was matted in a wedged shape as if he hadn't combed it since rising from his pillow. He still hadn't shaved, and his grizzled beard made him resemble a miner from the Gold Rush era. He removed his reading glasses and set them on the counter.

"You don't waste any time, do you?" he said in his sandpaper voice.

"What do you mean?"

A grin split his face in half like a puppet. "I invite you in for free coffee and here you are eight hours later!"

"I was in the neighborhood."

"So I guess you didn't find anything interesting last night."

"Actually, I did. Do you remember that rental house you told me was unoccupied? I checked it out, and there were two women living there. They said they were sisters."

His untrimmed eyebrows lowered until they were overhanging his eye sockets. "Really? That's odd."

"I figured you would have heard."

"Me, too! Stevie Nason—that's one of his family's properties—was just in here and I'm sure he would have said something if he'd rented the house. I remember him bitching last year about how he couldn't find a tenant. Sisters, did you say?"

"One of them said her name was Becky," I said. "I didn't get the other's name. But they were wearing identical red wigs."

Now both of his eyebrows shot upward on his forehead. "Really!"

"You sure they haven't stopped in your store before?"

"I think I would have remembered two young ladies of that description, Warden."

"Becky is about five-seven, bony-looking, and she had an unusual chin—very pointed." I made a gesture as if stroking an invisible Vandyke beard. "The younger one is dark and pretty with a mole on her cheek you can't miss. Are you sure they haven't come in? I would think that someone who lived so close would stop for gas or groceries occasionally."

Fales had eyes as black as anthracite and nearly as impenetrable. "I'm not trying to be argumentative, but it feels like you're accusing me of something. I hope you're not suggesting I'd protect a couple of criminals."

My curiosity was so intense it could sometimes verge on rudeness—as it had just now.

"I apologize, Mr. Fales. I was just surprised to find someone living there."

"My wife covers for me some days. She might have seen them. The coffee's in back, by the way. Help yourself."

He returned the reading glasses to the bridge of his narrow nose and set to taking stock of his cigarette supply.

I made my way to the coffee machine and filled the largest cup available. I took a day-old molasses doughnut out from under a bell-shaped lid and wrapped it in a napkin, then began making my way to the front of the store.

I passed a tower of beer. It was a special Fourth of July display with cases arranged in a pyramid with a life-size cardboard cutout of the Red Sox's ace pitcher at the center. Across his chest was an advertising slogan:

NATIONAL HOLIDAY
NATIONAL PASTIME
NATIONAL BEER

Boston baseball caps hung from a rack attached to the display, and souvenir T-shirts were draped over the boxes in different colors and sizes.

I nearly dropped my coffee.

I reached for the closest shirt, a blue one, and turned the collar over to look at the label: PRODUCT OF MAJOR LEAGUE BASEBALL. I hurried to the counter. "Do you have any of these in pink?"

Fales looked at me as if I'd just fallen on my head. "You want to buy a pink Red Sox shirt?"

"I'm asking, have you sold any in pink?"

"Beats me. It's part of a holiday promotion our distributor is doing. I know we have pink hats."

"So you don't remember selling a pink Red Sox shirt to a woman?"

"Are we talking about the ones in the red wigs again? No, I don't remember selling a pink shirt to a woman in a wig."

"You said your wife covers for you some days. Can you call her for me and ask if she recently sold one of the shirts in pink?"

His unshaven jaw dropped. "You want me to wake Connie?"

"Blame it on me."

"Oh, I will."

I returned the blue shirt to the display while Fales made his call. Even from across the store, I could hear that the conversation was not amicable.

"No, I don't know what it's about!" He covered the speaker with his hand. "She said she sold a couple—all to girls."

"Can I speak with her?"

"Better you than me." He handed me the phone.

"Mrs. Fales," I began.

"Do you know what time it is?"

"My name is Mike Bowditch. I'm a Maine game warden. I know this is going to sound bizarre—"

"Bizarre? How about crazy?"

"Please, ma'am."

"Yeah, I sold a couple of pink shirts and hats."

"Do you remember if any of the women who bought them was wearing a crimson wig?"

"Is this one of Eddie's pranks? Because if it is, you can tell him—"

"One of them might've had a mole on her cheek like Marilyn Monroe or Cindy Crawford."

"I'm hanging up now."

"What about a skinny woman with sun-damaged skin and a really pointy chin?"

There was silence on the other end of the line. "Maybe."

"So she sounds familiar?"

"If she's the bitch I am thinking of, I think she stole a couple of packs of gum when my back was turned."

"Do you remember what kind of gum?"

"Huh?"

"Was it Big Red?"

"How did you know that?"

The screen of the phone had become slick from the perspiration on my face. "If it's all right, I'm going to have a detective with the state police call you. Her name is Ellen Pomerleau."

"What's this about?"

"Detective Pomerleau will explain."

Or at least, I hoped she would. I handed Fales his phone back and tossed a five-dollar bill on the counter. He'd told me the coffee was free, but I had to assume that the aggravation cost extra.

Excited as I was, I almost called Pomerleau from the road, but since I was meeting Tate in minutes, I decided to hold off. My theory—about Becky's buying a pink Red Sox shirt to use as a winding sheet for a dead baby—was going to sound harebrained enough as it was.

I arrived at the hidden house before the sun had cleared the tops of the pines. I had expected Tate to call me before the appointed hour, assuming

107

that she would be eager to hear what I'd found. But it was nearly six thirty, and the phone had not yet rung.

I wanted nothing more than to go kick down the door, so sure was I that I had found the people who had abandoned that baby. But I knew I needed to wait.

Five minutes passed. Then ten.

Tate was one of the more punctual people of my acquaintance, or at least, she had been once.

I gave up and dialed her number. "I've been waiting for you to call."

"Yeah, well, I'm writing a speeding ticket."

I heard the sound of cars zipping past her. "A speeding ticket?" I said in disbelief.

"Guy was going fifty in a school zone. I pulled him over. He gave me lip. Now he's getting a citation."

She was doing her job. I understood that. She was right to make stopping a dangerous driver her priority over answering my cryptic text message. But it irked me nonetheless.

"I need you to meet me at an address when you're finished. Twenty-seven Rankin Road in Birnam. I'll be waiting in my truck so you can't miss it."

"Do you want to explain to me what's gotten you all worked up about this place?"

"This is the house, Tate. The mother of that girl lives at this address."

"How do you know for sure it's the right house?"

"I just do."

"Well, in that case . . ."

"The baby was buried in a pink Red Sox T-shirt. Fales Variety down at the corner sold one of those shirts recently. There's more to it, but I'll explain everything when you get here."

"I can't promise I won't be delayed, again." Tate ended the call.

I had never had a warm relationship with rank-and-file state police troopers. Too many of them looked down their noses at game wardens in general and (given my reputation for being a maverick) me in particular. It hadn't taken Tate long to adopt an elitist attitude. But unlike her new colleagues, she knew me well enough to have legitimate grievances.

I had glimpsed the other "sister" from a distance and for only seconds, but I could see her face clearly in my mind's eye. Among the wardens I knew, I had an average memory for faces: neither hopeless nor photographic. But there had been something about the younger girl in the house. I recognized her from some place. If I could only remember where.

I gulped down the last of my coffee and climbed out of the truck. I closed the door firmly but softly. No need to announce my arrival.

I crouched down behind the roadside lupines to

avoid detection and scanned the tire treads in the mud. I saw my own tracks immediately, one set heading in, the other set heading out. But there was a new set as well that had been made by a truck or an SUV. This other vehicle had come out heavier than it had gone in, considerably heavier. Overnight, someone had driven in to the house, picked up some seriously weighty items—and then hightailed it out of there. It couldn't have been coincidence that this activity had happened after a law enforcement officer had showed up unexpectedly on the doorstep.

I knew I should wait for Tate. But I had a sneaking suspicion that we would find the home unoccupied when we knocked on the door. The two women had called someone with a truck, gathered up their stuff, and fled in the night.

Without thinking, I rose to my feet and began walking in plain view up the drive. I focused my concentration, made myself sensitive to the slightest movement, the faintest sound.

Stacey's father, Charley, had given me a master class in bush craft when I was a rookie. He had suggested using a mental checklist when approaching a potentially dangerous situation. As a professional pilot, he was a firm believer in taking a strict inventory before embarking on any adventure.

What do I see? I asked myself.

A single light is burning in the upstairs window.

The others are dark. And all of them are closed tight. A patch of new cedar shingles on the back side of the house don't match the older ones.

What do I hear?

No mechanical sounds coming from inside.

What do I smell?

Just the faintly sulfurous odor of a nearby swamp.

What do I taste?

The chemical sourness of the swamp gas—or whatever it is.

What do I feel?

Utter stillness in the air.

I advanced to the kitchen door for a closer look. As I did, the smell of the swamp grew stronger. That made no sense; I hadn't detected a foul odor last night. Why should the place suddenly be giving off a reek like a henhouse full of rotten eggs?

A vehicle came rumbling down the road. I turned my head and recognized the smoky-blue shape of Tate's Ford Interceptor. I heard the door slam. Even heard her swear aloud. She knew I hadn't waited. She knew I had made my way alone up to the house.

I opened the storm door, but the inner door was locked tight. I pressed my ear to the inset window.

What do I hear?

Hissing.

All at once, I understood. The noxious odor, the shut windows, the hissing coming from the kitchen.

I leaped down the stairs and sprinted toward the drive. Tate was striding squarely toward me with a scowl. "You couldn't have waited?"

"Get back, Dani!" I waved my arms above my head like a madman. "We need to get back!"

She raised her hands in confusion. "What are you talking about?"

"Run!"

Seconds later the house exploded in a giant fireball behind us.

11

The shock wave sent me flying. It knocked me into Dani, and I landed on top of her. The instantaneous heat was like nothing I had felt before. For a moment I thought the clothes on my back and the cap on my head had burst into flame.

Then came the firestorm of burning wood and scorching pieces of metal falling from the sky. I dug my face into the wet dirt and pulled my arms up around my head to shield my ears. Some object hit me in the middle of the back—not hard. Later I would find that it was a twisted and blackened aluminum window frame. I heard glass breaking against trees and rocks. Finally I smelled the smoke.

I lifted my head cautiously and spat out the mud in my mouth. Ashes were falling in fat black flakes from the trees around me. When I touched the back of my head to feel for an injury, my fingers came away powdered gray from the sizzled hairs.

Dani squirmed out from under me, her eyes hugely white. The ground was smoldering where the debris had landed. I rolled over to look at what remained of the house and saw a glowing crater. The closer trees were all aflame. Burning pinecones snapped and popped. Embers drifted like fireflies down to the forest floor. When they touched dry leaves and logs, new flames leaped up from the ground.

Dani got to her feet as I pushed myself up onto my knees. She stretched her arm toward me, and we gripped each other's wrists. She was rugged for such a short person, and I let her help me to my feet.

"Are you all right?" I asked.

"I think so."

When I turned to glance back at the blaze, Dani said, "Mike, you're kind of on fire. Your vest."

Hurriedly, I began unfastening the heavy ballistic vest and dropped it to the ground. The olive fabric that covered the Kevlar had an expanding hole in the center that was ember red around the edges and smoking. I stamped on my vest like a man trying to kill a snake.

Dani gazed into the white-hot center of the inferno. "Was anyone in there?"

"I'm pretty sure they left last night. I think I scared them off when I showed up at their door."

"What happened?"

"It was propane. They sealed the house up tight and then turned on the stove. The gas built up until it reached the electric light upstairs."

"You think this was deliberate?"

"I know it was."

She began to cough into her fist. "I need to call this in."

The heat, even from this distance, was intense; the smoke poisonous and thick; the glare blinding. Dani got on the phone to Dispatch.

Birnam didn't have more than a single volunteer fire truck. The nearest department was probably in Fryeburg, twenty minutes north. If firefighters didn't get here soon, they might find themselves facing a genuine wildfire, the kind that had rampaged through these same hills in the late forties, laying waste to dozens of homes.

We could do nothing but wait for the engines to arrive. The fire was beyond our ability to battle.

"This would be a good time for you to tell me what you found here last night."

When I'd finished recounting my activities over the past twelve hours, she frowned and crossed her arms. "You should have called Pomerleau and told her about those weird sisters."

"Do you really think she would have raced out here based on one of my hunches?"

Dani considered the question for a while. "You could have been clearer in your e-mail to me, at least."

"I wasn't sure you'd take me seriously either."

For the briefest moment her stony expression

gave way and I saw real, raw emotion in her eyes. Was it disappointment? Or was it hurt?

"You really don't know me at all, do you, Mike?"

The first engine to arrive wasn't even the Birnam town fire truck. The local volunteers must have had trouble mustering at their station. Instead it was a brand-new Pierce pumper with the town crest of Fryeburg on the driver's door. The men who jumped off it wore heavy tan coats with fluorescent stripes around their chests. They wasted no time outfitting themselves in helmets and other gear and unspooling their fabric-covered hoses.

A compact, square-jawed man approached us carrying his fire helmet under his arm as if it were a football. He had a salt-and-pepper flat top and the confident bearing of a fire chief.

"Do we know if anyone was in there?" He directed the question at Dani rather than me. She was a state trooper after all, while I was a mere game warden.

"No."

He adjusted the helmet on his head and fastened the chin strap. "You said it was a propane explosion? How do you know?"

"The warden here smelled propane when he knocked at the door."

The chief finally made eye contact with me. "You're damned lucky you were able to get clear in time."

"Warden Bowditch's got nine lives," Dani said with uncharacteristic amusement. It revealed dimples I had forgotten she had.

She could come across as such a plain person, but she had one of the most beautiful smiles I had ever seen, one of those beaming grins that so thoroughly transforms the face, you can't believe it's even the same person.

"Maybe you could lend a few of those extra lives to my men," the chief said. He gazed up at the burning hillside beyond the remains of the house. As soaked as the forest was, the trees were still burning. "What about unexploded tanks?"

"I saw three propane tanks when I was here yesterday. I assume they all went up with the initial explosion."

"I can't afford to make assumptions when my men's lives are at stake."

Finally, the Birnam truck came rattling down the road. We watched the outdated engine and its ragtag crew, struggling with their clumsy coats and boots. The Fryeburg chief was going to need a lot more help if he was going to stop the fire from spreading up the hillside.

The summer had been damp so far, which was a help, but a fair number of dead and diseased trees were up on the hillside—ancient hemlocks plagued by adelgids, pines going rusty from some yet-identified scourge—and these caught fire easily. Great funnels of smoke rose into the morning sky. Sparks leaped like animate objects from one treetop to the next: a contagion of flame.

"You ever fought a forest fire before, Mike?" Dani said in a quiet voice as she gazed upon the burgeoning inferno.

"No. Have you?"

"Never wanted to. I had some bad experiences with fires when I was a kid."

It was the first confidence I could remember her sharing with me. Dani Tate wasn't the sort to open up about her past. Or anything else, for that matter.

"I guess we should block off the road," she said, "so we don't get curiosity seekers. You should stay here. Pomerleau's on her way over. She's going to want to hear the whole story from you. And don't leave anything out this time!"

More engines arrived, accompanied by an ambulance, and multiple cruisers from the two nearest sheriff's departments and the state police. Fryeburg even pulled some of their officers off the river to come help.

Pomerleau appeared half an hour later. The moment she saw me, she came over. She flushed so easily, being pale, and there was no mistaking her anger. "You promised me you wouldn't knock on doors."

"Technically, I promised that I would only ask about the pigs."

"Technically? You must have freaked them out if they decided to blow up their own house—if that's what happened."

"It wasn't their own house. It's a rental, owned by a company called Pequawket Properties."

Now her anger gave way to incredulity. "How do you know that?"

"I was curious so I did a property search. Ever heard of them?"

"Yeah, they're backwoods slumlords. You don't want to know how many calls we get to rental houses owned by the Nasons." She removed a ballpoint pen and a small notebook from the inside pocket of her blazer. "So at this stage, it could be that some drunk passed out and left the gas stove on, and God only knows how many people are dead."

"Or it was set up to look like an accident."

Her pen stopped in mid-scribble. "What are you saying?"

"The house was sealed tighter than a drum. Who closes all their windows on the muggiest night of the summer?"

"Maybe they had air-conditioning."

"I didn't see an AC unit."

"Maybe you missed it."

"I didn't miss it."

"So now you're auditioning to be a fire marshal, too?"

"It's no mystery what happened here. Someone sealed up the place and turned on the propane. Eventually the gas encountered an open electrical circuit. Then bang. The renters would have known it would take days or weeks for the fire marshal to determine that no one was inside at the time of the explosion. They burned the house down to destroy any DNA evidence that might have been inside."

"How do we know the house was empty when it went up?"

"I found fresh tracks leading into and out of the drive. They weren't there last night. The treads coming out were deeper—like the truck had been loaded up."

She shook her head in disbelief. "You wardens."

Evidently, even Ellen Pomerleau wasn't immune from the elitism that was so common among state troopers. It left me feeling more disappointed in her than aggrieved.

"We do our best," I said.

She coughed into her fist as a cloud of ash drifted by. "Tate told me you saw two women inside the house last night."

"The older one called herself Becky. I didn't get the other's name. Becky said they were sisters, but I don't think they were. And they were both wearing crimson wigs."

She stopped writing again. "OK. . . ."

"I don't think they were playing around with them. I think they were wearing them for real— like they put them on as disguises when they heard me drive up."

"Any obvious identifying marks? Aside from the fake hair, I mean."

I described them as best I could.

"So what made you so sure that the younger one was the mom of our Baby Jane Doe?"

"At first, I wasn't. I just knew there was something wrong with her. She seemed drugged. And she had this strange expression on her face when she looked at me."

"Do you mean she looked guilty?"

"No."

"Afraid that she might have been found out?"

"No."

"Remind me never to recommend you as a witness in court."

Out of frustration I blurted out what I hadn't even consciously realized. "She looked like she wanted me to rescue her."

She slid her pen behind her ear. "Explain to me what that expression looks like, please."

"She had this helplessness about her. Have you ever visited an animal shelter and seen a dog that no one wants to adopt?"

"So she reminded you of a mutt?"

"I'm speaking metaphorically."

"Metaphorically. Now, there's a word I've never heard come out of a game warden's mouth before. Hunches aren't leads, Bowditch."

I knew Pomerleau was only teasing me, but I felt a need to defend myself. "What convinced me that she was the infant's mother was a conversation I had this morning. I stopped at Fales Variety on my way over here and saw they had a display of baseball shirts with the same MLB.com collar tags as the shirt we found wrapped around the cadaver. I spoke with Mrs. Fales and she remembers selling a pink Red Sox shirt to a woman matching Becky's description. Does that qualify as a solid lead?"

The amusement melted from Pomerleau's face. "Yeah, I would say that qualifies."

"You might want to have someone interview Mrs. Fales. But what do I know? I'm just a game warden."

The detective studied me quietly for a while. "I was out of line before. It sounds like you found something that's potentially helpful. I'll talk with Mrs. Fales myself. Do you think you can describe these women well enough for us to get sketches using the Identikit?"

In an earlier era, police departments employed artists to draw the rough portraits of suspected criminals and missing persons. Now, as with everything else, they used computers to create facial composites. Some of the cops I knew didn't have much use for Identikits; they said the programs ended up making faces look the same. I'd seen "Becky" clearly enough and had confidence I could describe her features well enough to get a decent likeness. But her shy "sister" might be more of a problem.

"I think so," I said.

Just then Dani's cruiser came speeding back up the road, lights flashing, followed by a crystal-white SUV. The Cadillac SRX Crossover looked as if it had been washed and waxed only hours earlier. I noticed that it had a New Hampshire plate: LIVE FREE OR DIE. What Granite Stater was important enough that Tate would have provided the person with a police escort onto the scene of a fully involved fire?

Pomerleau seemed to know the answer. "How did they get here so fast?"

Both vehicles stopped. Dani emerged from her Interceptor and fastened on her campaign hat.

Then a chunky, middle-aged man climbed out from behind the wheel of the Cadillac. He paused a full minute, spellbound by the raging fire, before circling around the front of the SUV. He was dressed in a dress shirt that had come untucked in back, pleated chinos, and heavily scuffed work boots that didn't match his office casual outfit. Strands of black hair were combed across his mostly bald head and stuck there with some gluelike substance.

He opened the passenger door and stretched out his arm to the person behind the tinted windshield. I got a glimpse of jewels on the tiny hand taking his. Then a tight-faced woman stepped out from behind the door. She had blue-black hair styled like that of Michelangelo's statue of David, skeleton arms visible to her shoulders thanks to a sleeveless white blouse, tight pants that did nothing to flatter her skinny legs, and a neck no wider than one of my biceps.

"Who are they?" I asked Pomerleau.

"Deanna Nason and her son Steven. They own Pequawket Properties. This is one of their rental houses—or it used to be."

12

The mother required that her son hold her hand elevated as she walked, like a queen crossing a puddle with the assistance of a courtier.

As they approached us, Pomerleau leaned close to Dani. "Who called them?"

"I have no idea, ma'am."

"Well, someone must have called them." Pomerleau removed the pen from behind her ear and stepped forward to intercept the mother and son. "Mrs. Nason! I didn't expect to see you here so soon."

"Why not? It's our house." For all her gold jewelry and regal airs, her accent was pure trailer park. You don't see much plastic surgery among Maine people, but Deanna Nason had a face less expressive than a Halloween mask. Her gaze drifted disinterestedly toward the conflagration.

"I'm Detective Pomerleau with the Maine State Police. This is Trooper Tate and Warden Bowditch."

Deanna Nason had irises the color of a greenhead horsefly. Colored contacts, of course. "What a horrible, horrible thing. I hope the Cobbs weren't at home when it exploded."

"The Cobbs?"

"Our tenants."

Pomerleau flipped open her notebook again. "You wouldn't happen to know their full names?"

"Do you remember, Steven?" the mother asked.

His eyes were dog brown, with utterly no light behind them. "Frank and Rebecca."

Pomerleau made a note. "So they were a married couple?"

"Yeah, I guess," the son said.

"Well, if they weren't brother and sister—" The detective took a breath to stop herself from going down the rabbit hole. "Did they provide you with identification as part of the rental agreement? Social Security numbers? Driver's licenses? That sort of thing."

The mother stroked her son on the arm. "Steven, go get that file folder for the police officers that Mama asked you to bring."

He shuffled back to the Cadillac.

"You brought a copy of the rental agreement with you?" I asked, unable to contain my disbelief.

Deanna seemed perplexed—both by my official capacity here as a game warden and by the question itself. "When we heard about the explosion, we knew you'd need all the information in our files."

Pomerleau interceded before I could chime in again. "Who called you about the fire, Mrs. Nason?"

"I wouldn't know. My son answered the

126

phone." Deanna turned to us with an expression that begged indulgence. "Until recently all he handled for me was building maintenance. My younger son, Christopher, used to help with the business side of things, but lately I've been trying to pass responsibilities over to Steven." Her son returned with a thin manila folder. His mother cooed, "Baby, who called you about the fire?"

"A policeman."

Pomerleau, Tate, and I did a round-robin of glances.

The detective accepted the folder from Steven's hands. They were thick and callused from a lifetime of manual labor. "Do you remember the policeman's name?" she asked.

"He didn't say."

I could guess what Pomerleau was thinking: *Who would give the Nasons a heads-up that one of their rental properties had just gone kaboom? And why?*

Deanna removed a tissue from her pocket and pressed it to her nose as if the fumes from the distant fire might overwhelm her delicate constitution. "So were the Cobbs inside when it happened?"

Pomerleau said, "I'm afraid we don't know yet. The firefighters are still fighting the blaze, as you can see."

"Well, do you know what caused it?"

127

"That's for the fire marshal to determine, ma'am—again, after the fire has been extinguished."

"But it had to have been their fault. We maintain all of our properties above and beyond the fire codes. Isn't that right, Steven?"

"Yes, Mama."

Their reactions were so bizarre: Deanna Nason had barely acknowledged the dramatic incineration of her own property. Her son meanwhile kept staring at it with the mesmerized look of a Neanderthal gazing into the first man-made fire he'd ever seen.

Pomerleau flipped through the rental agreement. "This is everything?"

"What else would there be?"

"Copies of their driver's licenses. Credit-report information. Canceled bank checks. All I see here is a four-page agreement signed by Rebecca Cobb and you, Mr. Nason." Pomerleau pointed the tip of her pen at Steven's sternum.

The mother interrupted, "We don't require that sort of personal information if the renters seem like good country people. And as for payment, many of our tenants use money orders, so there is no need to keep copies."

"I would think the IRS would require receipts," the detective said.

"Are you implying something about our business practices? Because we run an ethical business. If you want to speak with our accountants, I can give you their names."

Pomerleau drew a breath. "This agreement is dated almost a year ago. Is that how long the Cobbs have rented from you, or is this a renewal?"

"I have no idea," Deanna said. "Whatever is in the folder is in the folder."

"Do you remember, Mr. Nason?"

The slow-moving man said, "I don't remember. You should ask Chris."

The suggestion brought a flash of color to the mother's immovable cheeks. "Steven, let's not drag your brother into this, please."

"What can you tell us about the Cobbs?" Pomerleau asked with a patience I found saint-like. "Do you know where they work?"

"She said he's in the merchant marine," said Steven. "He's at sea most of the time."

"Is that why Mrs. Cobb's signature is the only one on the lease?"

"Must be."

It was hard to tell if Steven was stupid or being deliberately unhelpful or both.

"Did you ever meet Mr. Cobb?" asked Pomerleau.

Steven turned his unfocused eyes from the blaze to the cluster of emergency vehicles—fire trucks, police cruisers, and ambulances—in the road. "No, I never met him."

129

The breeze shifted and pushed a cloud of pine-scented smoke in our direction. Pomerleau suggested we retreat down the road to get out of the way of the firefighters.

"Can you describe what Mrs. Cobb looked like?" she asked Steven Nason when we'd gotten clear of the fumes.

"Skinny. Brown hair. Your height."

No mention of a crimson wig, I thought.

Pomerleau turned to the mother. "What about you, Mrs. Nason? Did you ever meet Mr. or Mrs. Cobb?"

"I certainly did not!"

"Did I say something to offend you, ma'am?"

Surgery had left Deanna Nason's face unable to show anger, but you could hear the building frustration in her voice. "You have to understand that we own dozens of buildings and have hundreds of tenants."

"But you admitted the possibility that the Cobbs rented from you before? Would your other son—Christopher, is it?—know if they had? You said he used to manage the business end of things."

"I don't understand what it has to do with Christopher."

Pomerleau could no longer contain her exasperation. She clicked her pen a few times in obvious frustration. "We're going to need to talk to him."

Deanna Nason's mask finally slipped, even if her expression remained static. "What the hell for? He's a lawyer down in Portland. He's busy! He doesn't have time for this bullshit."

"Mrs. Nason—"

"I'm not going to be sued for negligence! We're not to blame for this. We keep our buildings up to code. If two deadbeats forget to turn off the gas burners—"

Pomerleau cut her off. "I'm sure it's a stressful situation for you, not knowing if your tenants perished. I should have waited until later to start this conversation. In fact, I think we should continue back at my office. Can you call Christopher and have him meet us at the Troop B barracks in Gray?"

"Why are you trying to drag Chris into this? He just got that job as an associate. What will his bosses think? Are you trying to get him fired?"

"No, ma'am. Not at all. And I don't think the partners at his new firm would find it suspicious for him to answer a few questions about his family's tenants. Meanwhile the fire marshal can go about his investigation—"

"Investigation? I told you we're not at fault here!"

"It's the formal term for a review of the incident scene."

"We came out here to be helpful and because we were concerned about Frank and Rebecca."

A few minutes earlier, Deanna hadn't even known their names.

Once again, I found myself unable to keep my trap shut. "Do you know Eddie Fales, who owns Fales Variety?"

"That shitty place at the crossroads?" Deanna said. "I wouldn't set foot in there."

"What about you, Mr. Nason?"

Steven was staring absently at a group of police officers—Fryeburg cops and county deputies—standing idly by their vehicles. A big man in a blue uniform was telling a joke that must have been hilarious based on how hard the others were laughing.

"Mr. Nason?" I said again.

His half-bald head turned slowly. "What was the question?"

"Do you know Eddie Fales? I spoke with him this morning and he said you'd told him the house was unoccupied—that you were having trouble renting it."

Steven had the blank expression of a person being asked to solve an algebra problem in the original medieval Arabic.

"He must have been confused," he said at last. "I was talking about a different house."

"When was the last time you came out here?"

"Last winter?"

That was bullshit. The cedar shingles I had spotted at the rear of the building were new and hadn't even begun to weather.

"Do you remember another woman living here

132

at the time? Early twenties? Attractive? She might have been Mrs. Cobb's sister."

Steven Nason stared down at his mud-caked boots without answering.

His mother, however, eyed me up and down as if she were taking the measurements for my casket. "And who are you again?"

"This is Warden Bowditch," Pomerleau said.

"What is he getting at?" Deanna asked, as if I weren't present.

"It would be helpful to the fire marshal to know how many people were living here," I said.

Deanna Nason finally let her artificially green gaze range up the slope to the fire raining embers from the sky. "I suppose that makes sense." She glanced at her son. "Answer the warden, Steven."

"I don't remember a sister. Mama, don't you have an appointment at the beauty salon?"

His mother seemed as startled by his sudden mindfulness as we were. "Yes, I do. Thank you for reminding me, baby."

He jingled the keys in his rough palm. "Shouldn't we go?"

"If the police will allow us to leave," Deanna said.

"Thank you for coming over here so quickly," Pomerleau said. "Here is my business card. If you can think of anything else about the Cobbs, don't hesitate to call me."

Deanna Nason accepted the card as if someone

had sneezed on it. "I can't imagine we will. As I said, we have hundreds of tenants and can't be bothered to get to know them all personally."

"You should expect that the fire marshal will want to have an in-depth conversation about your building."

Deanna Nason's fake eyes flashed. "I have to say that I resent the implication that we are at all at fault for anything here. I can't understand why we are being made out to be the bad guys. It's not like we wanted this tragedy to happen."

"I'm sure you didn't," Pomerleau said, letting sarcasm creep into her voice for the first time.

"Then again, maybe this is a blessing in disguise," the mother said almost wistfully. "With the insurance we should be able to build something nicer here. Maybe a multitenant building. What do you think, baby?"

"We could charge more for rent," he said.

People think that predatory landlords are city-dwelling monsters, but the Nasons proved that they can flourish in the backwoods, as well.

I don't know how we held our tongues until the Nasons had returned to their SUV and driven back down the road.

Then Dani let one fly: "What a bitch!"

Pomerleau turned her pale eyes on the young trooper. "Come on, Tate. You know that's not right."

"For all we know, two or more people died

134

in that explosion, and all she cares about is the insurance settlement."

"You don't understand. I wasn't disagreeing with you. I meant that you weren't using the right word. A woman like that requires the proper adjective. Deanna Nason isn't a bitch. She's a *goddamn* bitch."

13

Because Birnam had no municipal water, tankers had to be brought in, one after the other, to feed the hoses. I saw the fire chief hurrying past. His face was smudged with creosote.

"So who *did* call the Nasons?" I asked Pomerleau after she returned from a brief consult with the Fryeburg police.

"Deanna and Steven must have at least one friend who's a cop. Hard as it is to believe."

"Those slumlords need a friend on the force to look the other way on their infractions," said Dani. "You *are* going to interview them again?"

"Of course I am, Tate," Pomerleau said. "But I want to see what I can find out about Frank and Rebecca Cobb first. Weird that no one has ever seen the husband. Don't you think?"

"It's weirder that Steven lied when he told Eddie Fales the house was unrented," I said.

"What did I tell you about going on hunches?" said Pomerleau. A sheen of perspiration that shimmered like baby oil was on her translucent skin. "Obviously there are a lot of things here that don't add up."

"Did the Fryeburg chief know anything about the Cobbs?" Tate asked.

Reflexively, I glanced over at the spot where the idle police officers were gathered. The huddle was breaking up. I saw the Fryeburg chief and one of his men—an enormous specimen of a police officer—climbing into a garish cruiser. The Fryeburg prowlers were dark blue with orange and red swooshes along the side: a paint job that better belonged on a stock car, in my opinion, than on a patrol vehicle.

"The Fryeburg cops don't get down this way as a rule," said Pomerleau. "I've got to call the Oxford County sheriff's department. There's got to be a deputy who patrols this road and has seen the Cobbs coming or going."

I glanced at my watch. The crystal was smeared with dirt. I needed to call Stacey before she heard about the explosion from someone else.

"So now what happens?" I asked.

"Now you follow me back to Gray to help make a sketch of the two women you saw. If they really did blow this house up, it would be nice to have more than a couple of aliases to go on."

"I should call my sergeant, let him know what I've been doing."

Pomerleau grinned as if she had decided she liked me after all. "He must be under the misapprehension that it was warden's work."

"He knows me better than that."

"What do you need me to do, ma'am?" asked Dani.

137

"I want you to knock on doors from here to the crossroads. See what the neighbors know about the Cobbs. Go back to Fales Variety and hang out there a while. Ask questions of the customers."

"What about Mrs. Fales?" I asked.

"I want to be the one who interviews her," the detective said, "since she seems to be one of three people to have actually seen Becky Cobb in the flesh. Steven Nason, Connie Fales, and our own Warden Bowditch."

Being on such a short list made me uncomfortable, I had to admit.

I drove back out to the main road to get clear of the emergency vehicles and the general chaos. Two Fryeburg police cruisers were parked in the lot of Fales Variety. No doubt the officers were helping themselves to free coffee.

What I would have given to stop there myself. But Pomerleau would have skinned me like a mink if I started asking questions before Tate had even arrived. I didn't want to risk losing the detective's newfound respect for my judgment.

On a whim I made a pit stop at the Knife Creek trailhead. It was quiet there in the green light of the pines. I rolled down my window and took a breath of balsam-scented air to clear the foulness of the house fire from my lungs.

Two mourning doves alighted in the parking

lot, their wings whistling as they settled to the ground. I watched them strut along like animate bobbleheads pecking here and there for who knew what.

I tried Stacey on my phone, but the call went directly to voice mail. "So you know that house I told you about on Rankin Road?" I said. "It kind of blew up. It was a propane explosion. But I'm OK! I wanted to tell you before you heard the news from someone else and started freaking out. How did things go this morning with Barstow? I love you, Stace."

After I hung up, I wanted to kick myself. *How did things go with Barstow?*

I had nearly died—again—and instead of sharing anything real about my experience with the woman I loved, I had shrugged it off. Then I'd asked a perfunctory question about her job. Had I wanted her to be furious with me?

On the other hand, my question might have been perfunctory, but my concern for Stacey was sincere.

In Maine government, as in most bureaucracies, it is remarkably difficult for supervisors to fire a problem employee who is a member of the state union. In my early days as a game warden I had stretched the limits of acceptable conduct so far I'd begun to wonder if they were made of rubber. But if anyone could contrive to get himself or herself canned from the Department

139

of Inland Fisheries and Wildlife, it was the one and only Stacey Stevens.

The state police have three Major Crimes units. The southern division is housed at the Troop B barracks in the town of Gray. The building—a tidy structure as blue as a robin's egg—is within a stone's throw of our own Warden Service division headquarters. I thought of stopping in at HQ but didn't want to risk running into my officious sergeant.

I could always argue that Pomerleau had commanded my presence in her office to investigate a potential homicide. It would be hard for my superiors to fault me for that.

At the barracks door, I pushed a button and gave my name to a disembodied woman's voice that issued from an intercom. A moment later a buzzer sounded and an electronic lock opened. The door was heavy enough to have stopped a runaway cement truck.

"Detective Pomerleau wants you to go right to her office," said the receptionist.

The building was small enough that I had no trouble finding my way. When I got to Pomerleau's office, I understood why she hadn't come out to the lobby to meet me. She was seated behind her desk with a smile so wide I could see the amalgam fillings in her back molars. She'd switched her phone to speaker mode, and a man's electronically amplified voice was broadcasting from the console. She motioned for me to take a seat.

"You need to understand my brother," said the man on the phone. "You've heard of the spectrum, right?"

"I am familiar with autism, Mr. Nason." Pomerleau added the name for my benefit.

"Then you realize he processes information differently from you and me. You're attributing evasiveness to him because he couldn't describe one of our tenants. What you need to understand is that Stevie doesn't 'see' faces at all. I grew a beard once in college, and when I came home, he didn't even recognize me."

Pomerleau leaned forward and swung her computer monitor around on its stand so that I could see the screen. She'd pulled up the Web site of a Portland law office and opened the page dedicated to associates. Beside a brief column of biographical text was a photograph of a pudgy, thirtysomething man in a charcoal suit and burgundy tie. His black hair was in full retreat from his forehead. And he had a grin that would have scared a small child.

"What about your mother?" asked Pomerleau sharply. "Is she on the autism spectrum, too?"

"That comment is unprofessional. And I resent it."

"She didn't do much this morning to ingratiate

herself to us. For all we know, there might be bits of charred bodies in what's left of your rental house. Your mother acted as if the explosion was a business opportunity to build anew."

"I know Mama can come across as graceless. What you need to understand is that many of the people who rent from us—they're not paragons of virtue, all right? You and I both know that. But we provide them with an affordable place to live. Look, I know we could do better about alerting you to illegal activities we suspect might be taking place on our properties."

"I am going to stop you there," said the detective. "At the moment, I really don't give a crap about the drug dealing and prostitution taking place in your units. All I care about is finding the identity of a dead baby we discovered buried a quarter mile from your former rental house."

"Are you talking about the girl in the paper?"

"I am."

"I thought you were investigating the explosion this morning."

"No, sir. The fire marshal is handling that investigation. I am trying to find out who left a dead infant to be devoured by wild pigs."

"And you think there's a connection to the fire? And that the Cobbs might be involved?"

Pomerleau held a finger to her lips for me to

remain quiet. She didn't speak a word of response to Christopher Nason.

"Detective?" he said at last. "Detective, are you there?"

She sat quietly for a few seconds more, then said, "Mr. Nason, I apologize, but I have the marshal on the other line, and I really need to take the call. Can I get back to you in a few minutes?"

"Yes, of course. But what you really need to understand is—"

"We'll talk soon."

She hit the end button on her console and leaned back again in her chair.

"Are you sure that was a good idea?" I said.

"Giving the Nasons added incentive to provide us with whatever information they're withholding? I guess we'll find out soon enough."

14

No matter the building or the decade when it was constructed, law enforcement offices—at least in Maine—have a certain sameness. These elements are nearly universal constants: fluorescent lights that drain the color from every face, out-of-date computers humming because their internal fans never stop, government-issued posters and notices on the walls that no one actually ever reads, lingering smells of fast food hurriedly eaten at desks.

During Pomerleau's conversation with Chris Nason, I'd had a chance to study the room, looking for personal items that might help me understand her better. I saw a framed certificate issued by the FBI showing that she'd completed a course at Quantico. Also a beefcake fireman-of-the-month calendar that must have been a gag gift from her superiors because there was no way the office HR person would otherwise have permitted it to remain tacked to the wall. Lastly, there were two portraits on her desk: of a boy, who looked to be eight, and a girl, who looked to be four. The kids had caramel-colored skin that suggested Pomerleau—who was whiter than a ghost—and her husband might be of different races. I was fairly certain that they hadn't adopted the children since the first time I'd heard her name had been when she was on maternity leave and unable to work a case that involved me: a motorist had vanished after hitting a deer.

"Any hits on the Cobbs?" I asked.

"Not a one."

"What? They didn't even get gas at Fales Variety?"

"The Fales said they've had some people use stolen debit cards to buy gas before the cards were reported missing. We have a call in with their merchant processor. There might be something there."

"I don't suppose the fire marshal has had a chance to begin searching for bodies."

"Not yet. Which means we need to proceed with the idea that the Cobbs are still alive."

"Except no one has ever seen Frank Cobb, as far as we know."

"So let's start with his wife, then." Pomerleau removed her ballpoint from her blotter and began clicking it. "Tell me about her. Tell me about Becky."

"I thought we were going to do a sketch on the Identikit."

"We will. But right now, I'd like you to describe the encounter you had with her last night. What did you say to her? What did she say to you?"

I closed my eyes to bring back Becky's hard

face. I saw her keen eyes and her pointy chin. In my imagination her raggedy lips began to move.

"She said, 'What do you want?' "

"And what did you say?"

"I asked about the pigs."

It took me half an hour to summarize a conversation that had lasted all of a few minutes. Pomerleau didn't let anything slide; as far as she was concerned, no detail was unimportant. The process was trying, but it made me respect her even more as an investigator.

She tapped the pen against her teeth. "So this second, younger woman, Becky's so-called sister—she didn't speak at all?"

"Not a word."

"But you said she looked familiar. You think you might have met her before?"

"Not exactly. It's more like I saw her picture."

Pomerleau's screen saver had come up on her monitor while she'd been interviewing me. More photos of her children. The detective smiled as the images flashed before us. "And a picture is worth a thousand words."

"What are their names?" I asked.

"My kids? Isaiah and Imani."

"They're good-looking."

"They got their looks from their dad. Fortunately, they got their brains from me. You don't have children, do you, Bowditch?"

"None that I know about."

Her face went blank.

"That was a joke."

The detective raised her whitish eyebrows and pulled her computer keyboard out from the hidden shelf under her desk. "And on that note, we shall turn to the Identikit." Police used to employ actual artists to help witnesses create a likeness of a suspect (and some departments still did). Later, they moved to a system that was closer to a children's game. The witness would reconstruct a face using strips of preprinted paper that displayed a panoply of features—all manner of eyes, ears, chins, cheekbones, moles, eyeglasses, and facial hair—overlaid atop an oval shape. But as with everything else these days, computers had taken over from print. The current Identikit programs were so comprehensive they let you add facial jewelry and headwear to your composite. Not only could you decorate your purse snatcher with a do rag, you could choose the color and the pattern.

Pomerleau had planned to ask me questions about the women's faces and then call up options on the screen for me to approve or discard, but it quickly became apparent that it would be easier if I simply took her place behind the keyboard and mouse.

"Start with Becky," she said. "The way you described her, she sounds like someone who might've had a run-in with the criminal justice system before."

That was the ultimate value of Identikits in the modern world. Police had formerly used sketches to create wanted posters and mug books. Now we made images that could be scanned with facial-recognition software and matched against the photographs of thousands of missing persons and convicted criminals.

I have a decent memory for faces, as I said, but when you have a program capable of re-creating the physiognomy of any human being on the planet, the options become so overwhelming as to make you begin second-guessing every detail.

Eventually, I had an image that fairly well matched my memory of the hostile woman— right down to her crimson bangs. I tilted back in my chair to study the portrait, then showed it to Pomerleau. "I don't suppose you recognize her?"

"I think I would remember that devilish little chin."

The detective moved me aside so that she could upload the odd-looking facial collage to a database. She also printed a handful of copies to circulate around the barracks.

"You want to take a pee-pee break?" she asked.

"Is that how you talk to your kids?"

"It's how I talk to their father."

I stood up and stretched my arms. Being thrown to the ground by the explosion had done a number on my back and leg muscles. Sitting for an extended period had made them tighten up. I felt as stiff as I had on the mornings after high-school football games.

I followed Pomerleau's directions to the rest-room. It was my first chance since the morning to check myself out in a real mirror. I still had faint smudges at the corners of my mouth and beneath my nose from having breathed in smoke. When I glanced over my shoulder into the glass, I could see the singed hairs on my neck and the black-edged hole in the fabric of my ballistic vest. I cleaned up as best I could, then stepped back into the hall to check my phone.

I had a voice mail from Stacey: "You almost got blown up? Jesus, Mike! How do these things keep happening to you? And why didn't you call me immediately? You are such a . . . man. Well, thank God, you're all right. When I think about what might have happened—"

Pomerleau emerged from a break room with two bottles of Poland Spring water and two bags of salt-and-vinegar potato chips. "Ready?"

I would listen to the rest of Stacey's message later. "Yeah."

We settled back into our office chairs and opened our bags of potent-smelling chips.

"Have you heard anything from the medical examiner? Anything about the baby?"

Some detectives would have chosen to watch

the autopsy in person, but not Pomerleau. "You know Kitteridge. It's always a few days before Walt issues a report."

"In my experience, he's pretty loosey-goosey when it comes to speculating about cause of death."

Pomerleau grinned as if I'd just solved the riddle of the Sphinx. "Kitteridge had his anthropologist take a look, and they're certain it wasn't a stillbirth. She was about two weeks old when she died. Walt says it's too soon to determine cause of death, though."

"What about DNA results?"

"It always takes longer than you'd like." Pomerleau licked the grease from her fingers. "Let's have a look at the little sister."

We got back to work on the Identikit.

As I should have expected, the second face was more difficult to reconstruct than the first. I'd only glimpsed the younger woman twice and both times from a distance. Her eyes had been large, brown, and widely spaced. And she had that distinctive beauty mole on her cheek. Her lips were unusual, too. There was a term for their shape. What was it? A cupid's bow?

Piecing her features together made me realize what a pretty girl she was. Once again, I had that itchy feeling of having seen her before.

The image on the screen in front of me still wasn't right. It had a vague, anonymous quality that brought out the frustrated artist in me. Her face was full—she almost had a double chin but not quite—and there were sickly shadows under her eyes. She had heavy eyebrows, I remembered. Most girls her age plucked them down to delicate shapes, but hers were lush.

The last thing I did was to add the wig.

Pomerleau stood over my shoulder. She rested a hand absently on the back of my chair. She didn't speak, but after a few seconds I felt her grip begin to tighten. The plastic actually creaked.

"What?"

"Holy—"

"You recognize her?"

Without a word she disappeared down the hall.

While she was gone, I studied the image I had created. The sensation of having an elusive name at the tip of my tongue was stronger than ever, so much so that I began to doubt the girl I had made. Was she the actual person I had glimpsed or a model I'd seen in a magazine ad?

A minute later Pomerleau returned with a detective I'd never met. He had ginger hair and a cleft in his jaw that looked as if it had been left by a tomahawk. She introduced him only as Finch.

"What do you think?" Pomerleau's tone was pitched higher than I'd ever heard it. "It's her, isn't it? It's got to be."

Finch massaged his freckled chin. "Can you lose the wig?"

I removed the hair; for an instant, she was as bald as a Hare Krishna.

"Try her with dark hair—"

"Brown or black?"

Pomerleau broke in, "Black. Straight. Shoulder length."

I followed her instructions. Felt the two investigators go rigid behind me.

"Holy shit," said Pomerleau.

"What?" I said.

"The eyebrows are wrong," the male detective said, but without conviction, "and the face is too fat."

"That's her, Finch! Tell me it isn't her!"

"Isn't who?" I asked.

Ellen Pomerleau's eyes were filled with awe and fear. "A girl who died four years ago."

15

Finch folded his arms across his muscular chest. "I don't see it."

Pomerleau seemed ready to leap out of her skin. "How can you not see it?"

"It's not her, Ellen."

I swiveled around in the chair. "Not who?"

But Pomerleau's attention was fixed on her partner. "Tell me this isn't Cascy Donaldson."

And in that moment I realized why her face had looked so familiar.

Everyone in Maine knew the story of Casey Donaldson, who had disappeared on a rafting trip down the Saco River four years earlier: the college girl who had vanished in a thunderstorm under the most mysterious of circumstances and was assumed—after months of fruitless searching—to have been murdered; her body hidden somewhere far from where her friends had last seen her.

"I thought Casey Donaldson was dead."

"She is," said Finch.

"But what if she isn't?" said Pomerleau. "What if she's been alive all this time?"

Most of my friends in the Warden Service had taken part in the search. My former sergeant Kathy Frost had headed up the K9 teams that

153

roamed the banks for miles and even rode along in canoes, scenting the air for some trace of the missing girl. I alone seemed to have been excluded from the operation.

That year, I had been stationed 250 miles away in Down East Maine. During the previous winter, my career had reached its deepest, darkest bottom, and I was fighting every day to claw my way back into the sunlight. While most every warden I knew had done shifts searching for Casey, I'd been left to my daily duties, most of which involved driving long patrols while I brooded on the disaster that was my life.

I had seen pictures and videos of the missing girl, but she had remained as remote to me as a celebrity I knew only from television or movies, not so much a real person but a projection of one. Which was why I'd had such trouble recognizing her as Becky's dead-eyed "sister." If only I had paid closer attention to the story of her disappearance. Then again, self-absorption had always been my original sin.

"We need to tell Barrett," Pomerleau said.

"Tell him what exactly?" her partner asked, his face beginning to redden. "That the warden says he saw someone who looked like Casey Donaldson. What do you think the lieutenant is going to say to that? You know what he'll say, that it's one hell of a coincidence."

The two detectives were so intent on their

argument that they paid no attention as I leaned over the keyboard and opened the Web browser. I typed *Casey Donaldson* into the search field, and immediately a grid of images flashed onto the computer screen. I clicked on the first file.

The photograph showed an attractive black-haired girl with wide-set eyes and a mole on her cheek. Tan and athletic, she looked to be the picture of health. I opened a new window with the Identikit sketch side by side with the photo.

"That's her." I pointed at the illustration. "That's Casey Donaldson."

"There might be a resemblance," said Finch. "But that doesn't prove anything. All we're going on here is a game warden's unreliable memory."

"Thanks."

"No offense, Bowditch, but you know how worthless eyewitness identifications are. What were the results of that famous study? Seventy-something percent of all convictions overturned by DNA testing were originally made based on faulty witness testimony. Even cops have been shown to reconstruct their memories if they're biased toward a suspect."

"How can I be biased? I wasn't even part of the search for her."

"Yeah," Finch said, "but you've seen her picture before."

"I thought she was dead, too. Why would I

claim to have seen a woman who I assumed was murdered?"

The ginger-haired man shook his head. "I'm not going to delve into possible motivations you might have."

Pomerleau let out a burst of air from her nostrils. "We need to bring in Barrett and show him this, Finch. It's not for you or me to decide how this goes forward."

Finch glanced at his wristwatch. "Well, he won't be back for a half hour. He's at the meeting in Portland." Finch's face turned even redder. "Oh, shit, I just thought of something."

"What?" asked Pomerleau.

"Menario."

"Oh, shit."

"What if he finds out about this, Ellen? How do you think he'll react? Casey Donaldson was his case."

"His obsession, you mean."

"Wait a minute," I said. "Are you guys talking about Tony Menario?"

Neither of them seemed to hear me.

Maine State Police detective Antonio Menario was an old adversary of mine. He'd investigated two murder cases I'd been involved with early in my career where my methods had been called into question. Even though I'd been cleared of misconduct both times, he'd always seemed to look at me with the anger of a bull facing a red cape. But I had heard Menario had retired—or been forced to retire. The accounts of his departure from the force were unclear.

"Tony can't find out about this," Pomerleau said. "Not until we're sure."

"And when will that be?" asked her partner.

"When the DNA results come back."

"If they're conclusive, you mean. I'm going to go grab a sandwich before Barrett gets back. You want anything?"

"No thanks."

I massaged my bristly burned neck. "I'm telling you the woman I saw is Casey Donaldson. Let me talk to your lieutenant, and I can convince him. I'm even willing to talk to Tony Menario if you want."

The suggestion seemed to horrify Finch. "You do that and we'll have a repeat of the Dakota Rowe incident."

"Who's Dakota Rowe?"

"I know this is confusing," said Pomerleau. "It sounds like we have half an hour before Barrett gets back. Let's go outside, and I'll explain what happened—what wasn't made public during the search for Casey. At this point, I could use some fresh air."

There was a picnic table at the end of the building, in the shade of some red pines that gave a resinous aroma to the yard. Pomerleau and I sat

157

across from each other. The ground beneath our feet consisted almost entirely of sand, with a few wispy blades of grass drying in the sun.

"Casey Donaldson was a student at the University of New Hampshire when she died," the detective began. "Or maybe I should say when she was presumed to have died. She lived in Westbrook with her stepfather. He's a plumber. Her mom had died in a car crash when she was ten or eleven."

"I know the story, Pomerleau."

She shook her head so violently that a strand of ivory hair came loose. "Not all of it. Do you want to hear what really happened or not?"

"I do."

She began again. "The summer before Casey's senior year—four years ago this month—she decided to go rafting on the Saco River with some friends. You know what a party scene that is. Thousands of drunk and drugged-out kids canoeing and float-tubing for miles together. Camping out on the sandbanks. When I was a trooper, the same age as Tate, I used to get at least one call a night during bikini season—sexual assaults, regular assaults, lewd conduct, theft, vandalism, overdoses, at least one drowning every summer. July and August were two months of nonstop hell. But no homicides, though. At least not while I was patrolling that area."

I let her continue.

"You know that section of the Saco? From New Hampshire down to Great Falls in Hiram? I don't know how many miles it is, but it's got to be the most confusing river in New England. It's this maze of channels and oxbow lakes and horseshoe ponds. Not to mention you've got the Brownfield Bog in the middle of it all, which is like a labyrinth made of water.

"There was another girl and three guys on the trip. None of them from Maine, as far as I remember. Or maybe one of them was. It wasn't my case, either. I was still on maternity leave.

"What happened was that Casey and her friends had rafted up their canoes—tied them together to make them stable enough to stand up in. I've seen a few of those rafts with platforms that look like Thanksgiving Day parade floats. Or maybe Mardi Gras is the better example.

"So they're floating along on the third morning of their trip, letting the current carry them, when Casey realizes she's lost her dead mom's engagement ring. She freaks out—and this is where I think intoxicating substances played a role—and she starts raving about how she must've left it back at the sandbar where they camped the night before. Oxbow Island. The only problem is that it's three or four miles back upstream, and right in the middle of the marshes, so it wasn't like they could just drive back later to look for it.

"Anyway, Casey announces that she's going to take one of the canoes and paddle back to search for the ring. The problem is that none of her friends are in any shape to go with her. They want to because they're worried about her safety, but the guys are majorly hungover, puking in the river, and the other girl has tennis elbow or something and can't really paddle.

"They're all arguing about what to do when a 'Good Samaritan' comes along. His name is Dakota Rowe. He's a local boy they met at Hodge's Campground their first night on the river. Rowe was working for the Hodgkinses that summer. Casey's girlfriend says he was hitting on them both pretty hard when he came to check their campfire. 'He seemed harmless,' she said. But she was surprised to find him following them in a beat-up kayak.

"So anyhow, Rowe agrees to go with Casey. He stashes his kayak in a 'secret place' in some bushes, and the two of them set off upstream. Later, her friends claim they all had a bad feeling about this guy, but evidently, it wasn't bad enough to keep them from letting Casey paddle off alone with him.

"The friends decide to pull their canoes out of the water to wait. An hour passes. Then another hour. They notice black clouds on the horizon. Pretty soon, they're hearing thunder. The National Weather Service issued a report afterward that said it was a severe storm with sixty-mile-per-hour gusts and multiple lightning strikes: nothing you'd want to be outdoors in.

"So Casey's friends are all scared shitless and sobering up fast, and they decide to call 911. Of course everyone else on the river that day was doing the same thing. I know some of the camp-grounds and rental companies sent out boats to help their customers get off the water and find shelter. The Fryeburg police sent out patrols along the side roads to do the same.

"The storm passes after a couple of hours, and it doesn't look like anyone was electrocuted or drowned. But Casey's friends are more panicked than ever because now it's getting dark. They try to convince the Warden Service to send an airboat, but the wardens don't want to go on a wild-goose chase at night. 'Those two are prob-ably just curled up somewhere waiting for it to get light' is what they're told.

"The next morning, though, a couple of wardens show up at the landing and talk to the UNH kids. Casey's friends convince them to take an airboat up the river to Oxbow Island. Halfway there, what do they find? Casey's canoe stuck in some alders and half-full of water. So now they have two missing persons to locate—Casey and the Good Samaritan.

"The Warden Service sends in a second airboat, and pretty soon it's like the Everglades in there, with airboats roaring up and down the channels. The Forest Service is about to send over a helicopter. There's a massive search under way when guess what happens?"

I couldn't hazard a guess.

"Dakota Rowe strolls into work at Hodge's Campground for his evening shift as if nothing has happened and no one is searching for him. The Hodgkinses call 911, of course. The wardens show up, and the Fryeburg police send a couple of officers to get Rowe's statement.

"He claims that he and Casey paddled easily back up to Oxbow and she found her mom's diamond ring after about an hour of searching. They decide to turn around and go back downstream when the storm hits. According to Rowe, he suggests that they pull off at a path he knows that leads back to the main road because it's not safe to be out on the water during an electrical storm. But he says Casey is acting all weird—like she doesn't trust him—and wants to keep paddling. He says, 'Fine, good luck,' and has her drop him at the trail. And that was the last he saw of her, he says. His story is that he hitchhiked home and spent the night alone.

"Of course, the wardens want him to point out where this all happened, so they take him out on an airboat and he shows them Oxbow Island and the path where he claims Casey dropped him. But there's still no sign of her anywhere. Meanwhile, the Fryeburg cops are calling in the state police. One of their officers knows Rowe from having busted him on some juvenile stuff, and they all think the kid's story sounds fishy.

"Menario is the detective who gets the case, and right away he has suspicions about Rowe. He talks to Casey's friends and gets their take on the guy as a creep. Then he talks to the campground owners. They have nothing good to say about him, it turns out. Pretty much they accuse him of taking the kayak without their approval.

"By now, another wave of storms is coming through, so the wardens decide to postpone the search until the next morning. At this point, people are still hopeful that they'll find Casey hunkered down somewhere in the swamp. But Menario isn't so optimistic. He's already begun to form this hypothesis in his head. He has a hunch that Dakota Rowe killed Casey and hid her body somewhere.

"When the airboat gets back, Menario takes Rowe aside and starts grilling him. He asks the kid why he didn't stay with the girl if she was in danger, and Rowe says because he wasn't going to risk his life for some hysterical bitch he just met. Menario asks him why he didn't at least want to fetch his kayak, and Rowe has an answer for that, too. He says he planned on driving back later to pick it up, that he didn't figure anybody would find or steal it in a thunderstorm.

"That's when Menario plays his trump card. He asks Rowe again about what happened when they first got to Oxbow Island, how long the two of them were there together, where they found the missing ring, et cetera. He lets Rowe repeat his complete statement and then he says, 'I have proof that you're lying, Dakota.' And he pulls something out of his pocket. You'll never guess what it is?"

Pomerleau had planned on answering the question herself, but there was no need.

I had already figured it out: "A diamond ring."

16

Pomerleau couldn't hide her surprise. "How did you know? That information was never made public."

"I just had a hunch."

She let out a big guffaw that made me like her even more. "Touché."

"Where did Menario find the ring?"

"Casey's friend Noah gave it to him. It dropped out of a tarp in his canoe, and he was too embarrassed to tell anyone while the search was in progress. Menario swore the kid to silence, saying it would be the only way to secure a murder conviction since it was definitive proof that Rowe was lying about what happened."

An ant, foraging for crumbs, crawled across my hand. I shook it off. "And what did Rowe say when Menario showed him the ring?"

"He said Casey told him she'd found it. He had no idea why she would have lied. Maybe she was tired of his company. Menario told him he's been caught in a lie and had better come clean. That was a mistake, threatening him that way. The kid comes from a wealthy family. Lake cottage on Kezar Lake. Ski condo at Widowmaker. The Rowes, as it happens, have lots and lots of attorneys. He told Menario he wouldn't say another word until he saw one of them."

Anthills were everywhere in the soil beneath the table. I watched the tireless insects scurrying into the mounds with bits of food and then emerging with sand pebbles they'd excavated from some new tunnel. Something about their purposefulness was mesmerizing.

"Here's what I don't understand," I said. "How was Casey pronounced dead if they never found her body? I thought it takes seven years for a missing person to receive a death certificate in absentia."

Pomerleau applied a coating of zinc to her lips. The white lipstick made her look like a lifeguard. "Seven years is how long it takes for the presumption of death to be triggered. But it doesn't have to take that long. If there's a preponderance of evidence that leads the state to believe a missing person is deceased, the process can take as little as four years, which is how long it's been since Casey vanished. Menario has been waiting a long time to see homicide charges brought against Dakota Rowe, and it's about to happen very soon."

"Wait a minute. I thought you said Menario had retired."

"Let's just say he was encouraged to retire."

"What did he do?"

"He had a dustup with Rowe last year. The

colonel gave Menario the option to 'retire' instead of losing an appeal to the disciplinary committee."

"But you're saying he's still got a hard-on for the case."

"You've met Menario. The man is a walking hard-on. Before he retired, he arranged with his buddies in the AG's office for the arrest and indictment to go forward as soon as the state issues a death certificate for Casey Donaldson."

In my time, I'd met a few retired officers like Menario who walked out of their retirement parties with gold watches and boxes full of case files they'd never been able to close. Being retired, they had all the time in the world to chase loose ends. Some of these obsessed ex-cops made Captain Ahab look easygoing by comparison.

One of the ants was exploring the hairs of my forearm. This time, I let it roam.

"So the state hasn't declared Casey dead yet?"

"Legally speaking, she is still alive."

"Legally and actually."

Pomerleau let out a sigh. "Until we have physical evidence that your woman in a wig was Casey, we're going to have trouble convincing Barrett to open a new investigation. No disrespect, but the face you drew could be any one of a thousand women in this state. Haven't you ever run into someone who could be your doppelgänger?"

"You said *we*. Does that mean you believe me?"

"I know more about you than I've let on, Bowditch. Lots of people still think of you as the idiot rookie who almost let a cop killer escape. But your record of success since then is, well, pretty mind-blowing. But you made a bad first impression in the law-enforcement community that you might never outlive. You're like the Boy Who Cried Wolf."

"Only the wolf was my father."

"Honestly, I'm not sure what to hope for here. If you're wrong, we still have to find that infant's parents, which won't be easy, but it will be just another shitty case. But if you're right . . ."

Pomerleau didn't need to finish the sentence for me to grasp the ramifications of Casey Donaldson's having been alive all this time.

Since she had seemingly been a happy girl who would never have run off on her own, then the only conclusion one could logically draw was that she had been kidnapped and left for dead by Maine's finest. To be held captive while the world forgot about you; to be forced to give birth to a child and then watch it perish or be murdered; and then to stand by while your dead daughter is buried in the mud for pigs to eat—it was hard for me to imagine a worse nightmare.

I could taste the vinegar from the potato chips in my stomach coming up as acid in my throat. "Is Donaldson's DNA in CODIS?"

The acronym stood for Combined DNA Index System. It is the national database in which are stored the genetic markers of millions of suspected and convicted criminals, victims of crimes living and dead, missing persons, their family members, and probably many other unsuspecting Americans. The armed forces have a separate database for their 3 million members, nicknamed the Repository, whose stated reason for being is to assist in combat-death identifications, but only a naïf would believe it couldn't be covertly accessed by top-level law-enforcement agents in high-profile cases.

"I would think her DNA would have to be in the system," Pomerleau said. "Menario would have gotten hair samples."

"Then crime-lab analysts will be able to compare her DNA against that of Baby Jane Doe."

"They will."

"Casey Donaldson was the mother of that infant, Pomerleau. And there's no doubt in my mind that she's still alive somewhere, still waiting to be rescued."

Pomerleau sat up on the bench as an unmarked cruiser pulled into the lot. "There's Barrett. I'm not looking forward to the conversation we're about to have."

"Do you think he'll believe me?"

"I'm not sure I would."

We had to wait fifteen minutes before the lieutenant would see us. Then Pomerleau, Finch, and I walked in a solemn procession to his meticulously maintained office.

Barrett had a runner's build, thinning salt-and-pepper hair, and a no-nonsense demeanor. Framed photos of him in a U.S. Navy flight suit were on the wall.

Pomerleau went first, laying out the elements of the case, then asked me to take over. Barrett listened without interruption, examined the photograph of Casey Donaldson and compared it side by side with the Identikit sketch, then sent me out of the room while he conferred with his detectives.

He didn't ask me a single question. I found that ominous.

While I was waiting back in Pomerleau's office, my phone rang. It was Ricky Elwell.

"So I got your pork all butchered and wrapped up nice. You want me to throw it in the freezer or you want to pick it up today?"

A random thought thrust its way into my mind. The butcher boy seemed to be one of those connectors you find in all social networks: those uncanny people with the gift of knowing just about everyone. Ricky was a greasy-haired spider sitting at the center of a vast web that extended across the Saco River floodplain.

"I'll come pick it up. Tell me something, Rick. Do you happen to know anything about a girl named Casey Donaldson?"

"That college chick who disappeared? Dude, everyone knows that story."

I suspected that Ricky Elwell might know a few details others did not. "How long are you going to be there this afternoon?"

"Well, I got an appointment to get my nails done and my balls waxed at four. Otherwise my social calendar is wide-open."

"You aren't old enough to have hair on your balls, Rick."

"Dude, that is cold!"

After fifteen minutes, Pomerleau returned to her office. Now that we were back inside, she had removed the sunscreen from her lips, although white traces still showed at the corners.

"Well?"

"The lieutenant wants to wait for the DNA results. Also for the fire marshal's initial findings."

"So he didn't believe me?"

"Let's say he's withholding judgment."

"What about circulating my sketches at least? Someone might have seen Becky and Casey recently, especially if they're on the run. We don't even need to identify the younger sister. We can just share the drawings."

"The lieutenant doesn't want to open up a can of worms unnecessarily. What happens if other people notice the resemblance? What if Casey's stepfather does?"

I stood up. "This is bullshit."

"Think of it from Barrett's perspective."

What had I expected? I was the only witness to an occurrence so improbable that it belonged on the cover of a supermarket tabloid, right beside a picture of President Trump shaking hands with a gray-skinned alien in the Oval Office.

There was nothing to do now but go fetch my hog meat from Ricky Elwell.

I paused in the doorway to offer a final observation. "The fire marshal isn't going to find Casey's remains in what's left of that house. Whoever burned that place down took her with them. The girl is still alive and still being held captive. You know in your heart that I am right about this, Detective."

"I'll give you a call when I hear something."

When I left, Pomerleau was staring at the framed photograph of her own still-innocent daughter.

17

As usual, a crowd was hanging around the Elwell homestead. That butcher shop was the boondocks equivalent of a Boys & Girls Club.

I hauled my personal YETI Tundra out of the backseat and carried it into the darkened barn. I'd found I couldn't leave an expensive cooler in the bed of the truck without someone stealing it. I could probably have left a five-thousand-dollar computer back there and no one would have run off with it. But rednecks, I'd found, have a special fondness for coolers.

Ricky was seated on a butcher-block table, waving around an Old Gold and swinging his short legs as he held forth to a semicircle of acolytes. "Now, the thing about a bear is that it has this bone in its johnson. About as long as a pencil and just as thin. Same with a raccoon, but a coon's is smaller and shaped like a *J*. My old man had a jar of dick bones. He said the orientals ground them up into powder to put in their tea so they could stay hard all night long. Now, I ain't never tried bone dust because I never needed the help, but— Hello, Warden Bowditch!"

"You know, Ricky, there's a law against lewd conduct."

"I'm educating these kids to the facts of life."

"You should leave the sex ed to their teachers."

He thrust the lit end of his cigarette at me. "Those dried-up old prunes don't know half of what I know."

"How about ending the lesson for today and getting my pork chops."

"Do you got the money?"

"I do."

"OK, then. But you're going to need more than that cooler. There's a whole lot of pork in them fridges."

Ricky wasn't kidding. Before it had been dressed, the boar had weighed in at 222 pounds. Once Ricky had skinned it and removed the innards, it had tipped the scales at 180 pounds. After butchering, we were left with 160 pounds of shoulders, loins, belly, and hams. And that didn't even include the sow.

"I even threw in the pig's feet in case you want to pickle them. I always give my customers maximum meat so they don't feel like I'm ripping them off. With a pig, butchers say, the only thing you should lose is the squeal." The joke cracked him up and he fell into another hacking fit.

I pointed at the smoldering Old Gold clenched between his fingers. "You know those are called coffin nails for a reason?"

"Shit, dude. You sound like my mom."

For all his adolescent chatter, Ricky Elwell was a remarkably talented and thoughtful butcher. He had insulated shipping boxes loaded with the meat and packed with ice for me. Every individual package had been sealed and labeled. He even presented me with a surprisingly detailed receipt.

I wrote him a personal check rather than go through the hassle of making him wait for the state. Special reimbursement requests moved through the system like sap through a half-frozen maple. God only knew when I'd get my money back.

With the help of his entourage, we loaded the boxes into the bed of my truck.

"Hey, Rick," I said. "You remember how I mentioned Casey Donaldson before?"

"That girl who vanished? Did you guys find her skeleton or something?"

Knowing how the kid could gossip, I chose to play it coy. "I'm not allowed to say. What did you hear happened to her?"

"Cops say Dakota Rowe killed her." In true Maine fashion, Ricky pronounced the name "decoder."

"What can you tell me about him?"

The butcher dropped his cigarette butt onto the floor and reached into his shirt pocket for the pack. "Guy's a piece of shit. Rich as hell but likes to come across as a badass. He gets off on people being afraid of him. You want to hear a story—off the record?"

"You know I do."

"His folks have a cottage over on Kezar Lake. Someone on the other side had a dog that kept barking all night. So rumor has it, Dakota goes over there and scatters Raisinets up and down the road. I don't know how many dogs got sick or died from eating them. All to shut up one yappy schnauzer."

Chocolates can sicken dogs. Raisins can cause kidney failure. "Do you know where I can find him?"

"First off, I wouldn't go looking! But if you do, he still works at Hodge's in the summer."

"Even after what happened with Casey Donaldson?"

"The Hodgkinses are afraid to fire him because they think he'll poison their well."

"Why does the guy even work? I thought he was rich?"

"Yeah, but that river is a nonstop pussy parade in the summer—if you know what I mean." Ricky knocked a loose cigarette onto his palm and brought it to his lips. "Do me a favor if you run into Dakota and don't mention my name. I don't need trouble from that cock-sucker."

"I know, Rick. You're a lover, not a fighter."

He brightened up. "You got me pegged there."

"One more question before I go."

"Why are you asking me all these questions? I ain't Jimmy Neutron, Boy Genius."

"But you always know something we don't. Don't you?"

He smiled. "Pegged again!"

"You wouldn't know a couple named the Cobbs, would you? They live over on Rankin Road in Birnam. The wife has a pointy chin."

"They the ones whose crib burned down? Yeah, I heard about that explosion." He raised his eyes to the hazy summer sky and sucked speculatively on his cigarette. "No, I never heard of those people."

"Thanks, Rick. For everything."

"No sweat, Warden. Like my old man used to say, 'Service is our success.' "

I had forgotten about the kid's missing finger until we shook hands. Then I watched Ricky Elwell—all five feet two inches and 120 pounds of him—swagger back into the darkness of the barn, pants sagging below his waist, trailing a plume of smoke.

My plan was to store the meat in my freezer at home until we'd gotten a sample back from the lab saying it was safe for human consumption. Then I would distribute it to the food pantries throughout my district. I'd eaten wild boar at a fancy restaurant with my mother and stepfather and remembered it tasting juicy and succulent, almost like a cross between pork and beef, but at twice the price. The needy people who got first dibs on these chops and hams were going to be enjoying a rare delicacy indeed.

I found Stacey on the back patio, barefoot, and dressed in shorts and a MISS CONGENIALITY T-shirt that showed off both her sense of irony and her awareness of how she was viewed by all too many men.

She leaped to her feet to embrace me the moment I stepped through the sliding door. "I'm so glad you're all right!"

No one had ever hugged me harder than Stacey Stevens.

"I tried calling you from the scene," I whispered in her ear.

"I had my phone off because I was in meetings." She sniffed my uniform collar. "You smell like the inside of a chimney."

"My ears are still ringing from the explosion. Every muscle in my body aches. I need to sit down."

"Do you want some iced tea?"

"I'd prefer a beer."

While she went to fetch the drinks, I unstrapped my ballistic vest and examined the burn hole in the fabric. Then I draped my gun belt across the picnic table. When I collapsed in one of our

Adirondack chairs, I thought I heard it creak under the weight of every other damned thing I was carrying.

If only I had recognized Casey Donaldson when I first saw her.

I knew her face seemed familiar.

I shouldn't have walked away from Becky's belligerence. But I hadn't had any legal authority to push my way into the house, no warrant or probable cause of law breaking. In the old days that wouldn't have stopped me. I would have connived a way to do what I wanted to do and taken my licks for it later.

Instead I had acted "responsibly." And had abandoned Casey Donaldson once again to her personal hell.

And here I had just applied to become a warden investigator, a job I wanted more than almost anything else in the world. Some investigator I was. Some detective.

Stacey emerged from the house with two bottles of Molson. She dragged another heavy chair over to face me, scraped it across the slate. She reached out and grasped both my hands in hers. Her tan face made her jade-colored eyes all that much more vivid.

"Tell me what happened today, Mike. The explosion was all over the news, and people were talking in the office, but I didn't know what to believe."

"It's horrible, Stace. It may be the most horrible thing I've ever come across."

She squeezed my hands tighter. "Tell me."

There was nowhere else to begin except at the beginning.

18

After I'd finished my story and answered her questions, Stacey told me to go inside and take a shower while she put my smoky uniform in the washing machine. When I came out of the bathroom, I found her spread across the bed, naked except for some strategically draped sheets.

An hour later, I was sweaty enough for another shower. I lay on my back on the bed while she curled against me with her leg thrown over mine. Her hand was flat against my chest as if she were trying to detect my racing heartbeat through the nerves of her palm. I stroked her firm, sun-browned arm with the tips of my fingers. The positioning of our bodies was at once intimate and distant: lying that way, we couldn't see each other's face.

"I need to ask you a question," she said softly. "Please don't take it the wrong way."

"Go ahead."

"Are you absolutely positive that girl you saw was Casey Donaldson?"

"As positive as I can be. I'd risk my career on it."

She made a chuckling noise. "You've risked your career lots of other times, Mike."

I tried to twist my neck around to look her in the eyes, but my muscles were too sore. All I could see was the top of her head. She was sunburned where her hair naturally parted. "Yeah, well, I've never been this close to becoming a warden investigator. But if you want me to say I'd risk my life on it, I will."

She went quiet for a long time. I couldn't hear her breathing, but I could feel the air going in and out of her lungs. "I sometimes forget how ambitious you are."

"And you're not?"

"Not according to Barstow." She started playing with the hairs on my chest.

I had been so distracted by thoughts of Casey that I had forgotten about Stacey's own problems at work. "So what happened today? Did he ream you out for yesterday?"

"I never met with him."

My neck twinged again as I tried to make eye contact. "What?"

"Barstow and I were supposed to talk this afternoon. But then I heard the news. The governor wants to cut hundreds of state jobs to pay for tax cuts. You wardens are safe, but we may be losing five field biologists. Evidently, the department isn't going to rehire the positions that opened up when Graham and Marti died in the chopper crash. So that's pretty much the end of my moose study. Three years of scientific work down the drain so that a few dozen rich people can get even richer."

I finally disengaged myself from her embrace. I propped myself on an elbow and gazed down at her flushed face. "I hadn't heard. I'm sorry, Stacey. That really sucks."

"Yeah, it does. I ended up leaving early. I needed to get out of Augusta before I said or did something I would regret."

For my compulsively impulsive girlfriend this qualified as a hopeful display of good judgment.

"But your job is safe?"

"I'm not sure I really give a shit at this point."

"Stacey."

"Ever since my friends died in that crash, I don't even know who I am anymore."

"It's called survivor's guilt."

"You don't understand. There's more to it than that."

"So explain it to me."

"Have you ever heard that saying by Albert Einstein? I don't remember the exact words, but it's something like 'Men marry women thinking they won't change, and women marry men thinking they will. They both end up disappointed.' "

"I'm not disappointed in you, Stace." I smiled and touched her chin. "Besides, we're not married yet."

"I feel like I've changed. And not in the best way."

"That's not true."

"You know it is."

"People change. It's OK. I'm sure I've changed since we met."

She smiled for the first time since we'd begun talking. "You've become a better man."

A laugh exploded out of me. "Right!"

"I'm serious. My dad used to say that you might be the best man he'd ever met—or you could be if you worked at it—and I would think he was getting senile. You seemed like this immature, reckless, stubborn—"

"You can stop there."

Her smile grew wider, and she gripped my biceps tighter. "What I'm saying, Mike, is that my dad was right about you. I was focused on who you were, but he saw who you could become."

"I don't know what to say to that."

"Have you thought of getting out of here?"

"You mean moving to a different house?"

"I'm talking about chucking everything and leaving. We could go out West. Colorado, the Pacific Northwest, even Alaska. I could become a river guide again. Do raft trips through Cataract Canyon and the Grand Canyon. Or become a bush pilot. You could get a job with the U.S. Fish and Wildlife Service. You've always wanted to do undercover work."

At first I had thought she was kidding around, but her face was serious, her eyes gleaming with excitement.

"That's why I applied for the investigator position."

"You don't owe the Warden Service anything, Mike—not after the way they treated you."

"Colonel Malcomb gave me a second chance."

"And where has it gotten you? The state police still won't take your word about having seen Casey Donaldson. I hear things other wardens say about you behind your back, Mike. Your reputation isn't what you think it is. I don't think you should get your hopes up about that promotion."

"That's encouraging to hear."

She dug her nails into my arm now. "There's a big world out there beyond Maine, you know. Wouldn't you like to go be part of it? I don't want to be like my folks and grow old here."

"Your folks seem pretty happy to me."

"It was the right life for them: staying here."

"But not for you?"

"No," she said slowly. "I'm not sure."

"Maine is my home, Stacey."

"Mine, too. And trust me, it'll still be here—and still be the same—when we're ready to come back." She rose from the bed without covering herself. "Just think about it. OK? That's all I'm asking."

I watched her walk naked into the bathroom to take a shower. Then I went downstairs to begin typing up my report.

A warden friend of mine, Gary Pulsifer, the one who sent me the photos of Shadow and the other wolf, is a recovering alcoholic. He says that drunks have a name for the idea that moving to a new place will free them from their enslavement to the bottle. They call it "the geographical cure."

I could understand the impulse.

At many junctures in my life I'd wanted nothing more than to transform myself into a different person. If a genie had offered me the chance to become someone other than the damaged son of an emotionally abusive father, I wouldn't even have asked for two more wishes. But those days had disappeared in the rearview mirror. I wasn't the person I wanted to be—and certainly not the best man Charley Stevens had ever met—but I was inching closer. Which is all you can ask of yourself, I had come to believe.

Even at my lowest low, the idea of leaving Maine had never occurred to me. The state was as much a part of me as I was of it.

And I would be damned before I quit the place knowing that Casey Donaldson was still some monster's sex slave.

I preferred to interpret Stacey's proposal as a frustrated outburst. The governor was slashing

186

funds to her department, putting years of her hard work in jeopardy. She was exasperated; she was sleep deprived; and she was still in mourning for her dead coworkers. But Stacey was still Stacey, I told myself. Her dark mood would pass. And I knew in my heart she loved this place as much as I did.

Rain spattered the window screen as I sat at my desk, writing my report of the past two days. The room had grown dark as the clouds had gathered over the foothills until the only light was the bluish penumbra of the computer monitor. When a bolt of lightning flashed over Sebago, I considered shutting down the machine to avoid an electrical surge, but instead I jammed the window down and wiped the raindrops from the sill.

I was in a race against memory now. The formerly sharp images in my mind—of the half-buried infant, of the "weird sisters," of the foul-smelling house before it exploded—were already losing focus, growing soft around the edges.

For the longest time, I didn't even notice that Stacey was standing in the doorway. She had put on her MISS CONGENIALITY shirt and shorts again. Her long hair was a wet, dark tangle.

"You should open a window." She set another beer for me down on the desk. "It's stuffy in here."

"The rain was coming in."

187

"It's lightening up now."

"Is it?"

I turned to the window and saw a yellowish-gray haze above the treetops.

"I was only thinking out loud about leaving Maine. Don't take what I said too seriously. You know I would never leave here without you."

19

The fire marshal called while Stacey was making dinner. He wanted to interview me about the moments leading up to the explosion. My answers would help him to determine if the fire had been accidental or deliberately set. I expected he might ask me to walk the scene with him, but he said we could handle things over the phone. From the shortness of our conversation he had clearly already amassed more than enough evidence to make a decision.

"Do you mind my asking if you found any human remains?"

"I'd prefer not to comment while the investigation is still under way," he said, as if taking a question from a reporter.

"I understand."

He paused on the other end of the line. "I will say that I've found nothing to indicate the structure was occupied at the time of the explosion."

Just as I had expected. "Thank you."

"You're welcome. You were very lucky you weren't blown to smithereens today, Warden. I've seen a lot of propane explosions and few that were worse. The Lord was looking out for you, young man. If I were you, I'd say a prayer of thanks before going to bed."

I made a vague promise that I would do just that. Then I hung up the phone and went into the kitchen.

"They're alive, Stace! I knew that house was rigged to blow up after they left. I'm sure it was to destroy any evidence they might have left behind."

"Maybe it would be better if she was dead."

"You don't really believe that."

The tears in her eyes reflected the overhead lights. "You'd better rescue that poor girl is all I'm saying. Dinner's ready, by the way."

Stacey was a dreadful cook. It always amazed me how bad she was at meal making given the wonderful food her mother prepared. I'd found some bear meat when I'd been filling the freezer with the packages of pork, and she'd decided to make a chili with it. I doused my bowl with Tabasco until it was bloodred, and I still had trouble finishing dinner without choking.

Her culinary skills might have been nonexistent, but she had inherited her father's hawklike perceptiveness. "Should I have used another onion?"

I hid my mouth behind my napkin. "Two were plenty."

"More nutmeg?"

"I've never had nutmeg in chili before."

Her eyes narrowed. "You hated it."

"I'm not sure I would have thought of adding that particular spice to chili."

"I was experimenting. I'm a scientist. That's what we do."

Not on their boyfriends, I thought.

Fortunately, I was saved from any further discussion of the defects in her recipe by my ringing cell phone.

I didn't know the number, but it was a local prefix code. I stood up from the table to take the call. "Game warden."

"Bowditch?" said a man whose guttural voice I thought I recognized.

"That's right."

"This is retired State Police Detective Menario. You might remember me."

Someone in Barrett's office had reached out to the former detective, just as Pomerleau and Finch had feared. The chili churned in my stomach as I contemplated what my old nemesis might want from me.

"I think you know why I'm calling."

"I have a suspicion."

"I need to talk with you about the Casey Donaldson homicide investigation."

With that one word, *homicide,* he made it clear where he stood on the reliability of my testimony. He might not have been a trial lawyer, but he obviously viewed me as a hostile witness.

For four years, Menario had been circling like a vulture around the same theory of what had happened to the missing college student. Dakota Rowe had killed Casey and disposed of her body in the marshy channels of the Saco River, and so far her killer had escaped justice.

"And why do you need to talk to me?"

His tone hardened as if I had offended him by my question. "Because you need to stop spreading rumors."

"I'm not spreading rumors, Detective. I'm not doing anything."

"Bullshit."

"I suggest you talk with Pomerleau."

"I'm talking with *you*. I know you like playing detective, trying to show how much smarter you are than all of us in the state police. This time, I am not going to fucking allow it. Do you understand me?"

"Maybe you should wait for the DNA evidence to be tested. If I'm wrong, you can call back and insult me for as long as you like."

"Let me tell you something, Bowditch. Maybe it will change your mind if that's even possible. It has to do with my last day on the job."

"All right."

"There was no party. There was no cake. There were no speeches or toasts. Everyone I worked with knew I didn't want any of that shit. I worked a normal day, same as any other. I only did one

192

thing unusual, and that was, before I turned out the lights, I made a copy of a case file to bring home with me. Guess which one?"

"Casey Donaldson's."

"Bingo. I understand that Detective Pomerleau told you about my investigation. What she didn't do, I hear, is show you the complete file. I would like to do that. And from what I know about you, I suspect you would be extremely interested in seeing the documents that Major Crimes has never shared with anyone outside our unit. That's true, isn't it?"

Stacey began cleaning up the dirty dishes. I carried the phone out into the hall to escape the clattering plates and the running faucet. I stood under a deer skull I had found intact in the woods of my first district, up on the midcoast. I'd mounted the bones to a plaque and hung them on the wall as a memento mori. Not that I had ever needed one.

"Why would you show the file to me?" I heard the doubt in my voice.

"Because otherwise you're going to be running around saying the Donaldson girl is still alive. You're going to be sowing doubt where there should be no doubt. You're going to be jeopardizing my ability to secure a conviction against the scumbag, piece-of-shit lowlife who killed that poor defenseless girl. The reason I will show you the file—the only reason—is to shut you the fuck up. Meet me at the Good Life Café in Fryeburg at seven thirty tomorrow morning."

He hung up before I could squeeze in another word.

I wandered back out to the kitchen, where Stacey was scrubbing the burned chili pot.

"So that was your old buddy Menario? What's his beef now?"

"He doesn't seem too happy that I have found Casey alive."

She dropped the ball of steel wool. "What? Why? You'd think he'd be thrilled."

"He doesn't believe the woman I saw was really her. And he's worried that my sketch is going to spread enough doubt that this Dakota Rowe— the guy he believes 'killed' Casey—will walk if he ever goes to trial."

She rubbed her wet hands on the thighs of her jeans instead of using a dishrag. "So what are you going to do?"

"I am going to meet him, of course."

The next morning I rose before dawn again and got dressed without waking Stacey. Ever since the morning we'd shot the pigs, her insomnia seemed to have transformed itself into a deep sleepiness that was just this side of a coma.

But when I kissed her cheek, she batted her eyes open.

"I'm leaving to meet Menario. Don't be late for work."

She yawned into the back of her hand. "Remember that my folks will be here tonight."

Charley and Ora would be staying with us for the July Fourth holiday. Tomorrow was our first-ever house party. A bunch of our friends would be coming—Stacey's friends, mostly, since I had so few—and we weren't remotely prepared for the cookout.

She flopped onto her back and closed her eyes again.

"Don't fall back asleep."

I lingered a minute to look at her face, tracing it with my eyes as I might have with my fingers.

In the truck I took a few minutes to get myself organized before I set off for Fryeburg. Charley Stevens had taught me never to go into a possibly confrontational situation without some kind of a plan, even if I might need to change it halfway through.

"Always know why you're there," he'd said. "Know what you need to know."

Presumably Menario intended to show me some document—an interview transcript, an evidence report—that, in his mind, categorically proved Casey had been murdered. His goal was to convince me that I had sketched the face of the missing woman's doppelgänger by coincidence. In his mind, the real Casey Donaldson was long dead, her flesh rotting down to the bones beneath some undercut bank in the river, beneath a shroud of mud.

And what was my goal?

To have him fill in the gaps for me in Casey's story. To learn one new thing that might point me in the direction of finding her now.

The thunderstorms of the night before had broken off clumps of leaves and scattered green acorns across the road. I had to swerve around some larger branches that the winds had hurled onto the asphalt.

Halfway to my destination, I came upon several vehicles stopped along the roadside at the edge of Hancock Pond. Several people were wading in the shoals, some with their pants rolled above their knees, others stripped down to their skivvies. They were bent over and gathering floating objects from the water's surface and dropping them in all manner of containers. I pulled over beyond the line of cars and trucks and got out to have a look.

Lakes in the summer have a distinctive smell— froggy, but also heavy with algae and often gasoline fumes from outboard motors—but the warming air above Hancock Pond was close to overpowering with the odor of fish. The weedy shallows were full of floating corpses: large-mouth and smallmouth bass, hornpout, fallfish, even some brown and lake trout, not to mention red-breasted sunfish, pumpkinseeds, yellow perch, pickerel, and all manner of minnows.

The passing motorists had stopped to harvest the seemingly unexplainable bounty the lake was offering on this windless morning.

A man in an office-casual outfit, his chinos rolled up to his knees, waded toward me with an inane grin and a bucket full of fish. "Have you ever seen anything like this, Warden? It's like something out of the Old Testament. What happened here?"

"Lightning strike. A bolt must have struck the lake last night. Water is a good conductor of electricity. So the current radiates out from the point of impact, frying all the fish for dozens of yards."

"Really? That's wild!"

"I don't suppose you have a fishing license."

His grin dropped. "I don't need one to pick up dead fish."

"I'm afraid you do, and you can only keep the fish allowed under the state's regulations."

Some of the other gatherers had paused to listen to our conversation. "But these are just gonna rot!" said a leathery woman in yellow shorts.

"Rules are rules."

The foragers collectively groaned. Most dumped their finds back into the water. Those with licenses began sorting through their buckets and bags, tossing out the small fry and prohibited species.

Fortunately, several cormorants and loons had stealthily floated in from the deeper water to feast on the castoffs. I heard a family of ospreys chirping and whistling overhead, ready to dive as soon as the last humans cleared out. Better that the feathered scavengers ate their fill, I thought.

The unexpected stop delayed me close to half an hour. By the time I found a parking space in Fryeburg, I had begun to wonder whether Menario had even bothered to wait.

The Good Life Café was a bright little place with lots of hanging plants. The walls were plastered with posters from past years of the Common Ground Country Fair. Behind the counter and waiting on the tables were only women. Their mix-and-match uniforms consisted of kerchiefs wrapped around their heads, hemp shirts, ripped jeans, and sandals.

The people bunched up at the door, waiting for one of the six small tables, and those already eating, had a more upscale air about them, based, at least, on their clothing labels: Patagonia, Horny Toad, prAna, et cetera. Against this crunchy backdrop, I had no trouble spotting Detective Menario.

He was short for a cop, always the shortest guy in the troop photograph, and so always in the front row. He had compensated for his insecurities about his height through rigorous strength training that had thickened his neck and given his body the squat muscularity of a man who takes out his aggressions on a heavy bag chained to the rafters in his basement.

He wore a white polo shirt that was tight around his tanned biceps, charcoal-gray golf pants, and tasseled loafers without socks. A pair of aviator sunglasses perched atop his head. He looked grayer than the last time I'd run into him, and pouches had formed under his eyes. But he still wore a cop's buzz cut. Nothing about his appearance suggested he was the kind of person who frequented hippie cafés.

Menario didn't beckon to me; he expected that I would come over. Several dirty plates in front of him told me he had already finished breakfast. Neither of us moved to shake hands.

I sat down across from him. His white polo was so sheer I could see the curling black hairs on his chest through the fabric.

"Good morning."

"You're late."

An unsmiling waitress came over with two carafes. She seemed displeased by the heavy black firearm on my belt. As did everyone else in the establishment, judging by the frowns I was getting.

"Chicory coffee or Jasmine Sunrise tea?" she asked.

"Coffee. Thank you."

After she'd moved on to the next table, Menario smirked. "Have you ever had chicory coffee?"

I took a sip. It tasted like scorched hazelnuts. "So where's this file you want to show me?"

"In my car. It's not the sort of thing you open up in a place like this. Get the tab, will you? I'll meet you outside your truck."

The waitress seemed to be making a concentrated effort to ignore me—not a fan of law enforcement, I guessed—but I finally got her to deliver the bill. Menario's organic breakfast cost me twenty-three dollars, not including the tip.

20

Menario was waiting on the corner, wearing his mirrored shades and with a leather portfolio tucked under his gorilla arm.

"Now what?" I said.

"Open the door."

To make room for him in my patrol truck, I had to push aside the swinging laptop stand. He frowned at the muddy floor mats and pollen-covered dashboard. When he was finally inside, I waited for him to unzip the portfolio, but he fastened the lap belt across his chest.

"Start driving." His breath smelled of the strange spices in his breakfast.

"Where?"

"The river."

I turned on the engine and checked my mirrors. "What's with the cloak-and-dagger stuff?"

"You'll see."

We started off down Main Street, passed the prep school that was famous for attracting students from around the world, continued north till we came up on the fairgrounds, then kept going toward the bridge across the Saco. Two big canoe-rental businesses and campgrounds were there, on either side of the river, but before we reached the water, my passenger told me to take a right.

"We're going to Krasker Pond?"

"No."

Only after I saw the sign for Hodge's Campground and Canoe did I understand: Menario was guiding me to the place where Casey Donaldson and her friends had embarked on their ill-fated float trip. The retired detective had a flair for showmanship. We passed the pond and then he told me to take a left. The pavement ended abruptly and gave way to wet sand that I could hear sticking to my tires and gumming up my treads.

A livery van pulling a trailer meant to haul canoes and kayaks came barreling straight at us. The road was so narrow we passed each other with probably an inch of clearance, and even then I heard moose maples slapping at the right side of my pickup.

The entrance to the campground was coming up and I flicked on my blinker to signal the turn.

"Not here. Keep going straight and then veer right."

The right he'd indicated was not even a real road, just a cleared area in the underbrush that had been progressively beaten back by the passage of trucks and SUVs. The dirt was worn down into ruts between which long weeds sprouted. The grass blades bent and scraped the undercarriage, but at least they brushed off some of the sand.

I saw increasing light through the pine boughs and the oak branches, which told me we were approaching a clearing. It was a good thing I decreased my speed because a moment later a steep bank appeared before us. I braked hard but slid on the sand almost, but not quite, to the edge.

I pushed the transmission into park and gazed down at the tea-colored water of the Saco. "You could have warned me we were about to do a Thelma and Louise here."

"You don't know this road? I thought this was your district."

"If you're done busting my chops, maybe you can tell me why you brought me here."

He unzipped the portfolio finally, and a luxurious leather smell arose from within. The contents consisted of a single overstuffed manila folder secured by a fraying red rubber band. He removed the band and slid it over his wrist for safekeeping. Then he wetted his index and middle fingers and began leafing through the contents inside. He came to a stack of photos paper-clipped together.

"I wanted to start with the pictures. This is Casey."

He handed me a photograph that had been printed on regular copy paper. It showed a beaming, dark-haired girl with a spectacular tan, standing knee-deep in the river. Her eyes were hidden behind drugstore sunglasses in the shape of hearts. She was wearing a bikini top that showed off her cleavage, cutoff jeans around her waist, and that telltale diamond ring on her right hand.

I removed my own sunglasses and examined the portrait closely. She was certainly lovely. Her arms and legs were slender; she had none of the paleness or the doughiness of the woman in the crimson wig. This person was happy, healthy, and likely intoxicated. The one I'd seen reminded me of some bloodless creature that had evolved to live in dark caves deep underground.

There was, however, one significant similarity: the mole on her cheek.

"This is the woman I saw in the house."

"You are shitting me."

"I'm telling you it's her."

"Take a look at these." He began handing me photo after photo: Casey's high school yearbook page; a posed holiday picture of her and her stepfather, a flabby, bespectacled man who might have appeared in a child's picture book to illustrate his profession of plumber; Casey with her teammates on the UNH field-hockey team; Casey in selfies, both alone and with her male and female friends; and finally snapshots taken during that final float trip. Pomerleau had mentioned another girl had been along—a stocky blonde who might have been a fellow field-hockey player—and three guys. One was black, one might have been Latino, and the third was white or would have been if he hadn't been sunburned the most painful shade of pink I'd ever seen.

"I don't know what I can tell you." I handed all the photos back. "The woman I saw was Casey Donaldson. She's paler now, kind of sickly looking, and she's put on weight, but I have no doubt in my mind it was her."

Menario flipped to another photograph. It showed a young man who looked as if he spent serious time under a barbell. He had a hipster haircut and a waxed mustache that belonged on a bare-knuckles boxing champion from the nineteenth century. Unsurprisingly, the gym rat was shirtless. The picture revealed some truly artful tattoos on his arms and torso, not your usual redneck ink done by a self-taught artiste. A well-drawn hawk spread out on either side of his sternum, the outstretched wings covering both pectoral muscles, with the outermost pinions extending up to his shoulders. His arms were covered in full sleeves, the interwoven patterns so intricate I would have had to see them up close to pick out the individual images.

"This is Dakota Rowe?"

"Bingo."

"I was under the impression that you had

proof positive to convince me I was mistaken with my ID."

Menario rifled through his portfolio again, and this time he produced a folded document that he opened carefully across his lap. It was the most detailed topographic map of the Saco River I had ever seen. My guess was that the Warden Service had made it during the search using one of our sophisticated mapping programs. The detective stuck his index finger on an X at a place called Mad Tom Point.

"This is where Casey and her friends spent their second night." He traced a winding course along the river as it snaked its way to the south, often coiling back upon itself in channels and dead-water loops. His finger stopped on a second X. "And this is Oxbow Island, where they camped and went skinny-dipping the next day."

The island or sandbar was deep in the marshy area to the east of the main channel of the river. Finding it would have required intimate knowledge of the Saco. It was hard to believe a quintet of mostly out-of-state college kids would have ventured so deep into the backcountry to swim naked, especially when nudity was so common along the river.

"This is where Casey thought she lost her mom's ring," I said.

"It's where Rowe claims she found it, too." A

206

grin spread across Menario's face. "There was only one problem with his story."

"I know. One of Casey's friends found the ring in the bottom of his canoe."

Menario deflated like a pricked balloon. "Who told you that?"

He'd intended the disclosure to be his secret weapon. Surely, it would make me start questioning myself.

"It doesn't matter."

"Like hell it does!"

I stared out across the slowly moving river to the far bank. There was forest there and firm ground, but you wouldn't have had to paddle too far south to find the swamp. The question on my mind was how and where Casey Donaldson had escaped the maze and gotten off the Saco.

"Can I borrow this map?"

"Go ahead. It's a copy, anyway."

I folded the map and wedged it between the dash and the windshield. "Anything else you'd like to show me?"

To my surprise he zipped up the portfolio and set it at his feet. Then he opened the door and climbed down out of the truck. He slammed the door, gazed at me silently through the glass, and began threading his way through the trees, along the steep riverbank.

Seeing him from behind, I noticed he was hiding a pistol beneath his shirt, in a holster at the small of his back. Ever since the legislature had passed a law allowing pretty much anyone without a criminal record to carry a concealed firearm, I had gotten good at spotting *printing,* which is the term for the telltale shape a gun that has been inadequately hidden makes. Many ex-cops continued to pack after leaving the job. It shouldn't have surprised me that Menario, of all people, did.

I caught up with him thirty or forty yards along the forested cliff. He was standing in front of a white cross with Casey Donaldson's name written on it. A heart-shaped wreath of faded plastic flowers was looped over the top. Her sun-faded photograph was tacked to the center. At the base were a field-hockey stick and ball, a stuffed panda, a paperback copy of *Pride and Prejudice* with pages warped from the weather, and half a dozen bunches of dead flowers, some in plastic pots, others in crinkled cellophane wrappers.

The detective faced the memorial. He clasped his hands behind his back and began to rock back and forth on his toes. "Not a month has gone by since Casey died that I haven't come out here. Sometimes her dad comes with me. It's what we have to remember her instead of a grave."

21

Menario didn't speak again until we had returned to the truck. When we were both inside, but before I'd turned on the engine, he said in a softer tone than any he had ever used with me before, "You think I am so obsessed with Dakota Rowe's guilt that I can't even admit the possibility that Casey Donaldson is still alive. But here's a question for you to consider. Are you sure enough that the woman you saw was Casey that you are willing to risk a murderer going free? Because without a body there's already going to be plenty of doubt in the court that hears the case."

I knew what the retired detective wanted me to acknowledge: that I was being as obstinate, in my way, as I was accusing him of being. I had to admit it might all be some bizarre coincidence. I had been spectacularly wrong on a number of occasions, and real people had paid for my refusal to concede my fallibility.

"I didn't identify the person in the sketch to screw up your investigation, Detective."

"There's zero chance you're mistaken?"

"I understand the ramifications. If I am wrong, a guilty man might escape punishment."

"And you can live with that?"

"What I can't live with is the alternative."

His composure began to crack. "Which is what?"

"That Casey Donaldson has been held captive for years without anyone knowing she's alive. That she's been raped by her captor, been impregnated by him, and given birth to at least one child by him. That she was finally recognized by a potential rescuer, but he gave up without a fight. That because he didn't have the courage of his convictions, she was condemned to spend the rest of her life in hell. That's what I can't live with."

I saw his lips tighten as he tried to contain his emotions. "There's a term for your mental disorder. It's called a savior complex."

"I'll bring you back to your vehicle unless you'd prefer to walk into town."

He made a disgruntled noise deep in his chest.

When I had gotten the Sierra turned around, he suddenly leaned forward. "Take a right into Hodge's. There's one last thing I need to show you."

Compared with the famous campground across the river, which could play host to as many as sixteen hundred merrymakers on a Saturday night in July, Hodge's Campground and Canoe was downright genteel. The owners—"Hodge" Hodgkins and his wife, Sue-Ellen—had a reputation along the Saco for reporting intoxicated paddlers and underage drinkers quickly to the Fryeburg police. In consequence, they tended to have vacancies when their competitors were booked solid. The worst of the worst knew to go elsewhere to hold their bacchanals.

It said something about Casey and her friends that they had chosen to stay here rather than at one of the more raucous and freewheeling locations. (Unless they had merely been unable to get a reservation at one of the hot spots.)

The road rolled downhill through white pines that were older than the American Revolution. The brush had been cleared beneath the trees, and cars and trucks, many with out-of-state plates, were jammed between the massive trunks. Menario motioned me toward the office, which doubled as the camp store. I parked behind a cube-shaped Honda Element from Massachusetts. A beer-bellied young man in a bathing suit, flip-flops, and an orange T leaned against the lift gate. His shirt had a picture of the cartoon character He-Man with the words SUP LADIES? He was enjoying a cigarette while he waited for his companions to pay for their campsite.

Or I thought it was a cigarette until I stepped out of the truck.

As soon as he saw me, He-Man dropped the joint to the pine needles and mashed it down with the bottom of his sandal.

"Hey, Officer," he said preemptively. "You having a good day?"

"Not as good as you."

"Yeah, well—"

I could tell from Menario's demeanor that the ex-cop wanted me to harangue the guy, but I was of a different mind-set. With marijuana now legal in Maine, I rarely did more than offer a reminder that the provisions of the law didn't include toking up in public places. Besides, with opioid abuse rampant throughout New England—Maine was second in the nation in the number of babies born addicted—it seemed inconsequential to mess with every stoner I caught blowing a stick.

The store was a small wooden building made of stained-brown boards—the official color of all lean-tos and park signs—with green trim and a needle-strewn roof. A Pepsi machine hummed behind a stack of camp wood priced at five dollars a bundle. I followed the retired detective up the stairs to the screen door.

Inside, the place was packed with young bodies whose sweating skin smelled of sunscreen, bug repellent, and Axe body spray. A shirtless bronze giant in boardshorts stood at the counter signing the papers for a fire permit. Three girls in shorts and bikini tops inspected the merchandise hanging on the wall: pool noodles, cans of lighter fluid, folding beach chairs, dime-store fishing outfits, pound bags of candy. A huge sign over the registration desk warned that all fireworks were illegal on the Saco; the three exclamation points at the end suggested this message was infrequently heeded.

"Do you want a s'more kit?" I heard the woman behind the counter ask the giant.

"Absolutely!" said one of the girls.

Two older-looking rednecks—not college-aged and probably not even high school graduates but definitely here to hook up with coeds—jostled me against a rack of brochures, boating regulations, and river maps.

"Watch it!" said Menario.

The rednecks mumbled apologies and slipped out the door.

"Have a safe, fun float, de-ah," the woman told the giant. "Who's next?"

"We are, Sue-Ellen," said Menario, elbowing his way forward.

I finally got a look at the woman behind the counter. She was short, which is why I hadn't seen her, and thin with a heart-shaped face and close-cut gray hair, and she was dressed in a Hodge's sweatshirt and a brimmed straw hat.

An eclipse passed over the woman's face and all the light left her eyes. "Detective."

"Where's Hodge?"

"Down at the launch with Rusty repairing that sign that got burnt."

"How did it get burnt?" Menario asked.

"Vandalized. I suppose you're here for Dakota, but he just left to run the van down to Walker's Bridge to pick up some kayakers."

I hadn't spoken a word, and Menario hadn't introduced me, but the eyes of the young campers were all on me—and more specifically the gun on my belt. It was always the case when I met kids who didn't have routine contact with law-enforcement officers and were contemplating various misdemeanors.

Menario crossed his arms and teetered back and forth on the balls of his feet thoughtfully. "Tell Dakota I said hello."

"I thought you were retired."

"That doesn't mean I can't take an interest in him."

"I wish you'd leave him alone."

"You're a soft touch, Sue-Ellen. That's why I love you." Menario headed for the door as more campers were trying to come inside. They cleared a path when they saw my uniform so we could descend the steps.

"She's lying," Menario said. "That asshole is here somewhere."

The pine needles were fragrant and cushiony underfoot.

"Why do you think that my meeting Rowe will make a difference? I saw what I saw."

Menario treated the question as rhetorical and began beating a trail toward the riverside camping area. I hated leaving my vehicle where it was impeding the flow of traffic into and out of the registration center, but Menario didn't share my scruples.

I hadn't glanced at the campground map, but I sensed that the retired detective could have found his way around the property blindfolded and spun around three times for good measure. First, we checked a storage barn where scratched canoes and cheap kayaks were stored upside down on log supports. No one there. We made our way through a cluster of picnic tables and standing charcoal grills where a teenaged employee was picking up trash.

"Where's Dakota?" Menario said.

The boy just about leaped out of his skin, so stern was the detective's command. "Bravo Beach."

Wood smoke floated through the branches of the maples and the boughs of the pines. Hip-hop beats thumped. Laughter echoed. Something about the scene was surreal: so many partially clad people, faceless because of the smoky haze, drifting in and out of view between the trees. Wandering through that dreamland, my mind dulled from the oppressive heat, left me feeling a little drugged myself.

Ricky Elwell had said that the Hodgkinses still employed Rowe because they were afraid of him. I had detected a trace of that apprehension in Sue-

Ellen's tone. She seemed less concerned with Dakota's welfare than exhausted by Menario's visits.

We came out on an impressively wide expanse of sand, spread with blankets and beached canoes, where young women tanned themselves in folding chairs and young men hurled Frisbees at each other or splashed loudly in the shallow water.

Menario scanned the crowd with his hand flat over his eyes like a movie Indian. "He's not here."

"Yeah, I am," said a deep voice behind me.

In person Dakota Rowe looked even more imposing than he had when the detective had taken his picture. He wore only cutoff denim shorts and Teva water sandals. His deeply tanned and tattooed muscles glistened with perspiration. His hipster mustache had been recently trimmed.

He squinted at us, both on account of the sun, and because, I believe, it was part of his macho affect. "What do you want, Menario?"

"Detective Menario."

"Not anymore. You're a civilian now, Tony. Which means you can't be threatening my ass whenever you've got blue balls."

"Always the charmer. Dakota, I wanted you to meet Warden Bowditch. He's not a civilian so I'd watch your mouth around him."

To my surprise Rowe extended his hand at me. "Pleased to meet you."

Reflexively I shook it. I could feel the daggers Menario was sending in my direction. "Mr. Rowe."

"You were at the house that exploded," he said. "A buddy of mine is on the volunteer fire department. He told me all about it. So the cops think the dude who was renting it rigged the place to go boom? That's some crazy shit, man."

"What else did your buddy say?" I asked.

"Only that it was one of the Nasons' places. Serves them right, those fucking slumlords. Girl I dated lived in one of their shitholes and the pipes froze twice. Landlord said it was her fault for not dripping the water. I could tell you stories you wouldn't believe about that family."

So far Dakota Rowe was nothing like I had expected. I couldn't say that I liked him, but if Menario's intention had been to show me what a worthless character he was, the experiment was a failure thus far.

The detective seemed to gather as much. "You know what this month is? Don't you, Dakota?"

"I know."

"Four years from the night you and I first met."

"Worst night of my life."

"No, that one is still to come. It'll be your first night in prison."

Rowe spat in the sand. "Is that why you came out here from the old folks' home or wherever you're living? My lawyer warned me the DA is finally going to bring a bullshit case against me. He said I should avoid you like the plague, which is what you are, Tony."

"One last chance to admit you killed her," said Menario.

"Go fuck yourself."

"Once the attorney general brings the case before the grand jury, you're out of options. Don't think you'll plead your way out of it."

Dakota raised both palms at me in an imploring gesture. "Can you believe this guy? Four years he's been coming out here, trying to get me fired, or coming to my parents' home. You should watch out for them, by the way, now that you're a civilian. They don't like the way you're stalking me. And they have a lot of lawyers."

Menario seemed delighted by this response, as if it was what he'd hoped to provoke. "Is that a threat? You know it's against the law to threaten a law-enforcement officer."

"It wasn't a threat, Tony. It was a warning. Stop fucking with me. You're not going to like what happens if you keep it up."

"Sounded like a threat to me. And criminal threatening is against the law no matter who it's directed at."

"Detective Menario?" I said.

"This is the scumbag who killed Casey Donaldson, Bowditch." Menario was making a point to speak in his loudest voice so that the nearest campers could overhear.

Dakota Rowe shook his head. "And you're a totally crazy person. I said it before, and I'll say it until the day I die. I had nothing to do with that girl disappearing."

"Let's get going, Detective," I said.

"Listen to the warden, Tony. You need to get out of the sun. A man your age—it makes your head soft."

"That's not helping, Mr. Rowe," I said.

"How come it's not illegal for this guy to keep harassing me is what I want to know."

"Take out a restraining order against me if you want," said Menario. "Go ahead. I dare you. Go in front of a judge and tell him why you need it."

Dakota Rowe raised his face to the sun, as if it were God and he were praying to be delivered.

"Come on, Menario. You made your point." I took hold of the detective's arm and pulled, but he leaned his weight against me.

"Four years equals presumption of death in the state of Maine. Four years means we don't need a body to prove you killed her."

"Fuck you."

"Justice will be served, you piece of shit."

"Keep shouting, old man. Keep shouting." Dakota Rowe turned his back and began walking toward the waterline.

"You can't walk away from this, Rowe. Not

219

anymore. It's time to pay for what you did."

What happened next caught me off guard: Menario rushed at Rowe's back with his arms outstretched, intending to push him to the ground. Somehow Dakota sensed him coming and used a martial-arts move to divert the attack. The former detective landed on his face in the sand.

Rowe's laugh was sharp and cruel. "That was truly pathetic, Tony."

The next thing either of us knew, Menario had rolled over, drawn a revolver from his concealed holster, and had the snub-nosed barrel leveled at Dakota Rowe's chest. "Motherfucker! I should—"

My own hand went to the grip of my sidearm. "Menario!"

"He assaulted me!"

Rowe had both of his hands raised. "Take it easy, take it easy."

I thought a quiver of fear was in his voice, that he was genuinely afraid for his life, until he kicked sand into Menario's eyes.

Rowe then jumped on the blinded detective before I could take three steps. The two men began a wrestling match in the sand during which Dakota twisted Menario's wrist until he lost the grip on his pistol, while the former detective pummeled Rowe repeatedly in the ear. Sand was flying everywhere. Both of their bodies glittered with it.

My first thought was to kick the firearm clear; my second was to reach for my pepper spray.

But even before I could pull the canister loose, Dakota Rowe escaped Menario's grasp. He sprang to his feet, massaging his hurt ear, bleeding from scratches on his face, but laughing as if he'd just had the time of his life.

"You are so pathetic, Tony. Why don't you drop dead of a heart attack already?"

Menario rose to his knees and tried to surge forward, but I intercepted the ex-cop before he could grab Rowe's knees. For a man in his fifties, he was amazingly strong—which told me how rugged Rowe must have been.

"Stop it!" I said. "Just stop!"

"That son of a bitch assaulted me."

Rowe continued his campaign of humiliation. "Dude, you assaulted me first."

In my peripheral vision I could see campers gathered in the trees and along the waterline to watch the show.

"Detective," I whispered harshly into Menario's ear.

"Where's my gun?" he snarled.

"It's right there. It's right there."

"What the fuck, Bowditch? You were just going to let him—what the fuck is wrong with you?"

"This isn't the time," I said harshly. "People are watching. It's not what you want. It's not the way

221

you wanted this to happen. You need to let it go. For now. Just let it go."

Menario blinked and rubbed his forearm across his raw eyes. "You're a fucking coward, Bowditch. Did you know that?"

I ignored the insult. "Are you done, Detective?"

"Done?" His muscles loosened in defeat. I allowed him to peel my fingers off his sandy biceps. "I'm not even close to done. When he's finally rotting in a cell, that's when I'll be done."

22

Every police officer knows a cop who becomes so obsessed with solving a case that he loses all perspective. Maybe he has a child or a relative that reminds him of the victim. Or he gets too close with their family and begins to feel a blood bond that obscures his objectivity. The danger is always there in violent crimes against women and, especially, children.

Menario had accused me of having a savior complex. But he was something much more dangerous: an avenging angel.

Which didn't mean that Dakota Rowe was some put-upon innocent. The young river guide had played hard upon my sympathy while simultaneously provoking Menario to lose his temper. In my experience, the ease with which Rowe had manipulated us was rare among normal individuals but common among sociopaths.

I took the smug hipster aside while Menario dusted the sand off his clothes. "That wasn't helpful."

Grit was stuck in Rowe's mustache wax. "It's been four years, man. You seem like a solid guy. Imagine if you were me."

"He says you were the last person to see Casey Donaldson before she disappeared."

"Was I? How does he know? How do you know? I mean, who knows what happened to her after she dropped me off? She had her cell phone with her. She could have made it to the boat landing off the Denmark Road. Maybe the bitch called someone to pick her up."

"I don't appreciate your calling her that."

"Fuck you, man."

Now that I was staring into his hate-filled eyes, a thought was beginning to take shape inside my head. "In your statement you claimed Casey had found the engagement ring."

"She told me she did! Look, I won't lie and say I wasn't attracted to her. But if she was freaked out and lied to me, it wasn't my fault."

"You said you hitchhiked from the river back to your home. Who gave you a ride?"

"A couple of French Canadians from Quebec. I didn't get their names. What does it matter?"

"And you didn't see anyone until the next day when you went to work at the campground."

"I was tired. I slept."

"You grew up around here, didn't you, Dakota?"

"I went to school in Fryeburg. My family has a cottage on Kezar Lake. Does that qualify?"

"So I suppose you know the area pretty well."

"Well enough."

"What about the Rankin Road?"

"I already told you my buddy was at that fire. Why are you asking me these questions?"

Menario was so preoccupied with the notion that Rowe had murdered Casey that he had distracted me from another possibility. I couldn't believe I hadn't considered the idea until the creep was staring me in the face. Now I was at risk of giving away the game.

"I'm just nosy," I said.

"Then you'd better keep your nose out of my business."

Rowe walked off down the beach.

I went to fetch Menario from the river's edge.

"So how did that go?" I asked as I handed him back his revolver. "Did it work out as you planned?"

"Go fuck yourself."

In my truck, driving back to Fryeburg, I took the opportunity to explore my new line of thinking. "How much research have you done on Rowe?"

I didn't have to glance at Menario to feel him sneering at me. "So now you're having second thoughts about him?"

"Did you ever get a DNA sample from him?"

"On what grounds? There was no body, remember? No crime scene. Besides, it wasn't like his high-powered attorneys would have allowed him to volunteer a saliva swab."

"Do you know where he lives currently?"

"At his folks' place over in Lovell. They travel most of the year."

"He said he had a girlfriend who rented from the Nasons. Do you know who she is?"

"Why would I?"

"I'm wondering about his local connections."

It said a lot about Menario's lack of imagination that he couldn't see the implications behind the questions I was asking him. Dakota Rowe hadn't killed Casey Donaldson, obviously. But what if he had abducted her instead? A rich, handsome young man with sociopathic tendencies—Rowe had all the personality characteristics and financial resources to maintain a network of secret sex dungeons.

If the retired detective had been less of a hothead, I might have shared my half-formed theory with him. But I had already come close to alerting Rowe to my suspicions. The only person I could confide in now was Ellen Pomerleau. But even with her, I felt that I needed more than a spitball thrown against a wall.

We passed the fairgrounds and the academy and cruised back into town. Menario directed me to his car, a shiny new Mustang. It was an ex-cop's idea of a mighty fine ride.

"You need to stay away from Dakota Rowe," I said. "Seriously, you're going to screw things up big-time if you go looking for that guy again."

Menario slammed the door so hard my binoculars fell off the dashboard.

As I was driving east along Route 302, I spotted a state police cruiser parked across from the Jockey Cap. I slowed down until I could read the plate, then I hit the brakes. Dani Tate was waiting for speeders to come screaming out of New Hampshire.

I pulled my Sierra in beside her sedan so that our driver's windows lined up and we could chat. A warden I knew named Tommy Volk called this vehicular position 69.

She rolled down her window as I rolled down mine. We both kept our shades on.

"How's it going?" I asked.

"Living the dream."

"Boredom is what you get for joining the staties."

"For an extra fifteen grand a year, I can deal with it."

I had never before seen Dani Tate this relaxed. In the past, all of our attempts at conversations had been awkward at best, painful at worst.

"I just spent the morning with one of your former colleagues, Tony Menario."

"He retired before I was assigned to the troop. But I've heard stories. Let me guess. He wanted to bend your ear about Casey Donaldson."

"He's afraid that if word gets out that I saw her alive, he won't be able to make a case against the guy he likes for killing her. I don't suppose you've had a run-in yet with a raft guide named Dakota Rowe."

"Can't say that I've had the pleasure."

"Menario is right about one thing. The guy is seriously bad news. Has anyone reported sightings of the Cobbs?"

"Nope."

"Have you uncovered anything at all?"

"They didn't get mail or packages delivered to the house. None of the utilities paid the place a visit in over a year, either. Except for that one visit Becky made to Fales Variety, we can't find anyone at local stores who claims to have seen her. So either she did her shopping far from Birnam or someone was bringing in supplies."

"It seems like Steve Nason was their only point of contact with the outside world. What do you know about the family? I've heard some damning things about them from a couple of sources, but nothing specific."

"All I know is what I've heard around the barracks. I'm new in town, remember?"

"Tell me."

"From what I hear, the mother—Deanna—used to be a home health-care worker. But she was hot in a skanky way, and she managed to get a job caring for this old rich guy who had an estate on Sebago Lake. You know the one, the 'compound' at the end of Cape Casco. So she took care of this old codger for a couple of years. He was a widower and estranged from his adult children. You can guess what happened next."

"She married him."

"Nope. But she did manage to get herself written into his will. She inherited something like ten million dollars, not including the lakeside estate. His kids sued, of course, but she had a good lawyer on her side, her son. There was nothing the dead guy's family could do. She used the money to begin buying up rental properties. Her company owns dozens of buildings now, most of which are shitholes."

"So I have heard."

Dani reached across the space between us and offered me a copy of the morning newspaper. "Chris Nason is quoted in an article on the front page of this."

"Thanks."

She removed her sunglasses. Depending on her mood, her gray eyes could be as hard as flint or as soft as fog. At the moment they were the color of sea smoke. "So Kathy told me you applied for the warden investigator position."

"I'm still waiting to hear. When's the last time you saw her?"

"Kathy? We've talked on the phone, but it feels like I haven't seen her in ages. I want to meet her new puppy."

"Well, she's coming over this way tomorrow for a barbecue at my house."

Dani nodded. "Yeah?"

"You're welcome to stop by—if you're not doing anything. I'm sure she'd be thrilled to see you. Stacey wouldn't mind. She likes you."

"Sorry, but I have to work." Dani put on her sunglasses again. "Have a good holiday, Mike."

"You, too, Dani," I began, but she had already rolled up her window.

Her tires kicked up a cloud of dust that settled on my truck like ash as she accelerated out of the lot. I flicked the wipers, then squirted some cleaning fluid up on the windshield. The dirt became mud.

What the hell were you thinking, Bowditch?

The lead story in the *Press Herald* was the gas explosion on Rankin Road. The excellent photo of the burning crater and the smoldering trees brought back an emotion: the fear I'd felt when I'd realized the house was about to blow. The accompanying article held few surprises. The reporter hadn't connected the blast to the discovery of Baby Jane Doe the day before, which meant his source wasn't in the inner circle of the investigation. Pomerleau would be glad of that.

The focus of the story, instead, was on the phantom renters: "Frank and Rebecca Cobb." At the time the paper had gone to press, the fire marshal hadn't yet announced if he'd located human remains in the ruin. The culpability of the landlord for the propane explosion was yet to be determined. There was no mention of the wigged sisters.

The subtext, however, couldn't have been clearer: a shady couple had rented a house and they or someone else had blown it to smithereens to hide some misdeed.

I was mildly surprised that the reporter hadn't connected the fire to the discovery of the child corpse less than a mile away. But my respect for the deductive powers of the local media had been low for a long time.

The part of the article that interested me was the series of questions the writer had directed at Pequawket Properties. While it was legal to rent a house or apartment without a background check—including a criminal-records search and a credit-history report—other owners of rental properties were in disbelief that the Nasons had failed to do so in the case of Frank and Rebecca Cobb.

The Nasons' attorney was quoted in defense of his clients, who were also his mother and brother: "As a family who worked our way out of poverty ourselves, we are sensitive to the challenges facing people who have hit hard times through no fault of their own. Rather than engaging in intrusive inquiries into a prospective tenant's personal history, we prefer to have an in-depth conversation with those wishing to rent from us. We have found that the best way to gauge the measure of a person's character is to treat them as a fellow human being first."

Nicely done, Chris, I thought. The younger Nason had painted his family's negligence as a kind of virtue. They had been too trusting. As a result, they were victims themselves of the Cobbs' deception. It was good spin. I wondered how well it would hold up in the coming days.

23

After I left Dani, I took a detour back to Birnam. I had missed breakfast and I was starving. Fortunately, I happened to know of a store that sold decent molasses doughnuts and offered free coffee to cops.

When I arrived, I noticed that Eddie Fales's rusted Chevy C/K pickup wasn't parked in its usual spot alongside the Dumpster. In its place was a little Ford Fiesta scarcely bigger than the go-karts Shriners drive in parades. Other vehicles, too, were at the gas pumps and in the spaces in front of the building. Midmorning seemed to be the rush hour at Fales Variety.

The door gave its familiar chime as I stepped inside the store. I thought I spotted Fales behind the counter, ringing up a customer; all I could see was the top of his gray head. It was too hot for coffee, free or not. I decided to spring for a bottle of water to go with my doughnut. The Faleses hadn't bothered to install air-conditioning, and as a result the beverage coolers were absolutely opaque with frost; you couldn't see anything through the white walls of glass.

I waited in line with my purchase, listening to the conversations ahead of me, and noticed something strange about Eddie Fales's voice. It seemed pitched higher than normal.

Only when I arrived at the counter did I realize I had mistaken the wife for the husband. I had heard of married couples coming to resemble each other, but Connie and Eddie Fales might have been fraternal twins. Her gray hair was just as unruly, her nose just as pinched, and her lips just as narrow. She even wore similar reading glasses to those worn by her husband.

"Mrs. Fales?" I asked, as if I didn't already know who she was.

"You must be that warden."

"I'm afraid so."

"Did you ever find yourself a pink Red Sox shirt?"

"It wasn't for me."

"I heard about the dead baby. So the police think that woman who was in here bought that shirt to wrap the infant in? I wish I'd known. I would have done something if I had."

She reached under the counter and lifted out a long Colt revolver that would have fit comfortably in the hand of Wyatt Earp.

A woman behind me in line said, "Now, *that* is a gun, Connie!"

"It'll do the job." Mrs. Fales returned the six-shooter to its place of concealment.

"Have you remembered anything else about the woman who bought the shirt?"

"The detectives already asked me that question. I don't recall anything specific. But I could definitely pick her out of a police lineup. I've always had a memory for faces." She batted her eyelashes at me. "Yours I would definitely remember."

I ignored her flirting. "What about the car she was driving?"

"The cameras we got outside don't work. They're just for show. If we ever start making money, we'll get them fixed. I can't see anything out front unless I look out the window."

"Did you know she was living in that house on Rankin Road?"

"I already sat through one interrogation, handsome. Now, are you going to buy those items or not?"

I put down my money. "One last question."

"Here it comes," Connie Fales said to her friend in line behind me.

"You wouldn't happen to know a man named Dakota Rowe, would you?"

Connie's face became as stony as if she'd gazed on a Gorgon. "What about him?"

"Does he come in here?"

"Sure he does. All the time."

Now, why would that be? I wondered. Fales Variety was miles from the Saco. And Menario claimed Rowe was living at his parents' house on Kezar Lake, in the opposite direction of his place of employment at the campground.

"It doesn't sound like he's your favorite person."

"He dated our daughter—if you want to call it dating."

"What does he usually buy?"

"Aside from gas? The usual stuff: beer, chewing tobacco, protein bars for those muscles he's so proud of."

I offered her a smile. "No baseball shirts?"

My joke did nothing to soften her expression. "I can tell you what he bought the last time he was in here. Rubbers. He asked what was the largest size we sold, just to be cute. Wish he'd used them when he was 'dating' Alyssa. But don't get me started on that Dakota Rowe." Connie waved to the woman behind me. "Step right up, Norma!"

Next I went to see the burned-out shell of Casey's former prison. Over the past few days I hadn't done much warden's work, but I excused the diversion by telling myself I was on the lookout for feral swine.

The house had been well hidden when I'd first visited, but there was no missing the enormous clearing left by the fire. The surrounding trees that were still standing were as black as pipe cleaners, their branches having largely been burned off. The foundation at the center was a rectangle of ash-stained concrete. Unidentifiable bits of housing material lay scattered for acres about the place. Not to mention the damage done to the dirt road by the many emergency vehicles that had been squeezed onto the site. I could still see the marks of the fire hoses in the mud, like the slithering imprints of prehistoric snakes.

I supposed the Nasons would be on the hook for cleaning up the land. At least they had plenty of room now to build that profitable multitenant property that Deanna had mentioned.

As I stared around me at the disaster area, the same question kept running on a loop through my head.

Where have they taken Casey?

I wanted to believe she might still be nearby. The thought that she had been whisked far from here, beyond the ability of us to rescue, was too painful to bear. I couldn't remember the last time I had felt such a sense of urgency combined with such a sense of helplessness.

Steven Nason was the key. If he hadn't known exactly who was living here, and under what conditions, he must have had suspicions. Hopefully, Pomerleau would be able to pry some useful information out of him this morning, but I feared that Christopher Nason would use all the lawyerly arrows in his quiver to hold the detective at bay.

What was I to do in the meantime?

I couldn't very well start tailing around Dakota

Rowe in the vague hope that he would lead me to the next hidey-hole where the "Cobbs" were keeping Casey out of sight.

I hated waiting.

Waiting for the baby's DNA results to confirm what my heart already told me was true.

Waiting for the Cobbs to make a mistake and pop their heads up somewhere.

Waiting to hear whether I had gotten the warden investigator job.

Waiting for Stacey to get her life together—if she ever would.

When all you can do is wait, I had learned long ago, the best thing to do is work.

I spent the rest of that afternoon dealing with the mundane tasks, minor emergencies, and odd encounters that constitute my life as a Maine game warden. In short, it was a day of unique occurrences: it was a day like any other.

Stacey wasn't home when I pulled into the drive an hour before sundown. I changed into jeans and a T-shirt I'd gotten competing in the Tough Mudder Mud Run and Obstacle Race in the spring. My team of wardens, led by Captain Jock DeFord, had destroyed our archrivals from the state police. The troopers might actually become a threat to beat us if Dani ran the course next year: that little woman was an absolute beast.

What had I been thinking inviting her to our party?

Of course Stacey chose that moment to call me. "How was your breakfast with Menario?"

"It's a long story. I'll fill you in tonight."

"Can you stop at the grocery store on your way home? We need some stuff for the cookout."

"I'm already home."

"I guess I can pick it up."

"No, I'll do it." I grabbed a pen and jotted down the items she listed.

"I've been thinking. You know who we should give that pork to if it tests OK? The Cronks. Aimee can always use a helping hand. What's your name for those rambunctious kids of theirs?"

"The Cronklets," I said.

"They must be growing up fast."

While their father my friend—sits behind bars for manslaughter, I thought. Billy Cronk wasn't due to be released from the Maine State Prison for three more years.

"Maybe we should invite them," I said. "Aimee and the kids."

"It's late notice and a long drive from Washington County, but sure. Why not? There's all that jungle-gym crap in our backyard no one uses."

I hadn't yet figured out how to broach the subject of my conversation with Dani Tate. "Anyone else we're forgetting to invite?"

"You think about it. I've got a meeting with Barstow in five minutes. He probably wants to talk with me about what's going to happen with the moose survey now that there's no staff or funds."

End of the day before a holiday weekend. I didn't like the timing of this impromptu conversation at all.

"I almost forgot," she said. "You need to pick up my parents. They're flying over from Grand Lake Stream. You know my dad, he can't ever just drive when he can take the Cessna. They'll be tying up over at Dingley's Marina and need a ride from the lake to the house."

"Anything for your folks."

"And they'd do anything for you. You're like the son they never had."

24

The items Stacey had requested for the party weren't available at our local market so I had to drive down to the supersize chain store in Gorham to do my grocery shopping.

I have never been comfortable in crowds. My senses seem tuned to a higher frequency than those of most other people, and I am easily overwhelmed by the sights, sounds, and smells of so many human beings massed together in a confined space. Overstimulation is the curse that comes with the gift of heightened sensitivity. Anyone who has ever owned a cat will understand what I mean.

I clutched my shopping list and kept my head bowed as I pushed my cart down the fluorescent-lit aisles. Otherwise I knew I would start losing myself in distractions that might require nonstop interventions. *That man who lurched past me with a case of beer, on his way to his car—didn't his breath smell of liquor? The bruise on that child's face—didn't it have the shape of an adult's hand?*

I almost made it successfully to the checkout.

At the very last aisle, along the row of dairy coolers, as I was stocking up on cheese for our mooseburgers, I noticed a pale woman wearing a wig. It wasn't crimson. The color was somewhere between red and orange. But it was cut straight in the bangs and across the shoulders. She was skinny, dressed in oversize clothes, and wearing dark sunglasses that obscured much of her face; and she had her head down, as if trying desperately to go about her business without being spotted. Her shopping cart was heaped full of the sort of staples you'd buy to outfit a bomb shelter.

No way, I thought. *Impossible.*

She seemed to sense my staring because she turned her cart 180 degrees and began hurrying toward the checkout as if she expected to be chased.

I abandoned my purchases in the middle of the aisle. "Excuse me!"

She quickened her pace.

"Hey! You in the wig!"

She must have heard me because every other person around us did, but still she didn't pause. She turned a corner fast to escape me.

I began to jog. As I always did these days when I was off duty, I was carrying my backup piece, a Walther PPK/S, which I wore in a concealed holster inside the waistband of my pants. I was close to reaching for it.

I caught up with the woman as she was passing the pharmacy. I stepped around her and grabbed her shopping cart. The sudden stop nearly caused it to tip over sideways. The surprise made her whip her head around and her sunglasses fell off.

But she refused to look up. "What do you want? Why are you doing this?"

Instantly I realized my horrible, inexcusable mistake. "Oh, God! I am sorry."

I squatted down to retrieve her glasses from the floor.

She seemed reluctant to take them from my outstretched hand. But as she did, she lifted her head, and I saw her face. I recognized the gray complexion and dark-ringed eyes of a chemotherapy patient. My mother had died of cancer.

"I am so, so sorry."

Tears of fright and embarrassment were streaming down her hollow cheeks. She hid herself again behind her sunglasses.

The pharmacist, having witnessed my unprovoked assault, had come out from behind his counter and was standing over us. "Is there a problem here, sir?"

"It's my mistake. I apologize, ma'am. I saw you and thought you were someone else."

I offered to pay for her groceries, but she refused. All that poor, sick woman wanted was for everyone to stop looking at her. She wanted to become anonymous again.

I cursed myself all the way home.

If I could have mistaken a cancer patient for

Becky Cobb, was it any wonder that Barrett and the others doubted my identification of Casey Donaldson? It almost made me question my own certainty.

But no.

My idiocy in the supermarket was a by-product of the helplessness I was feeling. As I had just demonstrated, my fear for Casey's safety was eroding my judgment. I needed to collect my emotions and focus my thoughts.

After I'd put away the groceries, I poured myself some iced tea and sat outside with the map of the Saco River that Menario had given me spread across the picnic table.

Now that I had been assigned to patrol the Saco, I owed it to anyone I might have to rescue to familiarize myself with the endlessly zig-zagging watercourse. Stacey and I had once made the paddle from the boat launch at the covered bridges in Conway, New Hampshire, around Swan's Falls by portage, past the mobbed campgrounds at Walker's Bridge, through the insect-thick backwaters at Lovewell Pond and Brownfield Bog (where ducks exploded into the air around every bend), and come ashore above Hiram Falls: a multiday journey of thirtysomething miles. I put my finger on the *X* that marked the spot where Casey had last been seen. I couldn't even remember that particular crook in the river.

My phone buzzed on the tabletop. "Hello?"

"Is this Bowditch's Taxi Service?"

"Charley?"

"Why, hello, young feller! The Boss and I just arrived on Sebago. And my daughter said you might be available to chauffeur us to your domicile."

Stacey's father had grown up in logging camps in northwest Maine during the era of the river drives, and even though he had served as a pilot in Vietnam and had inhabited the civilized world from the Age of Aquarius to the Digital Age, he still spoke like the last of the old-time lumberjacks. Some of it was pure affect. Charley Stevens was one of the smartest men I'd ever met, especially when it came to sizing up other people, but as a warden, he had found it useful to have criminals underestimate his intelligence. I'd also come to see Charley's insistence on using the backcountry vernacular as a stubborn act of rebellion against an American culture that had no use for the wisdom of its elders. Stacey wasn't the only maverick in her family.

"Where are you? Have you landed already?"

"I'm not sure *landed* is the right term for a floatplane, but, yes, we've arrived at the lake. We're over at Dingley's chewing the fat with the man himself. Look for two old geezers and a beautiful young woman in a wheelchair."

"I'll be there in fifteen minutes."

As quickly as I could, I grabbed the keys to my personal vehicle, an International Harvester Scout, and set off for the marina on the northwest shore of Sebago Lake.

The "beautiful young woman in a wheelchair" Charley had mentioned was Stacey's mom, Ora, who could not be described as young but was certainly beautiful in a way that went deeper than her kind and radiant face. The Stevenses' relationship was my Platonic ideal of what marriage could be. Charley and Ora made it look so easy and natural. Why were Stacey and I having so much trouble?

I pulled into the marina as the first stars were appearing in the darkening sky above the lake. Down at the end of the longest dock, I could see a floatplane tied up and three silhouettes, a person in a wheelchair and two others. Ora waved at me from her chair as I strode down the floating walkway, my footsteps hollow and metallic in the breathless evening air.

"There's the man who wants to run off with my girl, Dingley," Charley said as I approached them.

"Looks like trouble to me," said the marina owner.

"Oh, Mike, it's so good to see you," said Ora.

She had snow-white hair cut at shoulder length and was wearing a pale green sweater, almost the exact color of her eyes, although it was too dark to see anything apart from her big smile. I bent over to kiss her cheek, but she wrapped her arms so tightly around me, I almost lifted her free of the chair.

As usual, Charley just about crushed my hand when he shook it. For a smallish man, he had the strongest grip. "Do you know Dingley, Mike?"

I shook hands with the marina owner. "Sure, Dingley calls me every time a drunk boater pulls up to one of his docks."

"Don't say that!" said Dingley. "I'll lose all my customers if that rumor starts going around."

Charley clapped him hard on the back. "Your secret is safe with us."

"There is no secret," pleaded Dingley.

"We were just talking about bats," said Charley.

"Did you see one?" I glanced at the lake, hoping to spot a flitting shadow. Out on the water the few remaining boats showed as bobbing green and white lights. But I saw no bats.

"No," said Charley. "That's what we were talking about—how you almost never see a bat since that white-nose syndrome wiped out most of their colonies. They used to be thick as mosquitoes up at Grand Lake Stream."

"I remember."

"I miss the bats," said Ora. "I miss watching them fly up the lake every night at dusk."

I felt a mosquito alight on my neck and slapped at it. "I miss the way they used to eat all the bugs."

"I suppose we should get going before we all come down with—what did the Penguin call it?—the Ziki fly?" said Charley.

"You know it's the Zika virus," said Ora.

The Penguin was Charley's nickname for our governor. "Someone should educate the chief executive," he said. "He clearly flunked biology."

We said our good-byes to Dingley, who promised to keep a close watch on the Cessna for the duration of their visit. Charley wheeled Ora up the ramp while I carried their luggage. I knew better than to offer to help them with the wheelchair. I stood back as the wiry old man lifted his wife effortlessly and set her down in the passenger seat of my vehicle.

As I settled myself behind the wheel, Ora took hold of my hand with hers and squeezed it. She seemed to have less strength than I remembered. I was afraid to apply pressure for fear of hurting her.

"Oh, Mike, it's so good to see you again."

"It's good to see you, too, Ora."

But as I raised her hand to my lips to kiss, I felt a pang—worry? regret?—that I couldn't explain.

25

S tacey's Subaru was in the garage and the door was open when we arrived home. She came out to greet us but did her best to hide the slight limp from her injured leg. She was barefoot, but still wearing her uniform. I was curious to hear about her meeting with Barstow, but I knew she wouldn't want to talk in front of her parents about being called onto the carpet.

"You're late," she said. "Did you take a wrong turn over Katahdin again, old man?"

Charley poked his big head out the backseat window. "If I did, it was because I didn't have my favorite copilot with me."

Charley and Stacey had been estranged for many years; she had blamed him for the accident that had paralyzed her mother. Every time they met each other now, it seemed to stand for a more profound reconciliation.

Dinner was venison loins that I had dusted with salt and pepper and wrapped with bacon before throwing on the grill. To ward off mosquitoes, we lit citronella candles that flickered as we ate. Besides the steaks, we had new potatoes and peas from the farm stand down the road. Stacey and I drank beer while Ora had a whiskey on the rocks.

Charley, as was his custom, consumed only milk, until we brought out the strawberry shortcake. Then he switched to black coffee. The man consumed so much caffeine I wondered how he ever fell asleep.

As we were about to collect the plates, Charley said, "What's that over there, flapping?"

I squinted into the gloom until I saw what he was pointing at. I had forgotten the map on the table, and it had blown to the edge of the yard where it had lodged against the fence. The old pilot had the eyes of an owl.

"It's a map of the Saco River." I used my palm to press out the wrinkles from the paper.

Charley brought his craggy face close to it. "I suppose this map has to do with that supposedly dead girl you saw."

Stacey tossed her head back in mock frustration. "I knew this was coming."

"What dead girl?" asked Ora.

Somehow Charley had restrained himself through dinner from bringing up Baby Jane Doe, the house that had exploded, and everything else he'd pried out of his many contacts in law enforcement. But the discovery of the map had given him permission to inquire. Not that he usually waited for permission.

"Mike's gotten into mischief again," said the old pilot. "Only this time he's involved our daughter."

Ora touched Stacey's arm. "What is he talking about, dear?"

"It's nothing, Mom. Come on, let's go inside. I want to give you that Louise Erdrich book I told you about. We can turn on the classical-music station."

"No, I want to hear."

Stacey shook her head sadly. "Go ahead, Mike. It's your story."

I pushed the smeared red plate of strawberries away from me, leaned my elbows on the table, and took a deep breath. "It all started with some pigs."

By the time I had finished, one of the candles had gone out and the last was guttering in a pool of citrus-smelling wax. The dancing light seemed appropriate for a ghost story. The expression on Ora's face was certainly one of horror.

"Why isn't every cop in Maine out there now looking for those Cobbs?" she asked.

"Where would they start, Mom?" Stacey said. "There are tens of thousands of buildings in southern Maine, assuming they didn't flee into New Hampshire."

Charley tugged on his big chin as he often did when he was trying to solve a puzzle. "Sometimes the best way forward is to go backward."

"What do you mean?" I asked.

"Assuming everything you said is true—about

251

her being abducted off the river—then it might be useful to figure out how she came to meet the Cobbs in the first place."

"There was an extensive search, Dad," said Stacey.

"But we know something now they didn't know back then. We know Casey's alive. And I'm inclined to agree with Mike that she's been held prisoner all this time. So where did she meet her kidnapper? He had a reason for being where he was that day."

"I see what you're getting at," I said.

"I sure don't," said Stacey.

Charley peered again at the map, held in place at the corners by our glasses and mugs. "So this is where she was last seen?"

"According to Dakota Rowe," I said. "But I wouldn't exactly trust his testimony on the matter."

"I'd like to meet that young man myself and take his measure." Charley picked at his teeth with a fingernail. "You're not working tomorrow, are you, young feller?"

Stacey placed her hands flat on the table. "No, Dad. Don't even think about it."

The old pilot had a grin that always reminded me of a jack-o'-lantern. He was one of those men who are so homely they are almost handsome. "But it's been years since I took a paddle down that river."

"It's the Fourth of July. We're having a barbecue here. Mike has to help me get the place ready for our guests."

"The warden and I can be on the river at dawn and back while the birds are still singing. Isn't that right, Mike?"

"Absolutely."

Stacey stiffened beside me. "But why? I don't get it. What point is there in paddling through that backwater? Casey disappeared on the Saco four years ago. Wherever she is now, she's definitely not there."

"That's true enough," said Charley. "But somehow that poor girl ended up in that house that blew up. If we can figure out how and where Casey got off the river, we might learn something about who it was who took her."

"Us? Who's us?" said Stacey. "The state police are investigating what happened to Casey Donaldson, Dad. They don't need your assistance."

His expression was all innocence. "What harm will it do? It's not like we're going to go knocking down those Nason folks' door."

She gave me a pleading look. "Mike? Can you support me here, please?"

"We can be back by late morning, Stace."

Stacey knocked a knee, hard, against the bottom of the picnic table as she rose to her feet. It was the leg with the stitches. She winced but continued to slide away from us. "Do whatever you want."

Stacey limped back into the house without another word, leaving us sitting around the table. The last candle hissed. Everything went dark.

Stacey stood at the kitchen sink, wrapping leftovers in aluminum foil. I came up behind her and wrapped my arms around her waist and pressed my face into her long dark hair. When she didn't pause in what she was doing, I took a step back.

"So you really are going paddling with my dad tomorrow?" She didn't look at me.

"We'll be back in plenty of time."

"No, you won't. You're going to find something odd that you need to 'investigate,' or you're going to have a confrontation with some random assholes you meet out there because that's what always happens when the two of you go looking for trouble."

She wasn't wrong in that regard, but her tone seemed unusually brittle.

"What happened with Barstow, Stace?"

"I don't want to talk about it now."

"Come on. What did he say to you?"

"That I've been pushing my luck, and I need to shape up, or there will be consequences."

"Maybe you should get ahead of this and call your union rep."

She turned on the tap to wash her hands. "I said I don't want to talk about it."

The sliding door opened. Charley pushed the wheels of his wife's chair over the doorframe. Neither of them looked happy. Ora cleared her throat and reached back with her hand, the veins blue beneath the pellucid skin, to tap her husband's.

"I owe you an apology," Charley said gruffly.

"Are you still planning on going canoeing with Mike?" Stacey asked.

Her father pushed his hands into his pants pockets. "I am."

"Then I don't want to hear it." She flipped the dishrag onto the wet counter. "I'm going to bed. I had a long day at work and need to get some sleep before the party. You should be all set in your room, but Mike can get you anything you need." She bent over to kiss her mother's cheek. "Good night, Mom. You know I'm not mad at you."

"Do you want to talk, honey?" Ora asked. "Just the two of us?"

"In the morning. I really am beat. Good night."

We listened to her quick feet on the stairs, then heard the bedroom door slam shut.

I couldn't think of a single thing to say.

Charley rubbed a hand through his thick white hair until it stood up. "It looks like I got you into some hot water."

"Mike is his own man," said Ora. "He's responsible for himself, just as you are responsible for yourself."

Her disapproval was like a knife in my heart. But the pain of disappointing that lovely woman wasn't enough to make us change our plans. Once made, bad decisions are so much harder to abandon than good ones.

26

I awoke in the dark to hear a cupboard snapping shut downstairs. Then the rattle of dishes. The clock beside the bed told me it was four-thirty. Stacey continued to breathe softly but steadily a few inches away. She had slept with her back to me all night.

I dressed in the dark, in the same dirty clothes I had worn the night before. I walked on the balls of my feet out of the bedroom and eased the door until I could hear the latch click.

In the kitchen Charley was fully dressed and making coffee. The former warden pilot always seemed to wear the same green shirt and the same green pants, as if retirement hadn't removed from him the desire to put on a uniform each morning.

"How's my daughter?"

"Asleep thankfully. She was still awake when I went up, but she wouldn't talk to me."

"It seems like a small thing to get her so riled up." The mug he offered me was a stocking stuffer Stacey had given me for Christmas. It was blaze orange with the drawing of a stag and the motto GETCHADEERYET?

"She's been having a hard time at work."

"My contacts in the department tell me

Commissioner Matthews is continuing her one-woman reign of terror."

I sipped my coffee. "Barstow is being a dick, too."

Charley leaned against the counter and held his steaming cup between his big paws as if to warm them. "Ora thinks it's something else that's bothering her, though."

"The helicopter crash really shook her up, losing three of her friends suddenly. And then finding that dead baby the other day."

"No. Ora thinks it's something else."

"Like what?"

"She thinks Stacey and you might be having problems."

I felt myself blush as if I'd been caught in a lie. "Really?"

"That girl loves you to pieces, Ora says, even if she doesn't always show it. But she's still struggling with herself. When she came back East after graduate school, we hoped she had put her problems behind her. In some ways she is as lost as ever. People assume Stacey's always finding fault with them, but it's herself she can't accept. That's Ora's theory, anyway."

"What do you think, Charley?"

"I think my wife is a hell of a lot smarter than me." He finished his coffee in one long gulp. "Let's get on the road. We need to be back in time to make amends to our better halves."

"Stacey and I aren't married yet."

He clapped me on the shoulder so hard I nearly spilled my coffee. "That's another thing I wanted to talk with you about."

We took two vehicles. Charley left my Scout at the lot below Birnam Bridge, then we rode together in my patrol truck up to Fryeburg. By road it was only nine miles, but the Saco was such a winding river we would be covering twice that distance by canoe.

The sky was the color of smudged charcoal when we passed the Fryeburg fairgrounds. The enormous complex of white buildings had a grandstand at the center, a harness-racing track, and agricultural barns, each labeled with the livestock that would be displayed and judged there in the fall. We turned down the side road that ran along the chain fence until we came to the campground at the end.

As early as it was, a few people were already wandering about beneath the pines. One shirtless, tattooed gent was walking a rottweiler with jaws big enough to take off your head. Someone else was frying bacon on a portable grill, making me wish we'd stopped for a real breakfast instead of raiding a box of granola bars I kept in the backseat.

I maneuvered the truck down the hill until I came to the parking lot below Swan's Falls.

Before we launched, I wanted to have a look at the river. The beach was quiet except for a big-bellied man sitting at a picnic table, looking out at the river slowly coming into view with the dawn. The first thing I noticed was his thick black pompadour. He wore a blue polo, poorly fitting dark pants, and black tactical boots. If not for the holstered pistol on his belt and the word POLICE printed on the back of his shirt, I would never have taken him for a law-enforcement officer.

"You can't park there," he shouted, loud enough to wake the campground.

Charley smiled at him. "We'll just be a minute unloading, young feller."

"The new launch area is back that way, Gramps."

Just then the cop caught sight of my own holstered sidearm. His arm jerked at his side, and I realized he hadn't recognized my black Sierra as a warden truck. Nor had he yet spotted the badge on my belt beside the weapon. I was out of uniform, and he took me for one of those open-carry enthusiasts who make police officers' lives so pleasant.

I made a gesture somewhere between a wave and a stop signal. "Game warden."

The fat man laughed to cover his mistake. "Hey, how's it going?"

"Finest kind," said Charley. The old Maine

expression translated, in this case, to "Very well, thank you."

"Couldn't see you guys clearly in the dark. Guess I should be eating more carrots. Didn't know you wardens were going out on the river today. You undercover?"

"Just going for a paddle," I said.

"For fun? No shit?"

In the few months since I'd been given this extra district to patrol I hadn't had many encounters with the local constabulary. The Fryeburg cops had a reputation for policing their sixteen miles of riverfront without compromise or mercy. For that reason I had been told that I could devote my energies elsewhere. I'd only met the regular patrolmen, but I knew the town employed close to a dozen reserve officers in the summer to handle the mobs who converged on the river. Fat Elvis here struck me as a seasonal hire.

My companion introduced himself first. "Charley Stevens, Maine Warden Service, retired."

"Mike Bowditch. I'm covering this district until you get a new warden."

"Jeff Nisbet. Fryeburg PD." Most police officers have firm handshakes, but this guy's was like rubber.

"They've got you out here early enough," said Charley.

"I been here since midnight. I like working nights. Besides, it's the Fourth of July weekend, you know."

"Any trouble?" I asked.

"The usual. Caught some teens drinking. Heard fireworks maybe a hundred yards down the river. They're illegal on the Saco. But the perpetrators were gone before I could run down there."

The man didn't strike me as someone who engaged in many foot chases.

"In a couple of hours it's going to be rush-hour traffic out on the river. You picked a crazy day for a paddle unless you're doing it for the scenery." He cupped his hands into imaginary breasts.

I'd met Fryeburg's badass new police chief and had a sneaking suspicion that Reserve Officer Nisbet might not be brought back the following summer if this conversation was representative of his attitude.

"Do me a favor," I said. "Keep an eye on my truck while we're gone. We should just be a few hours."

"You got it."

Charley and I lifted the upside-down canoe out of the back of my pickup and then walked it down to the beach. The river below the old dam had some chop, but it was hardly the millrace I'd seen here earlier in the spring when the snowmelt from the White Mountains came spilling down through this narrow passage.

We slid the canoe on the sand down to the water's edge and were getting ready to push off when Nisbet exclaimed from the high bank, "I realized who you are!"

Charley and I stared up at the heavyset man, uncertain which of us he meant and which of the many reasons for our notoriety he could have had in mind.

"You're the warden from that house that blew up."

"That was me."

"Thought I recognized you. I was at the scene that day with the rest of the department. Not that there was anything for us to do. That house belonged to my cousin's landlords."

"Pequawket Properties?"

"Yeah, the Nasons. Couldn't have happened to better people. My theory is that they blew the place up themselves for the insurance. I even bet money on it with one of the other guys at the station. Fifty bucks! Have a good paddle. Keep your eyes open for hooters." He cupped his imaginary breasts again.

27

The canoe was an Old Town Penobscot 164, forest green except where it had been beaten to hell on my voyages up and down the streams of Maine. The webbed seats were torn, the hull was scratched from long portages through alder thickets, and one of the thwarts had broken when a drunken duck hunter had attempted to sit on the brace. You might say that the canoe's many scars were the archaeological record of my career as a game warden.

Charley sat in the bow while I handled the boat from the stern. From his occasional over-the-shoulder glances, I could tell he found the arrangement not to his liking. The old woodsman was accustomed to steering.

The current was gentle, and it carried us straight downriver. It needed only an occasional J-stroke from me to correct our course. When I trailed a hand in the stream, I found it as warm as bathwater. The air was chilly in the shadows along the eastern bank, though, and the contrast between the cool air and the mild river raised a mist that dissolved when the sun touched it.

Neither of us spoke. Something about being out on the water in the early morning, the air fragrant with pines and woodsmoke, called for reverence. A few hundred yards below the falls, Charley pointed at a pine on the far shore. The top of it was lit up yellow by the rising sun. The glare made it hard for me to see the white head of the bald eagle until the massive bird lifted off a branch and, with slow and heavy wingbeats, set off before us down the Saco.

"When I was a boy, there weren't more than twenty pairs of those birds in the whole state," said Charley softly. "DDT just about wiped them out. What would it have said about us as Americans if we'd killed off our national symbol?"

Just then music began to blare from the shoreline. The song was "Here for the Party" by the country singer Gretchen Wilson.

"What in the—?" said Charley.

Downstream, the eagle shot forward as if someone had lit its tail on fire.

From the opposite bank another blast of music answered: "Gin and Juice" by Snoop Dogg. Someone must have been having screwdrivers for breakfast.

A naked young man came racing from a campsite and belly flopped into the water. When his head popped above the surface, he let out a pig holler. As if summoned, several of his friends (both male and female) came running down the beach, throwing off their clothes and screaming as if they were being chased by zombies.

"Welcome to the Saco," I said.

Within minutes we found ourselves passing through an obstacle course of skinny-dippers and float-tubers. Canoes slid down from the shore laden with coolers and barbecues, tents and folding chairs, cases of beer and cases of water, trash bags full of God knew what. Their occupants began tying the boats together to create rafts, which allowed them to stand up, boogie down, or leap from vessel to vessel to fetch refreshments.

Not a single person in sight was wearing a personal flotation device. At best, they'd stuffed their life jackets in their canoes' bows or sterns. But I wasn't on duty, and there were far too many boats for me to check.

"Hi, Grandpa!" a girl shouted at Charley, and raised her bikini top to flash him with her tattooed breasts.

"Haven't seen a pair like that in a while," the old man said under his breath. "Haven't wanted to."

A kid with a Super Soaker squirt gun floated by in an inflatable. He fired a stream of water at our canoe, catching me in the face.

"Hey!" I lifted my shirt to show the badge on my belt.

He giggled. "Sorry, Officer."

I sat back down and dug my paddle into the water to get clear of this particular scrum.

A few minutes later, someone in the rafted canoes had found a new song to play on their portable MP4 blaster: "Fuck tha Police" by NWA. Almost every cop in America knows the words of that rage-filled anthem by heart.

The floating orgy followed us for the next four miles. The party only grew bigger and louder as the temperature rose and we approached the campgrounds on either side of Canal Bridge, where tent cities extended from the dirty beaches, across the trampled fields, to the distant tree lines.

Some of the vessels were miracles of quasi-nautical construction. One enterprising group had built a platform, complete with a Persian carpet, atop a row of four canoes, using them as pontoons. They had a dance floor and a stack of firewood. In the stern was a tall thronelike chair on which sat a kid in a Speedo wearing a pirate hat and an eyepatch. The American flag drooped from a canted pole over his shoulder. What these rafters didn't have was a reliable means of steering their vessel. When it drifted into a sandbar, two dancers fell overboard from the impact. Captain Speedo cannonballed heroically to the rescue.

When we reached Hodge's Campground, I turned the canoe toward shore, and Charley hopped out and pulled us up onto the white sand beach.

"Well, this place has changed a mite since my last visit," said my friend.

In the shallows, people lounged in half-submerged lawn chairs while naked babies splashed unattended. Thick patches of poison ivy grew up the steep banks with footpaths leading through them. The local drugstores must have done a thriving business in calamine lotion. It being the anniversary of the nation's founding, we saw a great many flags: flying from poles; decorating muscle shirts, bandannas, and bikini tops; even taking the form of beach towels on which people lay sunning themselves.

I spotted a man in a Hodge's shirt carrying a paddleboard down to the river for a little boy.

"Excuse me!" I lifted my shirt so the man could see the handgun and badge on my belt. "Can you tell me where I can find Dakota Rowe?"

The man pulled up sharply. He fixed his wide eyes on my belt. Then he actually turned his whole body, paddleboard and all, in the direction of the campground; took a look at the pines; and then turned back. "Dakota's not working today."

"He's not working on the busiest day of the summer?"

"No." The man continued on his way to the water.

"I believe that young man was lying to us just now," said Charley.

"Do you think? Do you want to go looking for him onshore?"

Charley studied the position of the sun, which was the only watch he ever needed for telling time. "We should keep moving if we're going to get back before my daughter blows her top."

As we drifted from shore, I experienced a familiar sensation. The skin of my neck felt as if someone were blowing on it. That usually told me I was being watched by someone with hostile intent. It might have been Rowe, hiding in the trees, or it might have been one of the dozens of other merrymakers who'd recognized me as the enemy of their fun.

In time we could no longer smell the evergreens for all the cook fires. The air took on the greasy taste of frying burgers and bacon. Charley and I collected empty beer cans as they floated past. We even salvaged a half-full plastic bottle of Smirnoff vodka. Suntan oil left iridescent slicks on the surface of the water.

I had just turned twenty-nine in February, but I had never felt so old.

I had read somewhere that in the eastern United States only the Delaware River sees more boaters on a weekend than this short stretch of the Saco River. I had never believed that oft-quoted statistic—until now.

I had to give the Fryeburg police credit, though;

we saw uniformed officers stationed at every canoe launch and spotted police cruisers prowling slowly through the campgrounds. It came as a relief that the town had absolved us wardens of acting as ward monitors on this riverine asylum.

After another hour, we had passed through the logjam of boat traffic. We rounded a bend and found ourselves in the cool shadow of Walker's Bridge, listening to the *thump-thump-thump* overhead of cars speeding along the highway to Portland. We saw another eagle.

Upstream, it had been hard to imagine a sober person getting lost on the Saco. The brooks and creeks that flowed out of the swampy sections converged in the main channel, so it was only a matter of letting the current carry you back to the route. But increasingly now we were encountering forks in the river that would have forced Casey and her companions to make quick choices about which direction to go. Tall clumps of huckleberry and sheep laurel made it hard to see one's surroundings from the low vantage of a canoe seat.

"I think we go left here," I said as we came up suddenly on a wider channel arcing deeper into the bog.

"You're the pilot," Charley said.

In only minutes I started questioning my internal compass. The passage narrowed dramatically so that we brushed driftwood and felt leatherleaf slapping at our arms as we tried to paddle. Then the channel opened again, the bottom dropped off so that we could no longer see it through the brown water, and a perfect isle of white sand came into view dead ahead.

"This is it," I said with relief. "This is Oxbow Island, where Casey and her friends pulled up to camp."

"Seems like they didn't need to go so far out of their way for privacy."

I steered us into the shallows and heard sand rustle beneath the keel. "Menario said something about this being a lovers'-lane-type place."

"So, I see." Charley used the flat of his paddle to dig something out of the water and then held it for me to see.

A molted snakeskin? No. A used condom.

Four years had passed, the Saco had flooded this spit of sand many times, had probably even reshaped it. That didn't stop Charley from going exploring, though. The old man tramped back and forth across the island, which was probably thirty feet at its widest, with a crest of speckled alders in the center. He stopped occasionally to peer off across the bog. We were so low that no trees, hills, or any other landmarks were visible to help us situate ourselves. Finally he directed my attention to another channel on the east side of the island where the surface rippled from the strength of the flow.

"If you were a young girl with a canoe and you were trying to find cover in a lightning storm, which way would you go?"

"Back the way I came."

"I don't think so," he said, leaning on his paddle. "If it was dark and raining, and you were scared, wouldn't it be natural to mistake this creek here for the one you wanted? It's wider than the way we came in."

"You and your intuition."

"Intuition, hell! It's experience, young feller."

I followed my wise friend, stepping in his bootprints to make the going easier, back to the canoe.

28

Before long, we had lost sight of the island and the main channel. The disk of the sun seemed to become whiter and hotter as it ascended into the heavens. Charley stood up in the canoe so smoothly it didn't even rock. I sometimes forgot that he had been a river driver once, trained as a boy to balance on rolling logs and even run across a floating jam without ever getting his ankles wet.

He pointed to the northeast. "High ground up ahead."

We slipped our paddles silently into the stream and continued on. A great host of blue-bodied damselflies alighted on the canoe as if exhausted from some long migration and then, after a few minutes' rest, flew off en masse.

Now there was no current to speak of, just slack water. I noticed a frog staring up at me with eyes like copper beads.

I dragged my forearm across my sweaty brow. "Pretty easy to get turned around back here."

"Eyup."

The channel began to narrow. You could see all the way down to the mud at the bottom. Then the first treetops came into view.

"If you were a young lady from the city and

you saw those oaks after paddling way the hell up here in a thunderstorm, what would you do?"

"Abandon the canoe and try to make my way to dry land on foot."

And just like that Charley hopped out of the canoe. The water was only a couple of feet deep, but the muck was so thick he sank down to his chest. He let out a delighted laugh and slogged up onto firmer ground. His clothes, from his chest to his boots, were soaked and black from the rotting mire.

While I sat in the stern with my paddle across my chest, he grabbed the painter, pulled hard on the rope, and dragged us up into the tangled vegetation. The wiry old man was brawnier than wardens a third his age.

The clumps of cattails and leatherleaf only had the illusion of solidity. Hidden sinkholes were everywhere. One wrong step and you went in all the way to your thigh. At one point the mud sucked off one of my Bean boots and I had to go reaching down after it.

"Now I can see why Menario thinks Dakota Rowe might have hidden Casey's body here." I dumped out a quart of dirty water. "The way this bog reeks, even the best cadaver dog would've had trouble sniffing out a corpse if it was hidden under a few feet of this muck."

Charley offered me a hand. "It's mighty ripe. That's for sure."

I stood up and felt my sock squish against the cushioned insole. "I don't know that I'll want to get back in my truck smelling like this. We might have to drive home in our underwear."

"Doubt that'll be the first time it happened on the Saco."

Both of us fell in a few more times before we finally located a deer path. Unlike moose, deer will avoid soft ground since their slender legs and small hooves get stuck easily in mud. We followed the trampled trail through a scratching wall of alders, swamp birches, and red maples until we finally came to the tall trees beyond.

"Should have left some bread crumbs so we could find my canoe again," I said.

"You haven't noticed me snapping the heads off weeds to mark our way?"

We set off into the forest. I wished I'd brought along my GPS or at least my topo maps. I had a vague sense of where we must have been: on a peninsula of wooded land that rose out of the boggy floodplain. As best I could remember, there were no roads for at least a mile and certainly no houses that Casey could have gone to for help.

Which was why it was so surprising to see the cat.

It was black with white mittens, and it came mincing toward us through the forest as if we had opened a can of food for it.

"What the hell?" I said.

The cat rubbed itself along Charley's leg until he dropped down on one knee to pet it. Even fifteen feet away from him I could hear the cat's contented purring as he scratched its chin. "Now, where did you come from, little miss?"

Feral house cats are so common in towns and cities that most people don't realize why you rarely hear about populations of them flourishing far from humans. As effective predators as they are of birds and rodents, cats are excellent prey for all manner of larger creatures, from owls to coyotes to fishers to foxes. A big tomcat may seem fierce, but out in the real wilderness, he is no more than someone's afternoon snack.

"Do you think she's lost?" I asked.

Charley rubbed her drooping belly, always the telltale sign of a spayed cat. "She looks well fed."

"So where did she come from?"

"Maybe she will show us." The old man straightened up and waited for the cat to become bored with us, which took all of thirty seconds. She scratched an ear with her hind leg to dislodge a flea, cleaned her face with a paw, then gave us one more glance before setting off into the trees.

Charley and I followed at a distance.

Soon we smelled a cooking fire, not one made with charcoal briquettes: the smoke had the sharp, pine-scented odor of someone burning softwood.

A battered blue pickup was parked in a clearing up ahead. The vehicle had a white cap over the bed, and a family-size dome tent was set up beside the open passenger door. I heard a woman's voice making nonsense noises to a baby.

Charley and I froze in place as if we'd snuck up on a ten-point buck. Wardens are taught at the "school" we attend after graduating from the Maine Criminal Justice Academy how to walk quietly in the forest and use natural cover to hide ourselves. Not to mention that Charley had three decades of real-world experience in the art of concealment.

I couldn't see the woman from my position, but I gathered she was behind the truck. It sounded as if she might be changing a diaper on the tailgate. After half a minute a young man appeared, whistling tunelessly. He had a brushy beard and long golden-brown hair tied up in a man bun. He was shirtless with a pronounced rib cage. In his long arms was a stack of kindling he had picked up from the forest floor.

The cat trotted over to him as he dropped the firewood, which clattered onto the pine needles. "Sorry, Puddin, I ain't got no food for you. How come you didn't catch no mouse?"

"There ain't mice out in the woods," said the woman.

"The heck there ain't."

Their accents weren't southern exactly—but they definitely weren't from Maine.

Charley and I exchanged glances, then he stepped forward. "Good morning!"

We hadn't been more than fifty feet away, and not even that well hidden, but it was as if we'd cast off cloaks of invisibility. The man did a definite double take. I saw a young woman stick her head out from behind the blue truck. She had heavy acne and thick dark hair that made her look like a junior witch.

The bearded man raised a hand in a weak wave. "Howdy."

"You folks camping?" Charley asked as if the answer weren't self-evident.

"Yes, sir."

I decided to assert myself. "How did you get in here?"

The man stretched his arm off in a direction that I judged to be southeast. "Drove in on that road."

From the direction we'd come, we hadn't been able to see the dirt track leading back through the pines and oaks. It was completely covered with dead leaves and fallen needles, multiple autumns' worth, which meant it hadn't been plowed or graded in years.

I noticed their Pennsylvania license plate. The registration had expired months ago. "This isn't your property, I take it."

"What business is it of yours?" The woman was a cute little thing, barely five feet tall. She wore a white halter, stained with baby vomit, and bell-bottom jeans.

For the third time that day, I pulled up the tail of my shirt to show off the badge on my belt. "I'm a game warden. This is private land."

The woman stepped in front of her man. I had the feeling she was the assertive one in the family. "We got permission to be here."

"Permission from who?"

"The owner. He comes in to check on the place, make sure no one's burned it down. Lots of people camp here. We got the place to ourselves now is all. But there were three or four other groups here when we first came in."

Scanning the clearing, I saw old fire rings and brushed areas of ground where tents had been pitched. Tire marks in the dried mud, too.

"Really?" I had a bad habit of resting a hand on the grip of my firearm. It could be a menacing pose.

"We ain't done nothing wrong," the woman said, looking at my gun.

Things might have grown confrontational were it not for my friend's natural charm. "We should've introduced ourselves. My name's Charley Stevens. What's yours?"

"Prudence Smith."

"And yours?" Charley held out his hand for the bony man to shake.

"Jackson," he mumbled. "Jackson Smith."

"This is Warden Bowditch. We were out on the river and decided to come ashore. Found your little cat roaming around and followed her back here. Beautiful day, isn't it?"

"It's hot," said Prudence.

"The bugs been bad?" Charley asked.

"Manageable," said Jackson. "But they drove out the last folks who was here. Guess our skins were thicker."

"You have a baby, I see. What's his name?"

The woman darted behind the truck again and snatched up her naked infant as if we might have been aiming to steal him. The kid couldn't have been more than a year old but was already so long, he dangled past her hips.

"We ain't done nothing wrong," she said again. "We got permission, like I said."

"You didn't get the owner's name, did you?" I asked.

"John something," Jackson said. "His last name was unusual."

"How'd you two find this place?" Charley asked.

Prudence seemed to be relaxing her guard. "We were down in Portland for a while but didn't like the crowd. Drug addicts and thieves. Got kicked out of a couple of other sites. Lady working at a bakery outlet gave us directions. Told us which road to take. She said drive until you see the cellar hole, and that's what we done."

"You've had some bad luck then," I said, trying a softer tone myself.

Jackson looked at the ground as if with embarrassment. "I lost my job down in Pennsylvania. Then we lost our apartment. Almost lost the truck, too. So we decided, why not visit Vacationland?"

But the young woman had already decided she didn't like me. "Yes, we're homeless," she snapped. "No, we're not vagrants. No, we're not beggars. We just barely are making it." She gestured at the truck, the tent, the blanket spread with baby toys and picture books. "What you see is by the grace of God."

"You decided to go on the road," said Charley calmly. The cat had begun circling his legs again.

"Why not?" Prudence asked.

In my time as a warden I had encountered my share of illegal campers. It used to be that people parked their pop-up trailers at the ends of logging roads because they couldn't afford cabins of their own or were too cheap to pay for a campground site. And as long as they didn't start forest fires, the timber companies didn't mind.

But more and more, I was hearing stories of people like this couple who were living in the woods because they were homeless and had nowhere else to go. The city of Portland had razed much of the scrub woodland around its interstates for the express purpose of giving transients no place to pitch their tents. One of the effects had been to drive the displaced and the desperate into actual forests such as this one.

"And you said other people have camped here with you over the past month?" I asked.

"A bunch," said Jackson.

"So why're you hassling us?" the woman said.

Charley cooed at the baby. "What did you say this big guy's name was?"

"This is Carson." Prudence allowed herself the most tentative of smiles. "He's our little peanut butter and jelly."

"He's going to be a bruiser. Maybe he'll play for the Steelers someday."

The father grinned. "Wouldn't that be something?"

Charley nodded, but I could tell the compliment was a polite ruse to ask another question. "You mentioned a woman at a bakery outlet—"

"We don't want to get her in trouble," said Prudence.

"She told you to drive until you saw a cellar hole. Where would that hole be?"

Jackson, the proud father, waved for us to follow him. He was so gangly, he walked as if there were springs in his knees.

We ducked our way under some oak branches and stepped over a fallen pine that someone had used as an improvised commode. Flies buzzed excitedly around the dark pile beneath it.

Another clearing opened before us. The trees were just saplings along the edges. Hay-scented ferns grew in a verdant patch in the open sunlight.

"Never heard the term *cellar hole* before," said our guide. "The guy who owns the land said it used to be his dad's hunting and fishing cabin."

"Is that so?" Charley asked.

I wasn't sure what the old man's interest was in a vanished building unless it was just his natural curiosity. I trailed along behind them, wishing I hadn't left my water jug back in the canoe.

Jackson came to a halt and Charley stood beside him, looking down.

The cellar hole was a rectangle of burned timbers and charred shingles. There were shards of broken bottles, some crumbled masonry, along with more recent trash that displaced campers had thrown into the shallow pit. This seemed to be the local toxic-waste dump. If the landowner had no problem with people throwing dirty diapers and bags of garbage here, he was a better man than I was.

"John Blood!" Jackson exclaimed. "That's what he said his name was. Sounded like a comic book character to me."

And to me, as well. But the surname was not uncommon in Maine.

My phone buzzed in my pocket. I was sure it

was Stacey calling to ream us out for running late. But the name on the screen was Ellen Pomerleau.

"Guess what," she said.

I turned away from Charley and Jackson, who were musing over the question of when the cabin might have burned down. "What?"

"The DNA sample from your Baby Jane Doe came back from the crime lab."

"And—?"

"There's no question about it. The match was ninety-nine percent with the sample on file in CODIS. That little girl and Casey Donaldson share fourteen of twenty-two markers. You were right, Bowditch. I don't know how, but you were right. Casey Donaldson is still alive."

29

A heat shimmer was rising over the vast bog. The waves of distortion in the air made the hills along the far shore seem to ripple. I paused to get my bearings, looking for the trail of broken vegetation Charley had made to lead us back to the canoe. When I couldn't find it at first glance, he set a fatherly hand on my shoulder and led the way.

"There's no chance of it being a mix-up?" he said as we trudged through the huckleberry and sheep laurel. "DNA analysis came around late in my career. To me it's always sounded like something out of Buck Rogers."

"Sure, there's a possibility of a mix-up." I pulled my boot out of yet another sinkhole. "But it's like billions to one. The term the crime-lab analysts use is loci, but the easiest way to think of them is as points of comparison. The FBI database uses twenty loci. The more repeats that show up, the higher the probability there is of a match. The odds against the baby being the daughter of anyone but Casey are astronomical."

"I guess this news is going to ruin Detective Menario's holiday."

"Pomerleau is trying to keep a lid on it until she can bring in the FBI. But Menario will probably hear from one of his buddies in the department."

"What about the girl's family? Who's going to tell them?"

"Pomerleau thinks the Bureau will want to send an agent to her stepdad's house to talk with him. It's not the sort of news you break over the phone."

"Not unless you want to give the poor man a heart attack. So what happens next?"

"I assume Pomerleau will call a meeting of whoever worked the initial search for Casey four years ago along with anybody involved in the recent investigations."

"Sounds like you'll be leaving your own party early."

The party.

In the excitement I had forgotten about the backyard barbecue—just as Stacey had warned me I would. Our guests would be arriving in less than four hours. The only reason I could imagine that Stacey hadn't called to chew me out for being late was that she was plotting a more inventive punishment.

The thought of throwing a party, now that we had absolute confirmation that Casey was still alive, made my stomach burn. How could I enjoy myself when I knew that she was suffering nearby? But, as Dani had reminded me, I was a warden and not a state police detective, and this was not my case to work.

The breeze had picked up, and a northern water snake had somehow found its way into the boat and was curled up on my seat cushion. It was about four feet long and mocha brown with darker cross bands. As a boy I had acquired a respect for their surly temper and the sharpness of their fangs. But Charley reached in and grabbed the serpent by the tail. He hurled it into the channel before it could whip around to bite him. I watched the reptile swim away in S-shaped strokes, the motion reminiscent of the tail swishes of an angry cat.

Charley used the diversion to snag a seat in the stern. I had been right about the old woodsman; he couldn't bear to be in a canoe he wasn't steering.

We ended up following the serpent downstream. At first we couldn't dig the paddles into the water too deeply without raising clouds of mud from the bottom, but as the channel widened and deepened, we began to pick up speed. Soon we started hearing war whoops from rafters on the main channel of the river. Then the *rat-tat-tat* of thrown firecrackers in violation of the laws prohibiting them.

The island where Casey and her friends had camped, and where she thought she had lost her mother's diamond ring, came into view. We slid by it in silence, each of us absorbing the full weight of what had now been proven. Somehow, in seeking to find her way out of the maze of the bog, Casey Donaldson had found herself in another kind of labyrinth, one in which real monsters lurked.

"We can stop calling her Baby Jane Doe," I said as the sandbar disappeared behind a tussock. "She's the Donaldson girl now."

"That's not a proper name for her, either."

"It's a start."

The sensation I had experienced before—of an enemy watching me from some secret place—returned. Only this time I knew it was just the wind.

We wasted no time in getting off the Saco. For me, that meant ignoring a half dozen boating violations (principally absent flotation devices), along with other misdemeanors such as lewd conduct, littering, and almost certainly underage drinking, judging by the looks of some of the kids we saw floating along in tubes with cans of beer. I had to remind myself that I wasn't on duty today. Still, I hoped to God that no one drowned later on account of my inaction. When you are a law-enforcement officer, it is sometimes hard to accept that you can't save everyone from his or her bad decisions.

We arrived, along with a mass of other canoeists and tubers, at the sandbank above Birnam Bridge. By the time I had backed my Scout down the beach, Charley had somehow flipped the heavy boat over and was walking it up the ramp, the yoke braced against his shoulders, his oversize hands gripping the gunnels tightly. The sixteen-foot-long Old Town weighed seventy-five pounds. I gathered up the paddles and flotation cushions while he lashed the canoe to the top of my vehicle with trucker's hitches.

As we set off to Fryeburg to retrieve my patrol truck, Charley said, "I expect they'll bring the landlords in for another talk."

"The Nasons? The older son, Steven, seems to be the only person besides me and Connie Fales to have seen this 'Becky Cobb' in the flesh. He definitely knows more than he's admitting."

"You said he struck you as being empty between the ears?"

"His mother did all the talking."

"And she didn't seem too sharp, either."

"She was sharp enough to ingratiate herself with a rich, dying man and persuade him to leave her his fortune."

Charley rolled down his window to let out a deerfly that had pursued us into the vehicle. "I'm pretty sure Kathy Frost worked this search four years ago with her coonhound."

"She's coming to the barbecue tonight. Hopefully she can fill us in on what went wrong."

Now that it was midday, the Swan's Falls Campground was even more mobbed than it had been at first light. We had to wait in a line of slow-moving traffic to enter the grounds, only to find our new acquaintance from the Fryeburg police turning around cars since the lot was full.

Reserve Officer Nisbet even tried to turn us around before he recognized our faces. He stuck his face through my open window. His breath was horrible. "You're back!"

"So it seems," said Charley.

He pushed at his pompadour, which was losing its shape. "How far did you get?"

"Oxbow Island."

"That far?"

"We need to get into the lot to get my patrol truck," I said.

"Might be easier if one of you just walked in. There are cars jammed up every which way near the water. The chief is down there himself trying to sort out the parking situation so we can clear out some vehicles. What a shitshow!"

"Do you mind meeting me back at the house?" I asked Charley.

"Not at all. Any specific apologies you want me to make on your behalf?"

"Better I do it myself."

The campground was a human zoo with every subspecies of *Homo sapiens* running loose, out of their cages. One group of college-age rafters had painted their bodies bright blue, like ancient Picts going into battle against the Roman legions.

I saw many females wearing ill-chosen bikinis. Some fool scoutmaster had taken his Cub Scouts out on the river in the midst of the holiday chaos. Never had I seen so many young eyes opened wide in shock and fright.

It took me a solid fifteen minutes to nudge my Sierra out of its space and crawl back up the hill through the herd of vacationers. Finally I found myself back out at the campground gate, where Reserve Officer Nisbet was in a shouting match with a carful of frat boys.

I rolled down my window. "Hey, Nisbet!"

"Sometimes you want to strangle these punks," Fat Elvis confessed.

Death by throttling struck me as a harsh punishment for rudeness, but the reserve officer had a more draconian code of ethics than I did.

"Speaking of which," he continued, "Dakota Rowe came by looking for you. He'd heard you were asking about him at Hodge's. He must have guessed you put in here."

For years Rowe had only had to fend off Menario. Maybe my appearance on the scene had begun to trouble him.

"You know Dakota?"

"Every cop around here knows that piece of shit."

As I was about to leave, one last question occurred to me for Nisbet. "You mentioned that your cousin rents a house from the Nasons. Do you remember anything he said about them?"

"It's a she actually. Aside from never fixing anything? Not really. Look, Warden, no offense, but I've got work to do. I'm already up shit's creek with the chief."

"OK. Thanks."

Nisbet started to turn away, then stopped. "There is one thing. My cousin said she caught the dumb one peeping through her bathroom window once. I told her if it happened again to call me, and I'd personally drive out and shoot the son of a bitch."

So in addition to being a liar, Steven Nason was also seemingly a Peeping Tom. I wondered if Pomerleau was aware of that rumor. I looked forward to sharing it with her. It made me feel as self-satisfied as a cat dropping on its owner's doormat a dead mouse.

30

Even before I pulled into the driveway, I could see that one of our guests had arrived a full hour early. Kathy Frost had backed her bronze Nissan Xterra across the shaggy lawn and parked it in the shade of the pines, no doubt so that she could keep the tailgate open for her puppy in her crate. Every game warden and former game warden I knew made a habit of backing his or her vehicle into parking spaces—the better to pull out in a hurry if an emergency call came over the police radio.

Charley had beat me home, too, and had already untied the canoe from the top of my Scout and stowed it away in the backyard. Stacey's Subaru was in its usual spot, but I could deduce from its altered position that she had been out and back during the morning.

I heard voices in the backyard, so instead of going through the house, I circled around the side of the building.

Charley and Kathy were both sprawled on the grass, in the shadows thrown by the late-afternoon sun, playing with a honey-brown puppy: Kathy's new Malinois. When my former sergeant caught sight of me, she rose to her knees, a tall, fiftyish woman with a chestnut-

293

colored bob, hazel eyes, and a freckled face that was appealing more because of the personality that radiated from it than the symmetry of her features.

"Grasshopper!" She had given me the pet name when I was a rookie.

"Hey, Kath."

Several years ago, Kathy Frost had been shot in the line of duty and had lost her spleen and parts of other organs; she still carried steel-shot pellets inside her from the attack. The assault—followed by her forced early retirement from the Warden Service—had aged her, and for a long time I had worried about her health. But her cheeks were full of color this afternoon, and when she hugged me, I was afraid she might crack one of my ribs.

The puppy sniffed excitedly at my muddy pant leg.

"This is Maple," Kathy said.

"Nice to meet you, Maple." When I reached down to scratch the puppy's head, she bit my hand—not hard, but firmly enough to leave marks.

"Give a yelp," advised Kathy.

"A yelp?"

"So she knows she bit too hard."

I did my best to imitate a puppy in pain. Surprised, Maple released my hand.

"That was the sorriest effort at canine communication I ever heard," said Charley. He flicked a rope toy at Maple, and soon she was in a new tug-of-war. I noticed his hair was wet, and he'd changed into a fresh green T-shirt and Dickies. How had that old geezer managed to shower, too? I hadn't been *that* far behind him.

Kathy bent carefully over to lift her beer can from the grass. As healthy as she looked, she was still dealing with the long-term damage of the shotgun blast.

"So how goes the training?" I asked her.

"Great! Right now Maple and I are focusing on the basics. We won't start search-and-rescue exercises until she stops eating my shoes. She seems to have real aptitude, though. Her nose is excellent. Almost as good as—" She caught herself before saying the name of her dear, departed coonhound. Instead she addressed Charley: "How's Nimrod doing?"

"I swear that pointer is going to outlive us all. Fifteen years old and still full of vinegar!"

It didn't seem like the right moment to raise the subject of Casey Donaldson, but I was eager to ask Kathy about her memories of the aborted search. Pluto had still been alive then and was considered one of the best rescue-and-recovery dogs in the country—Kathy had taken him to New Orleans after Hurricane Katrina to assist in finding the bodies. How, then, had he failed to find any trace of Casey?

I glanced at the screen door that led into the kitchen. "Where are Stacey and Ora?"

"Making potato salad," Charley said. "Ora got the recipe from her mother, who was Waldoboro Dutch. It's good German-style salad. None of that mayonnaise-y stuff."

"I guess I'd better go face the music."

"Just a suggestion," Kathy said, "but you might want to change those yucky pants first. You smell like the Swamp Thing."

"Stacey's used to it."

I did, however, take off my boots and socks and hosed off the muck between my toes and under my toenails. In doing so, I found I had carried home an engorged leech. I flicked the little bloodsucker into the daylilies.

Stacey and her mother were preparing the salad at the table, which was the only surface low enough for Ora to reach from her wheelchair. The room smelled of fried bacon and caramelizing onions.

My bare feet left wet prints on the floor. "I'm home."

Stacey kept her back to me as she pushed the sizzling bacon around a cast-iron pan. "So we see."

"Charley said you had news." Ora said, unable to hide her anticipation. "He didn't want to spoil it."

Stacey turned around finally, but her expression wasn't annoyed, as I had expected, but tense; it was as if she were doing her best to keep a flood of emotions from bursting through some internal dam.

I plucked a piece of bacon from the paper towel on which it was oozing grease. "Detective Pomerleau called while we were exploring the edge of the bog where Casey was last seen. The DNA results came back from the crime lab. The baby we found was Casey's."

Ora made a swallowing sound and seemed to shrink in her wheelchair. But Stacey remained motionless. Her mouth tightened. Neither of them seemed capable of speech.

"Pomerleau's keeping it under wraps for now," I said.

"Have you told Kathy?" asked Ora. "Didn't she and Pluto work that case?"

"I didn't want to hit her with it first thing. Maybe after she puts Maple back in her crate. There's going to be a meeting tonight at the crime lab in Augusta to plan a course of action."

Ora fiddled with the hem of her sweater. "Are you going?"

"I don't know. I'm thinking that there will be people there who will want to hear what I have to say. But Pomerleau hasn't formally invited me yet."

"Of course you're going," said Stacey with no hint of anger. "It's not even up for discussion. That poor girl needs you."

I was having trouble reading her. "Is it too late to postpone the party?"

Stacey's smile was more of a wince. "I think my folks and I can manage to entertain people in your absence. It's not like you're a social butterfly."

I tried to keep things light. "More like an antisocial moth."

"Go take a shower, Mike."

In the bathroom, trying to shave in a foggy mirror, I realized how little I knew about Casey Donaldson as a person—what made her laugh, whether she was a good student, what her dreams had been before she was taken away like Persephone to Hades.

Too often that's the way it is with the victims of homicides or, in this case, a presumed homicide. Except for the investigators, who need to know everything about the habits of the deceased, most of us prefer to treat the victims of violence as icons. That's why we use their first names (Nicole, JonBenét)—as if they were members of our own family. We don't want them to be complex human beings. We want them to be flat screens on which we can project our outrage.

Stacey cracked open the door. "Our guests are wondering where you are."

"I'll be right down."

"I forgot to tell you. Allan called yesterday from the USDA-APHIS office. He got the results back from the lab and says our pork is disease-free and fine to eat."

"If we'd known sooner, we could have had chops instead of mooseburgers and salmon fillets."

"I thought we were giving the meat to Aimee. She just arrived with the Cronklets, by the way. I guess they stopped to see Billy at the prison in Warren on their way over."

I said nothing, but Stacey seemed to sense my pain.

"You have a life, Mike, a life beyond your job. You've worked hard to make one here with me. You should cut yourself a break and enjoy being with your friends for a few hours."

"It feels wrong to have a party when Casey Donaldson is being held captive."

Stacey studied me a while longer with those inscrutable green eyes. "So we're supposed to put our life on hold? For how long? What if she's never seen again?"

Again, I had no answer.

"You'll be all right, Mike. Pretend to enjoy yourself and most people won't even notice that you're faking."

After she'd closed the door, steam fogged the mirror again and I lost sight of myself in the looking glass.

I had never seen our backyard this crowded.

Stacey and I had been building a life together, and here it was in this collection of friends and family. With the notable exception of Billy Cronk, everyone we loved was here: Charley and Ora, of course; Aimee Cronk and her five tow-haired children; Kathy Frost and Maple (who, being a puppy, became the center of attention among the Cronklets); the Reverend Deborah Davies, chaplain with the Warden Service, and her ex-hippie husband, Burton, who ran an heirloom-apple orchard; Warden Cody Devoe and his shy new girlfriend, who clung to him the way a drowning animal clings to a log; Skip Morrison, recently promoted to chief deputy of the Knox County Sheriff's Department; and two of Stacey's college classmates from the University of Vermont, a married female couple named Jodi and Felice.

I had planned to station myself at the Weber as an excuse to avoid making small talk, but Charley kept offering suggestions about my barbecuing techniques until he succeeded in displacing me from my own grill. It was all the more galling that his burgers and fish turned out perfectly cooked.

To keep myself occupied, I took drink orders. Charley wanted black coffee (in eighty-degree heat), Ora wanted her usual whiskey and soda, the Cronklets wanted Moxie, the Reverend Davies wanted white wine, while her husband kept trying to foist off on us his homemade hard cider. Jodi and Felice insisted they could pour their own drinks, thank you.

I felt a hand on my wrist and found Aimee Cronk smiling at me. She was short and open faced, and she carried her extra pounds with such voluptuousness that she attracted admiring looks from men wherever she went. She had a glass of Burton Davies's cider in her hand.

"You tried this?" she asked.

"Not yet."

She leaned close to whisper. "Tastes like cat piss. And don't ask me how I know what cat piss tastes like."

I'd always adored Aimee.

"How is Billy doing? I heard you saw him on the way over." Just saying my friend's name made my mouth go dry.

"Oh, he says he's fine, but he really isn't. You know I can read that man like a book, and I'm not talking *War and Peace*, either. More like the Classics comics version of *War and Peace*."

The state of Maine does not have parole, which meant that Billy, having exhausted his legal options, would not be getting out of the Maine State Prison early.

"Aimee . . ."

"It's OK, Mike. He's too macho to say it, but it

301

means the world that you go visit him as often as you do. Stacey said you're giving us a freezerful of boar meat. I didn't even know that *Sus scrofa* lives in Maine."

"How do you know the Latin name for wild boar?"

"Animal Planet."

More likely she had been reading *Audubon* or *Smithsonian* or some other magazine left behind in the waiting room at the dentist's office where she was working as a receptionist. Aimee Cronk had never even graduated from high school, but I had always said she had one of the keenest intellects I had encountered and was more perceptive than the best FBI profilers I'd met.

Just then, Deb Davies's husband came along to thrust a glass of urine-colored liquid in my hand.

"You need one of these, Mike!" the orchard keeper said. He turned to Aimee. "So what do you think, Mrs. Cronk? Pretty good, right?"

"Purrr-fect."

I pretended to sip, murmured a compliment, and then excused myself. I passed through the busy kitchen (dumping the cider down the drain) and into my cluttered office, where I could think without being disturbed. I didn't realize that Kathy was following me until she appeared in the doorway.

Her face was dark with disappointment. "I just got a call from Ellen Pomerleau. She wants me up at the state crime lab at seven tonight for a meeting. That dead baby you found was Casey Donaldson's? You knew I worked that search. When did you plan on telling me?"

"After the party."

"You could have pulled me aside."

I said the first thing that came into my mind. "Where's Maple?"

"In her crate—which is where I'd like to shove you at the moment." Kathy stepped inside my office. "Grasshopper, you need to tell me what's been going on here. I don't want to be the only person in the room without a clue. Pomerleau said I am supposed to drag you along, by the way. I asked her if she meant that literally."

31

Kathy leaned against the door with her arms crossed and her neck tense enough for me to see individual muscles flexing beneath the skin. But as I told my story, the furrows in her brow disappeared, her lips parted, and her hands dropped to her sides. You could see the pain take hold of her. But she never came close to shedding a tear. Sergeant Kathy Frost had always been harder than her male colleagues—at least outwardly. It had been the price she paid for being the first female game warden in Maine history.

"I'm sorry. I should have said something as soon as I got home."

"Forget about it." She tapped the expensive Suunto GPS watch on her wrist. "We should get a move on. And you should change into a uniform. The bigwigs will take what you say more seriously if you're dressed like a warden."

"Can you answer one question for me, first? Four years ago, during the search, did you really believe Casey was dead?"

"I told myself I believed it. Pluto didn't indicate once out in that swamp. I should have taken it as a sign he might be getting too old for the job. I'm not the only member of the search team who is going to have to live with abandoning that girl." She reached behind her back for the doorknob and gave it a twist. "I'll see you in Augusta, Grasshopper. I'd normally suggest we carpool, but I need some time to wrap my head around this."

It hadn't hit me before what a neutron bomb this news would be when it exploded in the press. Kathy was retired on a disability pension, safe from consequences, but other wardens and police officers still on the job would be called to task for what they did and didn't do to find Casey Donaldson. Careers would end in disgrace. Or in lawsuits.

I slipped upstairs to change my clothes, then returned to the backyard in uniform.

The Cronklets were still swinging like gibbons from the monkey bars. I envied them their innocence.

The Reverend Davies stood up from the picnic table. "Is everything all right, Mike? Kathy said she had to leave."

"She had to run up to Augusta for a quick meeting."

"Now?" The warden chaplain always had her antennae up for accidents and emergencies that might require her ministerial services. "What's going on?"

"I'm not allowed to say. But I'll fill you in when I get back."

"You mean you're going, too?"

"My presence has been requested."

We both knew I wouldn't be back until long after the party was over.

I found Stacey in the corner of the yard watching the Cronklets at play. "I'm sorry about this."

"It's not your fault," she said with more resignation than I had anticipated. "It's part of the job. And the job is who you are. I've always known that." Then she hugged me good-bye with surprising intensity. "You need to find that girl, Mike. If she's still alive, you need to find her."

Charley was waiting for me in the driveway, hanging off my truck as if I had caught him in the act of trying to stow away.

"Don't forget to mention that cellar hole," he said.

"The one at the homeless camp?"

"That cabin burned down two or three years back—you can tell from the height of the willows growing up from the ruins. Now, it might be coincidence that it went up in flames the same as the house on Rankin Road. Or it might not. Either way, Pomerleau needs to check out this so-called John Blood who says he owns the land and find out why he's willing to let campers dump their garbage there."

And here I'd thought Charley's interest in seeing the cellar hole was another example of his crowlike curiosity. "We don't even know that Casey Donaldson left the bog that way."

"Like I said, it might all be a coincidence." He touched the brim of his cap to wish me good-bye and safe travels.

The Maine State Police Crime Laboratory is housed in an imposing brick building across the Kennebec River from the gold dome of the state capitol. Once it got dark enough, the national holiday would be celebrated with fireworks over the city. I doubted I would be out of the meeting in time to see the sky light up, let alone be in a mood to celebrate.

When I pulled into the parking lot, I spotted a clutch of troopers gathered around a sports car. Dani Tate—recognizable by her signature shortness—was among them. As I walked over to have a look, I realized that the onlookers were conversing in whispers.

The car was a brand-new Mustang Shelby GT. It had been a beautiful vehicle until someone had doused it with paint stripper. The caustic chemical had dissolved the clear coat and discolored the pigment underneath. If you had told me a flock of gulls had spent the night shitting atop the vehicle, I would have believed it.

I hitched my thumbs under my ballistic vest like an old-time farmer lifting his suspender straps. It was an unconscious habit of wardens.

The heavy vests did a job on your shoulder muscles, especially when you were paranoid like me and wore the ceramic plates inside.

"Isn't this Menario's vehicle?" I asked Dani.

"Yep."

"Dakota Rowe did this?"

"If he did, he's going to be number one on Troop B's shit list."

I looked around and spotted Kathy's Xterra parked at the shady end of the lot, once again for Maple's sake.

"So are you going to this meeting, too?" I asked Dani.

"I'm a material witness, thanks to you."

"What do you mean 'thanks to me'?"

"It was you who almost got me blown up the other day."

"Or you could say that I was the one who saved your life."

"Whatever you say, Mr. Hero." She had stopped using her fake gruff voice with me now that the others were out of earshot.

The receptionist had to buzz us in through the door. The lobby included a small glassed display of antique forensic tools: ancient microscopes and fingerprint pads, crime-scene cameras and tape measures. A painting on one wall depicted three forensic technicians examining a bloody room in which someone had taped the outline of a recently removed corpse.

I followed Dani into a brightly lit meeting room. Most of the seats around the rectangle of tables were already taken. Clearly this briefing was going to be more than an exercise in ass covering.

I recognized some of the faces but not all of them. There was Pomerleau's boss, Barrett, and her partner, Finch. The head of detectives for the state police sat beside them.

I saw Menario, wearing his golfing polo and slacks, with his head bowed over his dossier, like a monk studying holy writ.

Kathy sat against the wall, sipping a quart-size cup of soda through a straw. She beckoned Dani over to sit beside her, but there was no chair there for me.

The well-tailored suit of a slim man gave him away as an FBI agent. Most Maine detectives seemed to buy their suits at two-for-one sales and never bothered to have them tailored.

The Maine State fire marshal in his red uniform waited with his hands folded atop his report.

Beside him, the Fryeburg chief of police slouched in his chair, looking sunburned and exhausted from a long day keeping watch over the Saco. He'd brought along one of his people: a blade-faced woman, also in uniform, who was probably the town detective.

The medical examiner who had removed the dead baby from the pig wallow was conversing with two analysts from the lab downstairs. I expected to see the state forensic anthropologist, too, but he must have been granted a permission slip to miss the conclave.

I didn't know two men in plainclothes—obviously detectives from their demeanor—but imagined that they might represent the two counties where the search had taken place: Oxford and Cumberland.

Someone tapped me on the shoulder. "Bowditch?"

Turning, I was surprised to see the boyish face of Warden Service captain John "Jock" DeFord.

Before I could express my surprise at seeing him, he said, "I don't know about you, but this isn't how I planned on spending the Fourth of July."

"No, sir."

Normally, the current search commander—the head of what we called our Overhead Team—would have been present for this kind of briefing. But DeFord must have supervised the initial search for Casey Donaldson on the Saco four years earlier before his promotion to captain. Hence his presence.

DeFord rubbed his recently shorn scalp. "If you had told me last week that Casey Donaldson was still alive, I would have thought you were delusional."

"Four years without a sighting would have seemed conclusive to a lot of juries," I said.

"It doesn't matter. We screwed up, Mike."

"The good news is that we can still save her."

From behind me, I heard Pomerleau call out, "Is everyone here? Good. Let's get started."

The detective had dressed formally for the occasion, in a black pants suit and white blouse. You want to look smart when you are accompanied by the highest law-enforcement officer in the state.

I was startled to see that the Maine attorney general himself had chosen to join us. Hal Hildreth was small in stature but had great gravitas. He wore a seersucker suit, loafers, and a gold Rolex. His cheeks and hands were tanned from yachting off Mount Desert Island. His brushed-back golden hair was reminiscent of a lion's mane.

One of his female assistants—I was guessing she was the prosecutor assigned to the case—whispered something in his ear as they took seats together that had obviously been reserved for them.

The last person to enter the room was the sergeant who oversaw the crime lab.

Pomerleau waited for him to close the door before offering her opening remarks. "Thank you all for coming here on this holiday evening. I realize what an imposition this is for you to take time away from friends and family. But as you will hear, time is of the essence. Many of you were part of the search for Casey Donaldson four years ago. Others were part of the concurrent criminal investigation that explored, at the time, whether she was the victim of homicide."

Menario glanced up finally from the papers spread in front of him. We made eye contact. His mouth tightened as if the sight of me was enough to cause bile to rise in his throat.

"There are also people in this room who are only learning about Casey for the first time," said Pomerleau. "For that reason I think the best place to begin is at the beginning."

She stepped aside so the head of the crime lab could start his presentation. He touched a button on a laptop and video monitors flickered on around the room. In each screen was the same image: a smiling young woman with tousled black hair, white teeth, and a distinctive mole on her cheek. She was seated in a red canoe with a paddle across her bare knees. The sergeant pushed another button on the computer and the image became a video. Over the speakers in the room came the sound of running water, garbled background conversation, and then laughter from the man who had been holding the camera.

"Are you taking movies right now?" Casey said in a slurred but happy voice. "No, I'm not drunk!

I only had one shot. One and a half. How do you paddle this thing again? I'm serious! Tell me."

Then she collapsed into a giggling fit.

Pomerleau raised her hand toward the screen. "This is Casey Donaldson on what we'd thought —until earlier today—was two days before her death."

32

Never before had I been in a meeting with so many high-powered people. The vibe felt somewhere in between the White House Situation Room and the Council of Elrond.

"I'm not going to sugarcoat this," said Pomerleau. "In the scheme of nightmare scenarios that Major Crimes has to deal with, this is right there at the top. Doesn't matter how hard we worked or how thoroughly we searched for her—and I know many of you made real sacrifices looking for Casey—but there's no way around the fact that we failed in our jobs. You can be sure her friends and family will remind us of that. And there's a hundred percent chance this becomes an international news story. I'm talking about *60 Minutes*, CNN, Fox News, the BBC."

"Shouldn't our priority be finding Casey instead of worrying about damage control?" Kathy asked from the peanut gallery in back. No longer being a state employee had increased her already-considerable candor.

Ellen Pomerleau and Kathy Frost had worked together previously, but the rush of blood to the detective's pallid cheeks showed how little she appreciated the interruption. "That goes without saying."

"It seemed to me someone should still say it."

The attorney general, Hildreth, had a booming voice that belonged to a man twice his size. "I am going to ask that everyone refrain from interrupting Detective Pomerleau until she has finished the first part of her briefing."

"Thank you." She opened the top button of her blouse to release some steam. "I would like to start with a timeline of the initial investigation that began with Casey Donaldson's disappearance on the Saco River on July twentieth four years ago. As I did not work that case, I am going to call on some of the people in the room to provide supplemental information. In the assessment of the Major Crimes unit, recent events show with near certainty that Casey is still alive, is probably being held against her will in an unknown location, and recently gave birth to a baby girl whose cadaver Warden Bowditch discovered along Knife Creek in the town of Birnam."

Several heads turned in my direction when Pomerleau mentioned my name. I felt a desperate twitching in my stomach, as if I had swallowed a garter snake.

The detective continued, "From there, we'll move on to a discussion of our tactical plan, identify the officers in charge, delegate responsibilities to all of the participating agencies, and establish communication protocols between our teams. Lastly, we'll discuss how to control the dissemination of information to the public. Since we have a lot of ground to cover, I'm going to leap into the history so that we're all on the same page."

Casey Donaldson had been a good, if not exceptional, student; popular and fun loving, but not known to be a party girl. A drinker but smart enough not to get blackout drunk around boys.

"What about drugs?" asked the attorney general.

Menario leaped in before Pomerleau could answer. Retired he might be, but in his mind this was still his case. "The usual. Pot, of course. Molly sometimes, when she was going out. She tried Adderall but didn't like the way it made her feel, her friend Angie Gifford told me."

"This is the same girl who accompanied Casey on the float trip?" someone asked.

"That's correct. It was Casey, Gifford, and three male friends, all from UNH. Marcus Solomon, Noah Marks, Carlos Diaz."

"Would you describe any one of them as Casey's 'boyfriend'?" asked the attorney general.

"Diaz," said Pomerleau. "Although it was more of a 'friends with benefits' situation, based on his statement."

"Ah, millennials," said the attorney general with a knowing smile.

"So there were no arguments between them before she disappeared?" asked the state police head of detectives.

"No," said Menario. "And they were all together when she took the canoe that afternoon. Their alibis for each other were rock solid."

"What about at home?" asked the same officer. "Any problems with her stepfather?"

Menario seemed offended by the question. "Absolutely not!"

Hildreth's deputy, the female assistant attorney general, was scribbling furiously on a yellow legal pad. Without looking up she said, "Nevertheless, I'm assuming you explored the possibility that his daughter had run off intentionally?"

Menario's tone was like ice cracking. "She didn't run off."

The prosecutor paused in her note taking. "A day ago, you were telling everyone who'd listen that Casey Donaldson was dead. I don't think your certainties are worth a whole lot, Detective."

Everyone fell silent. Menario drummed his fingers on the table.

"Let's move on to the original search," said Attorney General Hildreth. "Captain DeFord, I believe you supervised the Overhead Team. Can you fill us in on the details of your operations? It would be helpful to see maps of the area."

DeFord lifted a laptop bag onto the tabletop. "I need a few minutes to hook up my computer."

"In that case, let's take a five-minute break," said the attorney general.

"Thank you!" said the elderly Fryeburg police chief, who seemed intent on being first at the nearest urinal.

I found myself fourth in line at the coffeepot, right behind Dani, who was filling a carafe from the tap.

"What do you think so far?" I asked.

"I think we should be spending less time on how she disappeared four years ago and more time on where she might be now."

"What if the two are connected?"

"We should be circulating that sketch of the other woman—Becky. Someone's bound to have seen her buying groceries or whatever."

I felt the blood leave my face. "But people will want to know why we're looking for her."

"Because she blew up a house!"

"The story about Casey being alive is bound to get out. Pomerleau can't keep it from her step-father. Major Crimes needs a plan if he goes running to the press with it."

Dani had spilled water on the burner and it was sizzling under the coffee pot. "She should have brought in Steve Nason and raked him over the coals. Obviously, the guy is lying through his teeth. He knows something about who was living in that house."

"His brother also happens to be a lawyer. I doubt Chris Nason would have let his brother answer a single one of Pomerleau's questions."

Dani poured coffee into a mug for me. "I hate it when the system protects scumbags."

"The system is *designed* to protect scumbags, Dani. You were a game warden and now you're a state trooper. How have you not managed to learn that yet?"

"Maybe I'm just an idiot."

"I know that's not true. I think what you are is an idealist."

In the other room the meeting was being called back to order.

I'd sat through dozens of search-and-rescue mapping presentations, so little of what DeFord had to say or demonstrate surprised me. I was gratified, however, by the response of the other cops in the room to the highly detailed maps the wardens had developed during the initial investigation into Casey's disappearance. Any suggestion that the wardens had conducted a half-assed operation and missed swaths of territory was belied by the thoroughness of the captain's presentation.

I paid particular attention to the channel Charley and I had followed earlier that morning. A team of wardens had tracked it to its source and conducted grid searches along its banks, closer to Oxbow Island, where Casey had last been seen.

The attorney general gave another of the explosive coughs he used to call attention to himself.

"Who was the warden investigator assigned to this case? And why isn't he here?"

"The investigator was Wesley Pinkham," said DeFord.

The room went silent. Every law officer in Maine knew that Wes Pinkham had died horribly in the line of duty two years earlier.

Hildreth adjusted the knot of his power tie while he collected his thoughts. "I'd like to ask Captain DeFord how and when the decision was made to abandon the search for Ms. Donaldson."

"We made the decision—in consultation with the state police—to suspend the search that fall," said DeFord.

"Suspend?"

"It is my understanding that Casey Donaldson has continued to be listed in the FBI database as a missing person."

The federal agent confirmed that was indeed the truth.

"So in summary, Ms. Donaldson disappeared and was presumed dead," said the attorney general. "An active criminal investigation has remained open, headed by Detective Menario until his retirement. His working theory of the case was that the girl was murdered and her body hidden, presumably far from the river based on the lack of evidence found by the wardens."

Menario chose that moment to sit upright in his chair. "I'd like a chance to speak."

Hildreth shook his leonine head. "It seems to me that your conclusion that Ms. Donaldson was the victim of a homicide has been rendered moot, Detective."

"Just because Rowe didn't kill Casey doesn't mean he's innocent. For all we know he's the one who kidnapped her. He might be holding her now!"

I rarely agreed with Antonio Menario, but for once we were on the same page.

"We'll get to that hypothesis shortly, Detective. At the moment I'd like to bring in Warden Bowditch."

But the neurons in my brain had chosen that moment to misfire. Charley had mentioned something I should bring up about our outing on the river. For the life of me, I couldn't recall what it was.

"Bowditch?" Pomerleau said.

Everyone in the room was now staring expectantly at me.

"You have our attention, Warden, even if we don't have yours," the attorney general said. "Let's hear what you found at Knife Creek."

I faced fewer questions than I had anticipated. The DNA results fully supported my story, said their forensic analyst. Casey Donaldson was the newborn's mother. Of that, there could be no doubt.

After the forensic technician had finished giving his testimony, the medical examiner was asked to present his findings on the cause of the baby's death. He said that the half-eaten body of the infant had been too mangled, the small bones broken in too many places. It was impossible to determine whether the child had died by human hands before it was interred. He ended his presentation by noting that in the judgment of the state anthropologist, her bone development suggested the girl hadn't been more than a few weeks old.

"Can you bring up the photograph again of the initials in the tree?" Lieutenant Barrett asked.

There was the inevitable technological delay. Then the picture came up of the carving Dani had discovered on the beech tree, beside the shallow grave.

"KC," said the attorney general. "I'd like to hear ideas on what those letters might stand for."

"Maybe they're a kind of homonym for *Casey?*" said the medical examiner, who seemed to have a mind for puzzles. "Maybe it was a playful way she signed her name?"

"Why would she carve her own name in a tree?"

"As a signal to us? A cry for help?"

Attorney General Hildreth turned in his chair to Menario. "Detective, I assume you have an opinion."

"I found no evidence that Casey ever referred to herself by those initials or that her friends ever did."

"It's on my list of questions to ask her step-father," Pomerleau said.

"Her stepfather." The attorney general groaned. "We need to discuss how we reach out to Mr. Donaldson with this news. We can't predict how he'll react. Most of us in the room are parents."

I didn't catch what was said next because at that moment my brain finally rebooted and Charley's parting words came back to me:

Don't forget to mention that cellar hole. That cabin burned down two or three years back. Now, it might be coincidence that it went up in flames like the house over on Rankin Road. Or it might not. Either way, Pomerleau needs to check out this John Blood person who says he owns the land and find out why he's so willing to let campers dump their garbage there.

I actually raised my hand like a know-it-all kid eager to answer his teacher's question. "Can we pull up the map of the search area again?"

The attorney general looked at me with bemusement. "Warden Bowditch?"

"That peninsula of land to the east of the Oxbow. Charley Stevens and I were in there earlier this morning. We met some homeless people camping near the cellar hole of a hunting cabin. They said they were living there with the

323

permission of the owner." From the expressions around the room, I could tell that no one, with the possible exception of Kathy, was following me. "This couple, Prudence and Jackson Smith, said the owner of the land introduced himself as John Blood. It sounded like a made-up name."

The Fryeburg police chief perked up. "Did you say John Blood?"

"Why?" I asked. "Do you know him?"

"Sure, I know him. He's a Korean War vet from East Fryeburg. Friend of my old man. But he wasn't driving around Birnam anytime recently, that's for sure. John Blood has terminal dementia. He's been in a nursing home in Portland for the past six years."

33

The FBI agent asked the question everyone in the room must have been thinking, judging by the blank faces around the tables. "What makes you think this is relevant to Casey Donaldson? Someone pretending to be the owner of a random woodlot?"

"Casey had to have come off the river somewhere that night," I said. "Either she found her way onto land or was taken onto land. The hunting cabin on that point burned down in the past few years, just like the house on Rankin Road."

The attorney general cleared his throat. "I think I understand where you are going with this."

Menario scowled. "You do?"

"You're suggesting the possibility that our supposed kidnapper has used a similar method. He holds Casey—and perhaps this Becky woman—prisoner in one isolated house for a time under an assumed name, and then when he fears he might have been discovered, he burns the place down to destroy evidence and moves somewhere else."

In fact I hadn't gotten that far in my thought process, but I was quick to answer, "Yes."

The AG addressed the Fryeburg police chief.

"Do you know if this John Blood is the actual owner of that property?"

The chief turned to his female detective, who said, "I believe his family is waiting for him to die to put it up for sale."

"Was it being rented out four years ago—after Mr. Blood went into the nursing home?"

"Possibly."

"Well, can we find out?" asked the AG.

"I can look into it," said Detective Finch.

"Where do we stand on distributing the sketch of Becky Cobb that Warden Bowditch created?" asked Lieutenant Barrett.

"We should wait until after we meet with Mr. Donaldson," said the FBI agent.

"I'd also like to take another crack at Steven Nason," said Pomerleau.

"Does anyone know of any connections he might have with Dakota Rowe?" I asked.

This time, AG Hildreth ignored me. "Ellen, you need to get Nason in for an interview first thing tomorrow. I'd prefer to act quickly. If he is complicit in Casey's kidnapping and can lead us to her whereabouts, we have a chance to get out ahead of this."

In Maine, the attorney general is appointed by the state legislature, but that didn't make Hildreth any less of a politician. He knew that there would be nuclear fallout from the admission that state investigators had mistakenly given Casey up for dead. He also recognized that the damage would be mitigated if the announcement was accompanied by news of her rescue.

Menario couldn't contain himself. "So you're going to write off Dakota Rowe as a suspect?"

"Not at all," said Hildreth.

"Don't patronize me," said the retired detective. "Casey is still alive because I fucked up. That's going to be the official line. You're going to make me the scapegoat."

The attorney general rose ceremoniously to his feet. "I'm going to suggest we take another five-minute break."

It was hard not to interpret Hildreth's response as confirmation of Menario's suspicions.

Within a minute, the room began to clear. Menario continued to brood over his papers—representing years of work—with a look of shock, as if he'd failed the biggest test of his life. Which, I supposed, he had.

When he caught me staring, the muscles in his neck twitched as if he was readying himself to vault across the table and grab me by the throat.

"Congratulations," he said.

"For what?"

"For making me look like a fool."

"I thought you'd be glad to learn that Casey Donaldson is alive."

"Is she? Or did her captor kill her when he

realized the police might be onto him? Your theory is bullshit, by the way."

"I don't have a theory."

He laughed through his nostrils. "I've known Stevie Nason for ten years. The man is border-line retarded. There's a reason he still lives with his mother. He's not mentally capable of masterminding a scheme like the one you've described."

"You're giving me too much credit."

"You're the one who's secretly congratulating himself on having reopened the case of the century. I bet you think you're a shoo-in for the investigator position now. Yeah, I heard you applied for the job. I wouldn't be so sure about that." Menario began collecting his documents with no care for their condition, shoving the papers into his portfolio. "You make a lot of assumptions, you little punk. Someday they're going to catch up with you."

As he left the room, his dossier wedged under his arm, I knew that he would not be returning. I never got to tell him that I had begun to share his suspicions about Dakota Rowe.

A voice behind me said, "He's right about that, Mike." Dani, seated quietly in the corner, had heard every word.

"Right about me being a punk?"

"You make too many assumptions. Not just at work, either."

328

"I've been in trouble my entire career, Dani."

She gave me a look that bordered on pity. "That's not the kind of trouble I was talking about."

I stepped outside to get some air, but the night was as humid as ever. It felt as if I were trying to breathe through a wet towel draped over my face.

I checked my cell, but there were no messages from Stacey. Why had I expected one? What would she have told me—that the party had been a huge success despite my absence?

Under the bug-fuzzed glow of the parking-lot lights, I saw Kathy checking on Maple in her crate.

I wandered over. "How's the pup?"

"Sleeping like the baby she is. You and Stacey should get a dog."

"I almost did."

"That's right. Your wolf dog. Whatever happened to him?"

"He's found a lady wolf according to Pulsifer. Some woman up in Chain of Ponds has gotten pictures of the two of them at a bait pile."

"No shit." Kathy smiled for the first time in hours. "It's a good thing that animal was neutered. I'm not sure how the public would react if they heard that a Maine game warden had accidentally reintroduced wolves to the state."

"Kath, I am really sorry about not telling you earlier about Casey."

"It's not that." She corrected herself: "It's not entirely that."

I waited for her to continue.

"If you had worked that search four years ago, you would understand better." She lowered the tailgate as quietly as she could so as not to wake the dog. "With some searches, you have a bad feeling from the start. There's this fear that you might never find the missing person. But no one felt that way about Casey. We were all *positive* we'd recover her body from that swamp. It was a river, and dead bodies wash downstream. How many thousand people paddle around that river system? The odds of someone stumbling on something . . .

"You always want closure, right? I never spoke directly with the stepfather. But I saw him around the command post, and he came across as such a strong, reasonable man. He never panicked or broke down once, according to DeFord. His response was always 'I understand that didn't work, so now what do we do?' You want closure for a parent like that—because he's acting the way you hope *you'd* act in his position. I remember saying to Pluto in the truck, 'OK, bud, we gotta find this girl today. We gotta do it for her dad.' I'd go into someone's office— one of the cops on the case or another warden working the search—and there would be a picture of Casey on their desk. People felt like she was their daughter or little sister. You don't just want closure for the family, you want it for yourself."

"Menario clearly did."

"He was a good detective before Casey. Did you know that saltwater crocodiles have a bite pressure that's something like thirty-seven hundred pounds per square inch? Well, that was Menario back then, he would bite down and not let go."

"It sounds like he might have gotten his teeth stuck."

"The man had a distinguished career. It's not fair what is going to happen to him now. The press is going to nail him to a cross, while the people who were in that room stand by and watch it happen."

The front door of the crime lab opened behind me and slammed shut. A car engine started. But I didn't turn to look.

"It doesn't help to know that she's still alive?" I asked.

"If we find her, it will. But what if she slips away again? Christ, if that happens someone should put Menario on a suicide watch." Kathy took a breath. "You know that Pluto and I searched the area between the swamp and that cabin. We didn't get as far as the building itself.

What if he was just getting too old and losing it and I didn't recognize the signs?"

"Frost! Bowditch!"

The captain was coming toward us across the lot, stepping into and out of the bright circles made by the arc lights on their steel poles. He moved with the loose-limbed ease of a natural athlete. No one ever believed me when I said Jock DeFord was in his midfifties.

"Is the meeting over?" I said.

"Pomerleau and her team want to get busy chasing some leads. Thanks to you, Mike, we might actually have made some progress tonight."

"Why don't you give him the investigator job already?" said Kathy pointedly.

DeFord pretended he hadn't heard the comment. "I'll call you both in the morning with an update."

Kathy gave me a long hug good-bye that reassured me that, no matter what, she and I would always be the best of friends.

As she was about to drive off, a question sprang to mind. I knocked on her window and she pushed the button to roll it down. "I wanted to ask you about Tate again. What made her quit the Warden Service? You can tell me, Kathy. You know I can keep a secret."

"It would be best for Dani to tell you herself."

"What makes you think she'll tell me?"

"Warden's intuition. Dangle loose, Grasshopper."

Kathy had picked up this curious expression in southern Louisiana, when she and Pluto were sniffing through the flooded streets of New Orleans and dragging corpses out of the bayous, after Hurricane Katrina had given us all a foretaste of the Apocalypse.

Driving home, I took the back roads instead of the turnpike. At one point, a mink bounded across the asphalt—eyes shining green in the headlights—and disappeared into the fading lupines beyond the sand shoulder.

I told myself that I needed some time to process all the information that had been dumped into my brain. But deep down, I knew that I was looking for an excuse to delay my return to Stacey. She had seemed understanding about my having to leave the barbecue in a rush, but I had a feeling that an argument might be waiting for me tonight behind our bedroom door.

What I hadn't expected to find was an empty house. Not only were the vehicles of all of our guests gone, but Stacey's Outback was nowhere to be seen. Had there been some sort of emergency?

In the living room I found half-finished bottles of beer and dirty plates on the coffee table. In the kitchen I found a sink full of crusted casserole dishes and unwashed pots.

My voice only echoed up the staircase when I called Stacey's name.

I slid open the kitchen door and stepped onto the patio. The night sky was a uniform brownish gray. Not a single star was bright enough to pierce the humid haze. The air was calm, but I felt something like a breeze raise the hairs along my bare arms.

In 1872 a British brig spotted a ship adrift on choppy seas, east of the Azores. When the crew boarded the wayward craft, they found the table set for dinner, nautical charts scattered about, the single lifeboat missing, and not a single soul on board. My house had become that ghost ship of legend, the *Mary Celeste*.

Before I could send a distress call to Stacey's cell, I heard a car pull into the driveway.

I met her at the front door. "What happened?"

"I didn't expect you home so soon."

"Where is everyone?"

Her shirt was untucked and her hair was tied in a halfhearted ponytail. "Gone home. The party ended hours ago."

"What about your parents?"

Her eyes were intense with anger. "I took them back to their plane."

"What?" The plan had been for Charley and Ora to stay another night.

She swatted a mosquito on her cheek. "Can I come inside, please?"

She strode down the hall to the kitchen, where she immediately filled a tall glass with tap water and drank it down in four gulps. The mosquito bite was already raising a red welt on her cheekbone.

"My dad and I had another fight," she said at last.

"Over what?"

"He got a call from Barstow after you left."

"He got a call from your boss?"

"Barstow didn't want him hearing the news that I'd been fired over the grapevine. I'm thirty-one years old. Where does he get off calling my father?"

Only now did I remember that she hadn't said a word about her end-of-day meeting with her superiors. "Wait a minute. You were fired yesterday?"

"I was going to tell you tonight, after everyone left. I didn't want it hanging over the party."

"How could they fire you? What cause did they give you? Have you called your union rep?"

"What cause did they give me?" Her voice rose. "I deserved it. I've missed I don't know how many days. I wanted to be fired. I'm glad I was fired."

"But why?"

"I need to get out of here, Mike. I need to start my life over."

I felt the same wooziness I might have experienced having donated blood. "Does that mean leaving me, too?"

"No! God no! I told you before. I want you to come with me. Your mom left you enough money. We can go to New Zealand or the Amazon. We could drive across Canada. We could do anything we wanted—together."

I couldn't imagine how bad an argument she must have had with her parents for them to have packed up and left before I'd returned home. I could see it happening with Charley, but not Ora. I really had boarded a ghost ship adrift on a dark sea.

"Stacey, it's late. Let's talk about this in the morning. You're still worked up about what happened with your dad."

"You have no idea. My old man still treats me like I'm a teenager, but you walk on water."

"This isn't about me."

"Mike, don't you see? With him, it's always about you."

That night, I slept again on the sofa.

34

While I was tossing and turning on the couch, Dani Tate was returning to her overnight patrol.

I have read the reports and heard from officers who were on the scene, and this is what I imagine happened. Not having been there, I can't make any claims to its accuracy. But some-times imagination can be a touchstone.

Shortly before midnight, Trooper Danielle Tate got a call from Dispatch. The owner of a convenience store said his wife was late returning home after working the closing. He'd tried calling her for the past hour but had gotten no response and, being too intoxicated to drive himself, wanted a trooper to check in at the business.

"Where is it?" Dani asked.

"Fales Variety in Birnam. I can give you the address."

"No need." She switched on the light bar in her cruiser. "I know where I'm going."

As she raced to the scene, pushing her Interceptor well past the speed limit, she'd had a strange feeling—almost a premonition—that she was going to hit a deer. It was all she could think of as she rounded every backwoods corner: that there would be a doe in the road ahead, about to come crashing through her windshield.

But she arrived in Birnam safely without having seen so much as a single animal anywhere along the darkened, tree-strewn highway.

Dani knew to turn off her pursuit lights before she got near the store. She needed to be stealthy to scout out the situation. She didn't want to spook someone inside into making a bad decision.

The building was completely dark except for the token security lights outside the entrance. A CLOSED sign hung prominently in the window. But a Ford Fiesta was parked next to the side door: Connie Fales's car, according to the information Dani had gotten from the dispatcher. There were no other vehicles on the premises.

Dani radioed in her location and reported that Mrs. Fales's car was still parked in the lot, but that the business appeared to be closed for the night, and there was no sign of forced entry. The dispatcher asked if Dani wanted backup.

Everything about this situation had alarm bells ringing in Dani's head. Connie Fales was a witness in an important investigation, capable of identifying a dangerous fugitive. Under the circumstances it would be foolish not to wait for backup.

Dani knew all these things, but still she said no.

She was a rookie state trooper, and a woman, and the last thing she wanted was to start her new career with the reputation as someone who easily panicked.

She removed her flashlight from her duty belt and approached the entrance from an angle that would keep her from being seen by someone inside. She took a deep breath at the threshold, reached out for the handle, and pulled. The unlocked door swung open.

Then she lost her grip and it swung shut again under its own weight.

A car passed along the Saco Road, heading toward Fryeburg, but didn't slow down.

She waited until the sound of its engine had been replaced again by the peaceful piping of frogs in the marsh across the highway. The night was warm with a gentle breeze that felt like a lover's breath on the back of her neck.

She hadn't been this afraid in years.

She removed her .45 from its holster. As a warden, she'd carried a .357, and she'd had to relearn how to shoot using this unfamiliar weapon. She'd always thought of herself as a crack shot, but that had been at the practice range.

Taking a deep breath, she opened the door again, just enough this time to slide half of her body in. She felt with her fingers for a light switch on the wall but found nothing. An eerie blue glow radiated from the back of the store where a wall of refrigerators and freezers hummed.

To call out or not? To risk being shot by a startled store owner or by a drugged-out robber lying in wait?

This time, she obeyed her training. "Mrs. Fales? Police officer! Are you here? Are you all right?"

There was no answer. Not that she had expected one.

Dani stepped inside. She flashed her light around the store in a broad arc, illuminating shelves of canned goods and racks of potato chips. She saw the beer display with the Red Sox pitcher she'd heard so much about. The flashlight beam touched another darkened doorway behind the counter, the entrance to an office.

The darkened interior smelled of coffee grounds and dried-out pizza slices dumped in an unemptied trash can. Connie Fales was the kind of owner who would have bagged up the garbage before she turned out the lights for the evening.

At that moment Dani finally admitted to herself that she should retreat to her cruiser and call for backup. True, Mrs. Fales might have suffered a heart attack in the back room. It was equally plausible that an armed person was crouched out of sight, waiting to rise up and begin blasting away at the careless police officer who'd dared walk into his—or her—gun sights.

The register was fifteen feet away. Dani could close the distance in less than a second. How could she turn back now without looking over the edge at what might be beyond?

Dani made her fateful decision. She rushed the counter.

An hour later Detective Finch arrived at Fales Variety to find the store lit up from within and without. He had just fallen asleep when he'd gotten the call about the homicide in Birnam. With Pomerleau assigned to the Donaldson investigation, he had caught the case.

Trooper Tate's cruiser was parked at an angle, as if she'd come in when the lot was empty, before all the other cruisers converged on the scene of the shooting. The Oxford County sheriff had sent two deputies and the Fryeburg police had sent one of their units. An ambulance had initially been called for; then it had become clear that it should be the medical examiner who responded. He was bringing the van he used to transport corpses to his autopsy table.

Someone had propped the front door open with a cinder block, and now all manner of insect life—moths, caddises, and mayflies—was swarming inside.

Finch unzipped his nylon jacket and entered the glowing building.

One of the deputies was conversing with the

sole Fryeburg officer. "Imagine burying a baby in a souvenir baseball shirt. Isn't that the sickest thing you ever heard?"

"Disgusting," agreed the local cop, an enormously overweight man.

Both officers stopped their gabbing and straightened up when they caught sight of the detective. The deputy was gray around the temples and should have known better than to hang out at a homicide scene, chewing the fat. But at least both of these bozos had known enough to put on gloves lest they touch anything.

Trooper Danielle Tate stood silently behind the counter, staring at the floor with a look of shocked sadness.

"You two, outside," commanded Finch.

As he approached the register, Tate raised her eyes. She had only seemed dazed. In fact, she had been studying the corpse at her feet while enduring the jabbering of her fellow officers.

Connie Fales lay like a flung doll behind the counter. The ragged hole in her forehead left no doubt as to the cause of death.

"Whoever killed her used her own gun to do it," said the trooper.

Tate pointed to a big Colt revolver lying on the warped linoleum, next to a toppled stool. The gun looked as if it had been tossed there after being fired.

Finch saw all the usual signs of a botched

armed robbery. The register drawer was open. The cash was gone with only an unwanted roll of pennies left behind.

"How do you know that was the gun that killed her?" Finch asked.

"I smelled the barrel." Tate added quickly, "Don't worry. I didn't touch it."

He glanced around the store. "Maybe she got a shot off herself."

"I don't think so."

Tate squatted down and with the tip of the pen she used to write traffic tickets indicated a tiny cut in Connie Fales's throat.

"I'm not following you, Tate."

The trooper pointed the pen at one of the dead woman's breasts. "There's also a bloody tear in her blouse."

Finch blinked his tired eyes. "I'm still not following you."

Tate seemed mystified by his inability to understand. "She was shot with a Taser. One electrode hit her neck, the other dart pierced her blouse and hit her breast. It's how her killer got the jump on her. She was electrocuted into submission and then shot, point-blank, in the head before she could recover her muscle function."

"That's a new twist. A robber using a Taser to incapacitate the person he's robbing."

Tate's voice couldn't hide her disbelief at her

superior's stupidity. "This wasn't an armed robbery, Detective. This was an execution. Becky Cobb did this to eliminate one of the only witnesses who could identify her by sight."

35

The next morning I awoke with a start when Stacey touched my arm. I nearly rolled off the couch.

In the half-light of the living room I saw that she was dressed in a sleeveless T-shirt, shorts that showed off her long legs, and fluorescent-yellow running shoes. She'd pulled a Red Sox cap down over her head and threaded her ponytail through the hole in back.

"Dani Tate is on the phone."

I felt a jolt of energy as Stacey handed me my cell. "What's happened? Did they find Casey?"

"I wish." Dani inhaled and exhaled. "Connie Fales is dead, Mike. She was murdered last night in her store. Shot with her own gun."

Without thinking, I rose to my feet. "Jesus!"

Stacey put a hand to her mouth. Cell phones being as loud as they are, she could hear both sides of our conversation.

"It was the Cobbs," Dani said.

"Of course it was them. Who else would have done it?"

"They tried to make it look like a robbery that had gone wrong. Someone waits till closing time. Then when the owner's getting ready to lock up,

345

they make their move. Things go wrong. The owner gets killed."

"Right. As if anyone would believe that."

"Finch almost did."

"You are shitting me."

"He would have figured it out. Here's the weird element in all this, though. They tased her first. That was how they were able to get the drop on her."

"Finch told you that?"

"Mike, I was the one who found Connie Fales." I sat back down on the sofa and heard the springs creak under my weight. "You need to tell me what happened, Dani. You need to tell me every detail of what you saw."

"That's why I am calling."

We were on the phone for close to an hour. My questions were like a Hydra. Dani would answer one, and then I would have two more that needed answering. She hadn't known what Finch was thinking when he arrived, but she could imagine, based on his inability to see what was in front of his face.

"I need to go over there this morning," I said at last.

"Pomerleau knew you were going to say that. She doesn't want you anywhere near the place. Besides, the ME has taken Mrs. Fales away. And Finch has closed everything until the techs finish their work. There's nothing to see."

"What am I supposed to do with myself?"

"Keep your head down."

"What do you mean?"

"As far as I can count, there are three people who have seen Becky Cobb in person. One of them, Steve Nason, is probably an accessory. The other was just murdered. That leaves you."

Not for one second had I considered myself in danger. I still had trouble believing that these people would be so foolhardy as to target a law-enforcement officer for execution when doing so would rain hell down on their heads. But I appreciated Dani's concern.

"Thanks for the warning."

"Pomerleau said she'll call you later to keep you in the loop." I heard Dani yawn on the other end of the phone. "And now, I should get some sleep. I have another patrol later."

"They're not even giving you the day off?"

"I'd prefer to work."

I knew the feeling.

Stacey had heard much of what Dani and I had said to each other. She had stayed for most of my questions. But in time she had gotten distracted by her own thoughts and left me alone.

I found her in the kitchen, drinking orange juice.

"At least we know they're still in the area," I told her.

"And that's a good thing? I keep thinking about

that poor woman. Gunned down for selling a T-shirt. It makes me worried for you."

"They're not stupid enough to come after me. If there's one thing the Cobbs have demonstrated, it's that they're not careless. So how do you plan to use your newfound freedom?"

"*Freedom* is a nice euphemism for being unemployed. I thought I might go for a run before it gets too hot."

"How far are you going?"

"I was thinking of doing half the Mountain Division Trail. What's that? Seven miles? Not very scenic but—"

"I might not be here when you get back."

She looked frightened. "What?"

"I just meant I have to work."

"Oh, right."

"Are you going to tell me what happened with your folks last night?"

She pulled the brim of her cap down over her eyes. "Ask my dad. He's the one who started it."

After she had left for her run, I cleaned myself up and put on my uniform. I noticed that Stacey had forgotten her cell phone on the kitchen counter. I hoped she wouldn't need it today.

While I was eating breakfast, I decided that I would try to find the dirt track that led from the East Fryeburg Road down the peninsula to the homeless camp and the burned-out cellar hole

Charley and I had visited the day before. I wanted to speak with Prudence and Jackson Smith again and have them give me a physical description of the man who'd called himself John Blood.

The FBI agent had dismissed the idea that there might be a connection between the impostor who'd claimed to own that land and what had happened to Casey, but my instincts told me otherwise.

Besides, interviewing the Smiths was as close as I could come to taking part in the investigation while maintaining the pretense that I was going about my usual routine. If pressed by my superiors, I could always claim to have been poking around the dark corners of my new district.

Even with a GPS unit and a bunch of maps, finding the road that led to the campsite was trickier than I'd anticipated. I had assumed that it branched off the main drag that zigzagged along the edge of the bog from Route 302 down to the Denmark Road. Instead I discovered that it branched off not just one but two unpaved fire lanes, so small they appeared to have no names.

A house was under construction at the second fork. If I hadn't slowed to look at it, I would probably have missed the peninsula road altogether. The home had the look of a place that the owner had started to build and then run out of money halfway through construction and was waiting for his coffers to refill before he could put siding over the TYPAR walls and nail shingles to the exposed roof decking.

Rural Maine was dotted with these sorts of structures, many of which would start to decay before they were ever finished—not just abandoned buildings but abandoned dreams.

As I drove down the peninsula, going slowly since the trail was as ridged as corduroy, with exposed rocks waiting to rip a gash in my oil pan, I marveled at how the Smiths and their fellow drifters could ever have found their way here. I concluded that the inaccessibility of the place was its greatest virtue. If you're a squatter looking to hide from anyone who might evict you from your makeshift camp, it paid to go past the point where a sane person would turn around.

I hadn't gone far, however, before I noticed a troubling sign: fresh tire marks led out of the woods but none went in.

Sure enough, when I finally arrived at the clearing where the Smiths had parked their truck and pitched their tent, all I found were trampled weeds and a pile of dirty diapers. Cans of Dr Pepper lay scattered about the crushed bracken and other ferns. The only conclusion I could reach was that, for reasons unknown, the Smiths had felt they needed to clear out of these woods in a hurry. Maybe Charley's and my arrival on the scene had panicked them.

I wandered over to the cellar hole.

A wood-pewee, a species of flycatcher, called from a stand of pines nearer the swamp. Based on the mosquitoes and deerflies that immediately descended on my exposed skin, the bird was about to enjoy a banquet.

I didn't see the cat until I felt her rub against my pants leg. The white-mittened feline had silently snuck up on me while my attention was fixed on the garbage dump.

"Hey, Puddin." I squatted down to stroke her spine from head to tail.

She purred contentedly.

"How could your people abandon you?"

The cat continued to vibrate beneath my hand.

Now I was certain that the Smiths had fled in a hurry. If they had been willing to abandon their pet to certain death at the talons of an owl or the fangs of a fisher, then the couple had been seriously spooked.

I couldn't leave the poor thing here to be eaten. I reached down carefully, afraid she might bite or scratch, but she allowed me to pick her up without resistance. Ever since the prior winter, I had carried a kennel in the bed of my Sierra, in case I had to transport some strange animal, wild or otherwise. Puddin started to struggle when she saw the jig was up, but I got her inside the crate and closed the cage door before she could slip past me.

I had just started the engine and was turning

the pickup around when my phone rang. It was Pomerleau.

"Did Tate get in touch with you?"

"She did."

"So you know about Connie Fales?"

"I don't suppose Finch found anything helpful? Mrs. Fales told me the security cameras outside the store didn't work. It had to have been the Cobbs, you realize."

"Finch and I are proceeding from that assumption."

"It means they have another hiding place nearby."

"Where are you?"

"Birnam."

I expected her to launch into a series of questions to determine what I was up to. Instead she said, "I need you to come over to the barracks in Gray."

"What's going on?"

"Tom Donaldson is here. When we told him we had news about his daughter, he wanted to come in rather than have us visit him at his house. We've just informed him Casey is alive."

"How did he take it?"

"Not the way we expected."

"What do you mean?"

She lowered her voice. "The bottom line is he wants to see you."

"He wants to see me? Why?"

"Because you're the only one of us who saw his daughter. I think he has questions only you can answer."

The truck gave a jolt as I hit a rock. What choice did I have but to go face the man?

"It's going to take me an hour if he doesn't mind waiting."

"Based on the conversation we had, I don't think he'll mind."

"I'm on my way."

I did pause, however, at the fork in the road. I put the transmission into park and tapped a text message to Dani Tate:

> Talked 2 Det. Pom. Can u do me favor? Can u keep eyes peeled for blue Toyota T100 w/ a white cap and PA plates: FAR4401? Owners IDed themselves 2 me as Prudence & Jackson Smith.

It took Dani less than a minute to reply:

> Yr squatters? What's up?

Me:

> Went looking for them but they cleared out FAST. Think they're scared of someone. Like 2 get description of man who called himself John Blood.

Dani:

U and yr hunches!!! Can't promise anything.

Me:

10-4.

Dani:

Anything else?

I listened to the yowling coming from the back
of my truck.

Don't suppose u want 2 adopt a cat?

36

I dropped the cat at an animal shelter on Route 302. Puddin was the most obliging feline I'd ever encountered. She accepted the handoff with such graceful resignation it made me wonder whether being passed from person to person had been the story of her life.

Half an hour later, the receptionist inside the Troop B barracks again buzzed me through the security door, but stopped me from proceeding past the lobby. She made a quick call to Pomerleau, whispered into the speaker. A moment later, the detective, wearing the same blouse and slacks she'd had on the previous night (the wrinkles were new), appeared in the reception room. Her hair was a hopeless mass of whitish-blond tangles.

"Thanks for coming."

Anxious as I was, I tried to open with something light. "Sooner or later, you're going to need to talk to my colonel about the time I spend on this case. It feels like the state police should be the ones cutting my paycheck."

But Ellen Pomerleau hadn't heard a word I'd said. "So I've got Donaldson in my office. I wanted to talk with you before I bring you in there. He knows the details—most of them—and

I've gotten him to promise he won't go to the media since it might jeopardize his stepdaughter's life."

"Mission accomplished then."

"Not exactly. It seems that Menario called him after the two of you had breakfast the other day. Tony wanted to warn the guy that there was a rogue warden jeopardizing the case against Rowe."

"So what are you saying? That Menario has convinced him not to trust my testimony? What about the DNA evidence?"

"Donaldson hasn't told us what's on his mind. The man is remarkably hard to read. All he said is 'I would like to meet this warden, please.' "

"Haven't you been able to explain to him that this is all good news?"

"It's potentially good news," she corrected me. "His stepdaughter was alive four days ago. But she's spent the past four years in a living hell. And there's no guarantee that her captors won't kill her if they fear we're onto them."

"What do you want me to say to him?"

"Just answer his questions. Be candid but discreet in your answers. The most important thing you can do is give him hope. But don't overpromise!"

"Piece of cake."

"And no sarcasm."

Unconsciously, I checked my uniform. I repositioned my gun belt on my hips. I tried rubbing off a spot of pine pitch on my ballistic vest with no luck.

Tom Donaldson had the dazed appearance of a person who was having trouble waking up from a deep sleep.

"Mr. Donaldson," said Ellen Pomerleau. "This is Warden Bowditch, who identified your daughter."

"It's a pleasure to meet you," I said.

The plumber used the chair arms to push himself to his feet. He was nearly as tall as I was, maybe six-one, but fifty pounds heavier. His small blue eyes were set close together behind his glasses. His strawberry-blond hair was very fine and in need of a trim. He wore a red-and-green-striped polo and pleated chinos. Only his powerful forearms and his heavy work boots hinted that he worked with his hands for a living.

"You're the one who saw Casey?"

"Yes, sir."

"Detective Menario called me about you. He told me you were making trouble." Donaldson had a Chicago accent I hadn't expected. But it matched his deferential, Midwestern demeanor.

"Mr. Donaldson—"

"No, I need to finish. I had given Casey up for dead, you understand. I'd buried her in my head. I took down all of the pictures of her in the house so that my fiancée would stop asking about her.

I put them in a drawer in my bureau. I wanted to move on, but Tony had told me the declaration of death was coming. He wanted me to be prepared when the state police arrested Dakota Rowe and the TV cameras appeared outside my house. And then to get a call from him, telling me about you and your history—"

The big man was standing so close to me I could feel his body heat. I could see the beads of sweat between his nose and his lip. His eyelashes were as pale as any I had seen.

"I understand."

"No, I don't think you do. I don't think you can."

Before I could so much as flinch, the burly man reached out and wrapped his arms around me. His bear hug felt like literally being embraced by a bear.

"Bless you," he said, tucking his head into my neck. "Bless you, bless you, bless you."

Once Tom Donaldson was done hugging and thanking me, he started in with the questions. What did Casey look like? Did she seem healthy? Did she do anything to signal she needed help? Did she say anything? Not even a single word? What about this Becky woman? Why didn't Casey rush past her? Might someone have been holding a gun on Casey from the other room? Had I heard anyone else in the house?

I tried my best to be circumspect. But there was no getting around the fact that none of my answers was encouraging.

Donaldson had started the interview leaning toward me with his big hands gripping the armrests, but the longer we spoke, the more he slouched back into the chair. He kicked his legs out in front of him. It is heartbreaking to watch hope drain like blood out of someone's face.

"The thing is," Donaldson said, "I really had resigned myself. Tony Mcnario would call me or want me to drive out with him to the memorial on the river, and he'd talk my ear off the whole time, about how we could get a proclamation of death soon—or whatever you call it—without having to wait the whole seven years, and about how he'd been keeping tabs on Dakota Rowe because he was worried he might hurt another woman or run off to Europe. The kid is rich, you know. Every morning, Tony seemed to wake up thinking about Casey—and I didn't. It made me feel like I was this horrible man who had failed Claire. She was my late wife, Casey's mom." He removed his steel-rimmed spectacles and pinched his nose between his thumb and forefinger. "Do you think I am a bad person?"

Why ask me? "It seems to me that you have been incredibly brave, sir. I am not sure how I would have behaved in your position."

"Do you have children, Warden Bowditch?"

"Not yet."

I thought he was going to warn me against becoming a parent and risking having my heart shattered like glass.

But again Tom Donaldson surprised me. "I hope you do someday. Casey and I fought all the time after her mom died. But that girl kept me going through the worst days of my life. I hope I did the same. The priest at my church says love is a mystery. He got that right."

Pomerleau, I noticed, kept glancing at the photographs of her two kids.

"I guess the shock of it still hasn't registered," the plumber said. "That Casey is still alive. That she had a baby who died. I'm afraid how I'm going to feel later, when it starts to sink in. I'm afraid of the emotions I might have."

"We can suggest people for you to talk with," offered Pomerleau.

"Maybe you should call your priest?" I said.

He tugged on an earlobe. "That's probably what I should do. The thing that I keep thinking is, what if this was another cruel joke God is playing on me, like when Claire died, and then Casey disappeared? What if she turns up dead this time?"

"Have faith, Mr. Donaldson," said Pomerleau.

Without thinking, I said, "We're going to find her."

Immediately I knew I had messed up. I had

made a promise, on behalf of other people, that I couldn't necessarily keep. I didn't have to meet Pomerleau's gaze to feel the heat of her disapproval.

There was knock at the door. Detective Finch stuck his head in. "Ellen, can I have a word?"

She seemed relieved to step into the hall.

"I should get to work," said the plumber. "Are you going to need me for anything else? There's nothing I can tell you that I didn't tell Tony Menario four years ago."

"Do you want someone to drive you home?" I asked.

The big man rose from his chair with a tired smile. "Thanks for the offer. Please thank Detective Pomerleau for me."

"I'll walk you out."

It wasn't even midmorning, but the sun was already raising mirages off the hoods of the vehicles parked in the lot. The air had the bitter taste of ozone, which reminded me of Maine's location as "America's tailpipe," downwind of the pollution billowing from Midwestern highways and coal-burning power plants. Every summer, tourists came to my scenic state for the clean air. No one warned them about the smog.

I worried that Tom Donaldson might hug me again, but this time we just shook hands.

"How did a game warden get caught up in this?"

"Trouble has a way of finding me."

I raised my hand in a wave good-bye as he pulled out of the parking lot. He smiled and nodded.

As I returned to the barracks, I noticed the Nasons' Cadillac SRX parked in a handicapped space near the door. Beside it was another brand-new Caddie sedan. The two vehicles had identical bumper stickers supporting the reelection of the current governor: the blowhard politician Charley Stevens had nicknamed the Penguin.

Now I understood why Finch had called Pomerleau away so suddenly. Was it possible that Christopher Nason had convinced his mother and brother to come in for an interview?

How?

Why?

Any lawyer worth his salt—and Nason had impressed me as a capable attorney—would have kept Steven Nason as far as possible from a police interrogation room. So why had they come in to be grilled?

37

I had become such a fixture at the Troop B barracks that none of the troopers or detectives even glanced at me as I roamed the building. I found Pomerleau's office unoccupied. I settled down in a still-warm chair to wait.

I heard heavy footsteps hurrying down the hall.

Detective Finch stopped in midstride. "You're still here? We thought you'd left."

"I figured Pomerleau would want to talk with me. Anything new on the Fales homicide?"

"We're exploring a few leads." He seemed in an inappropriately cheery mood for a man investigating a murder. "If you're planning on waiting for Ellen, she's going to be a while. We've got the Nasons in the conference room."

"I saw their vehicles out front. Is Steve Nason confessing?"

"You're not going to believe this, but Brother Stevie has disappeared."

"What?"

"His mother and brother say he must have taken off last night. They don't know where he went. They want our help finding him. They're *worried* about the son of a bitch!"

No wonder Finch was so animated. By running off, Steve Nason had done his best to incriminate himself. Theoretically, an adult American citizen is free to go where he pleases when he pleases without informing his family, let alone the authorities. Practically, however, the state police could use Nason's sudden, unannounced disappearance to begin searching for him—"out of concern for his mental state."

"That's wild," I said.

"It gets better. Chris Nason brought in another lease agreement he said they discovered in a file cabinet. Brother Steven rented a different house to the Cobbs last year!"

I wanted to ask where, but Finch was already on the move again.

I sat in the empty office feeling like Elmer Fudd after he has been clobbered in the head. Little birds were circling my skull.

I had to hand it to Chris Nason. It wasn't often you saw an attorney switch his defense strategy from obstruction and straight-out stonewalling to preemptive damage control. He must have realized the danger to his family's reputation if the existence of the other lease was leaked.

Where had Steve Nason gone? Where did he think he could hide? Menario had described the man as having a double-digit IQ. The police were bound to find him soon enough.

Or would they? All along, the investigators had operated under the belief that the older Nason brother lacked the smarts to abduct and imprison women as sex slaves without being caught.

But in well-documented cases, monsters had secretly jailed women and girls for years on end: the man in Cleveland who'd held three women as slaves in his basement before one escaped to alert authorities; the convicted sex offender who kept Jaycee Dugard in a series of shacks on his Antioch, California, property for eighteen years; the Austrian engineer who'd forced his own daughter to give birth to seven children in the twenty-four years he held her in a homemade dungeon. None of these men had been described by the police as a criminal mastermind.

They had been smart enough to outwit the authorities, however.

Maybe Nason was more cunning than anyone gave him credit for being.

I wasn't as confident in my belief in God as Tom Donaldson. My prayers tended to bounce off some invisible wall between the earth and the heavens. But I prayed now that Casey would survive the coming hours.

I felt an impulse to share the news of Steven Nason's flight with Stacey. Then I remembered that she had left her phone at home, on the kitchen counter.

Instead I leaned across Pomerleau's desk and scrawled a note on her sticky pad: *Congratulations.*

I felt both frustration and relief as I stepped

outside. Frustration that my part in this bizarre and horrific case might be drawing to a close. Relief that I would be freed to focus on doing the things I'd joined the Warden Service to do. I planned to keep the police radio turned up loud, in any case. Who knew what strange twist this uncanny day might take next.

Sebago Lake—water supply to most of Greater Portland and playground to thousands of boaters—represented the eastern edge of my district. It is the deepest lake in Maine; also one of the largest. In the summer I patrolled Sebago whenever I could. Given the heat and humidity, I thought I might haul my Jet Ski down to the water. Drunk boaters and unethical fishermen tended to watch out for wardens in patrol boats. Posing as another yahoo on a Jet Ski, I could sneak in close enough to catch them in their illegal acts.

On the drive home, I put in a call to Dani. I wanted to be the first to tell her that Steven Nason had taken flight. "Wait till you hear this."

"Sorry, I can't talk."

"What's going on?"

"Menario drove out to the Rowe family compound on Kezar Lake to confront Dakota over what he did to his Mustang. Shots were fired."

"Was anyone hurt?"

"Menario got winged in the arm. And Rowe took off before we could respond."

"So he's on the run, too? What's going on this morning? Why isn't this all over the radio?"

"It will be soon."

"Jesus."

"We're all thinking Rowe's lawyer will walk him into a police station before the day's done. It sure looks like he acted in self-defense. Menario is in deep shit, Mike. I think he'll go to jail for this."

Despite our many clashes, I derived no pleasure from the prospect of the retired detective's being prosecuted. What I was witnessing was the complete disintegration of a human being, not a man I'd call my friend, but someone who had devoted his life to public service. For a cop, even an ex-cop, to go to jail represented a uniquely brutal form of self-destruction, since the punishment inside the walls had the potential to be far more severe than that suffered by other inmates. For the first time I could remember, I found myself pitying Antonio Menario.

"Steven Nason has gone missing, too," I said. "That was the reason I was calling."

"What?"

"His family says he took off in the middle of the night."

"When it rains, it pours."

"I know. It's pretty damning."

"You realize this makes you the only person who can identify this so-called Becky Cobb."

The thought hadn't occurred to me. "I'd been thinking of taking my Jet Ski out for a lake patrol. With all this craziness going on, maybe I should stay on dry land. Just in case one of these chases turns into an all-units event."

"Probably a smart idea."

"Every once in a while I have one of those. I take it you haven't located that couple I told you about, Prudence and Jackson Smith."

"Not yet, but I've got my eyes open. Listen, I've got to run."

"Be safe, Dani."

She mumbled something as she signed off.

I turned up the radio and waited for the broadcast alerting every available officer to be on the lookout for Dakota Rowe in whatever vehicle he was thought to be driving.

Chances were, though, that Dani was right. If Rowe had acted in self-defense (despite having provoked Menario), then he would have called his family's attorneys right away, and they would be negotiating with prosecutors for their client to turn himself in.

What a day.

Ask any cop about the so-called lunar effect, and he or she will tell you it's for real. The science is disputed whether crime increases during full moons, but as far as I am concerned, the theory is grounded in stone. Maybe it's that there's more light on nights when the moon is full, and more light means more opportunities to commit crimes. Or maybe it goes deeper than that. Maybe the moon exerts some sort of pull on the human soul, the same way it does with the ocean tides. All I know is what I have seen firsthand. Visit a precinct lockup or a hospital ER on a night when the moon is at full power, and you're probably going to find it crowded with hairless werewolves.

Sometimes you don't even need the moon to be full for things to go haywire. Kathy Frost called these "what-the-fuck days," because there was no making sense of why unrelated people decided to melt down at the exact same moment.

This seemed to be one of those days.

On WTF days it paid to be ready for anything because anything seemed liable to happen.

Even though I no longer planned on fetching the Jet Ski, I decided to stop in at the house for a sandwich and a talk with Stacey. I wanted to tell her about all the insane things going on. A deeper discussion about our future together could wait for a calmer afternoon.

What surprised me, on pulling into the driveway, was that there were no signs she had returned from her run. Her Subaru wasn't there. Her phone was still on the counter where she'd left it. I even poked around the clothes hamper to check for her sweaty running clothes.

Nothing.

We had plenty of groceries and leftovers, so there would have been no reason for her to stop at the store. She should have been home. She should have been home hours earlier. It made no sense.

38

My phone rang as I was brushing bread crumbs from the cutting board into the sink. I wiped mustard from the corner of my mouth and answered the call. The number came up as blocked.

"Game warden."

"Is this the number to call if I've seen a feral pig?" It was the voice of an old woman. She spoke so softly it might as well have been a whisper.

"That's right."

"I saw a wild boar, I think."

"Where?"

"In a field behind my house. At the edge of the field."

"What's your address?"

She gave me a number on the Horseshoe Pond Road in Birnam. The location wasn't far from the Knife Creek Trail. I wondered if the animal she'd seen might be a pig from the same sounder as the one we'd eliminated at the wallow. The odds were good, given the proximity. If another hog was roaming around, separated from its group, how had I missed seeing the signs?

"When did you see this pig?"

"About an hour ago."

"I'll try to get over there this afternoon, but I can't promise it. Will you or anyone in your family be around if I come by?"

"I'll be here."

"What's your name?"

"Martha Tarbox. Do I get a reward if you kill it?"

I recognized the name. Tommy Volk had warned me against Mrs. Tarbox as a lonely old widow who made baseless calls to the Warden Service in order to receive visits from handsome wardens. "There's no monetary reward, but you will have the gratitude of the state of Maine."

"Gratitude won't pay the rent."

"I'll try to get over this afternoon. Don't approach the hog if you see it again. Feral swine can be dangerous, Martha."

"OK."

It made no sense to drive out to the Horseshoe Pond Road now. Big mammals such as deer and moose don't move around much in the heat of the day. I had to suppose that feral pigs displayed the same behavior. Yet she said she'd just seen it.

I had thought of waiting around until Stacey arrived home. I could only think that she had pushed herself to go for a longer run. Stacey ran half-marathons regularly. Maybe she was taking out her anger with Barstow on the trail.

Still, I felt an urge to drive over to the trailhead to check for her car. I went upstairs and changed my undershirt, buttoned the same short-sleeved uniform shirt over it, then tightened the Velcro straps on my ballistic vest again. Between the time that I left the house and the time my truck's air-conditioning kicked in, I was already soaked in sweat.

The Mountain Division Trail was a rehabilitated railroad line. Unlike most rail trails, this one continued to carry freight trains from Portland to the White Mountains. Conservationists had built an exquisite gravel path along the tracks to be used by runners and mountain bikers.

Given the heat and the time of day, it didn't surprise me to find the parking lot empty. If Stacey had been here, she had moved on. It annoyed me that she hadn't taken her phone when I had so much news to share.

As I was swinging my truck around, the phone buzzed on the console. It was Captain DeFord. Had Casey been found? What about Steven Nason? Or Dakota Rowe for that matter? I tried to keep the excitement out of my voice as I pressed the answer button.

"I heard from Pomerleau about what's going on down there," he began.

"It's pretty nutty."

"I also heard that Stacey lost her job. It's unfortunate." His tone and his word choice did not signal that he disagreed with the commissioner's decision.

"Yes, it is." I was waiting impatiently for him to break some kind of news about Nason or Rowe.

"I'm actually calling on another matter."

My heart dropped in my chest. "Oh?"

"The colonel and I would like you to come up to Augusta in the morning to discuss the investigator's position."

The events of the past few days had distracted me from thinking about the promotion I'd applied for.

"Absolutely! Sure! What time?"

"Eight hundred hours."

"I'll be there."

"We'll see you then." He hesitated before he spoke again, as if debating with himself whether or not he should tip his hand. "Congratulations, Mike."

As soon as I tapped the end button, I shouted out my happiness. Thank goodness no one else was within sight of my patrol truck. They would have thought me a lunatic. After five rocky years in the Warden Service, I had climbed out of the seemingly bottomless pit I had dug for myself.

My first thought was to share the good news with Stacey—until I realized that I had no clue where she was.

My second thought was even more crushing than the first: if Stacey really felt she had to leave Maine, I wouldn't be going with her.

Not knowing what to do with myself, I decided to go check out Martha Tarbox's feral pig sighting. Tommy Volk had warned me the old woman was a loon. He used to laugh about the time she had summoned him to deal with an injured "seagull." What he'd found, when he'd arrived, was an injured bald *eagle*. A naturalist, Martha Tarbox was not.

The Horseshoe Pond Road was little more than a wide, barely maintained ATV trail. The town of Birnam hadn't bothered to grade the frost heaves and fill the potholes after the spring thaw. I doubted if the public works department even plowed the road in the wintertime.

The first residence I passed was a mobile home with a junker on cement blocks in the drive and plenty of signs posted on the property warning about a dangerous dog. I never saw the canine, which must have been locked inside the trailer. But from the volume of its guttural barking, I judged the signs to be understated in their message.

My GPS said that the address Martha Tarbox had given me belonged to the next house. I drove a couple of hundred yards down the corrugated road. Then the woods opened up into a field of vivid wildflowers—pink lupines and orange daylilies and purple loosestrife—with an old farmhouse and barn in the center.

Even by the low standards set by many homes in the area, this place seemed to be a shambles. The clapboards had shed the last flecks of paint someone had once applied to them, and the roof had the scabrous appearance that develops when the shingles start blowing off. But the barn door was yawning open and I saw a little red hatchback parked inside, in the shadows. After all these years in rural Maine, it shouldn't have surprised me to see falling-down houses that were haunted by the living and not yet the dead.

I pulled into the rutted drive and turned off the engine. The ragged tree line behind the building was a hundred yards away, and the Saco River was probably another hundred yards beyond the edge of the forest. I could imagine a feral hog ranging happily in that narrow tract of wet, sandy woods.

I adjusted my gun belt on my hips and my ballistic vest on my shoulders as I climbed out into the midday heat. I headed for the mudroom door of the house, but was stopped by a creaky female voice calling from the barn.

"Hello!"

I changed course. I could see the outline of a Toyota Corolla hatchback where the sunlight met the dark. A woman moved in the shadows as I approached. Roosting pigeons cooed overhead, unseen in the rafters.

Why was she hiding? What exactly was going on here?

Suddenly my own words came back to me: *They're not stupid enough to come after me.*

Instead, they had tricked me into coming to them.

I reached for my handgun. My thumb pressed the button that released the heavy SIG P226 from its molded holster.

Just then, the girl stepped into the sunbeam. At first I didn't recognize her. Without the wig and with her dark hair a mess of knots, she seemed an entirely different person. Then I saw the mole on her cheek.

"Casey?"

She lifted her right arm and I saw something metallic flash in her hand. Reflexively I pulled my sidearm, but it was already too late. From a distance of ten feet, Casey Donaldson sprayed me full in the eyes with a burning blast of pepper spray.

39

A rite of passage for all cadets at the Maine Criminal Justice Academy is to be shot in the face with oleoresin capsicum, a chemical derived from chili peppers and pressurized as an aerosol to fire accurate blasts from a canister at distances up to twenty feet. The purpose of the exercise isn't just so future cops will appreciate the excruciating pain they can inflict if, in the line of duty, they pepper-spray a noncooperative person. It is also to prepare you in case you yourself are attacked with capsaicin.

I remember my instructor standing five feet from me, screaming at me to hold my eyelids open while he emptied an entire canister in my face. The sensation was instantaneous and unbearable. It felt as if the fluid inside my eyeballs had begun to boil. My tear ducts opened like floodgates, as did my sinuses. The skin on my face burned as if I'd pressed it against a hot plate. I remember doubling over, choking and coughing, while my instructors and fellow cadets shouted my name.

The exercise only began with being sprayed. Part two was to make my way, half-blind across the yard, to a tackle dummy, which I was expected to pummel into submission. Next to a mat where a teacher was playing the part of a resisting arrestee. Through commands and wrist locks I needed to subdue him and take him to the ground. The last stage, for me, was the hardest. Suffering, sputtering, spilling fluids from every orifice north of my pelvis, I was commanded to recite the specific legal language regulating use of force by police officers.

What the instructors at the Maine Criminal Justice Academy had never prepared me for was the possibility that I would be pepper-sprayed by the kidnapped woman whose life I had hoped to save.

Nor had they prepared me for a simultaneous sneak attack.

As I bent over in mental and physical shock, gushing tears and snot, coughing through a windpipe the size of a soda straw, I had the presence of mind to raise my handgun up into my "workspace," which is the area close to the face and chest from which you are taught to start your target acquisition.

Casey was just a bloodred blur now. I think I saw her stutter-step away from me, retreating into the shadows once her canister was empty.

Holding my weapon in both hands, I extended my arms in her direction.

Then came the shock of the Taser.

I felt the barbed electrodes pierce the back of my pants legs like two darts. A millisecond later a charge shot through my body. Every single one of my muscles went rigid. My motor skills left me as fifty thousand volts short-circuited my nervous system. I dropped forward onto my chest like a statue pushed off its base.

Being tased was another rite of passage at the academy. Odd as it might sound, being electrocuted is much better than being pepper-sprayed because the moment the Taser shuts off, you regain control of your central nervous system. The torturous effects of oleoresin capsicum can last for hours.

Between the chili pepper in the eyes, the shock of being immobilized by the Taser, and then having the wind knocked out of me as I fell chest-first onto the hard-packed earth, I was utterly helpless. It was enough time for the person behind me—whoever had shot me full of electricity—to club me hard in the back of the head.

Being knocked out isn't like in the movies. It's not as if someone gives you a love tap on the jaw or at the base of the skull and you suffer a fleeting moment of unconsciousness. You don't just wake up minutes later, dazed but more or less functional. When you are hit with real force in the head, the blow sends a shock wave through the tissue in your brain. Your gray matter sloshes around the inside of your cranium. There is significant cell death. Just ask a boxer what it feels like to take a KO-quality punch.

I don't remember anything from the time I was clubbed until I eventually "woke up," handcuffed and blindfolded.

It is likely my assailants hit me in the head again during transport. To keep me docile.

They must have had trouble moving my heavy, limp body as well. Some of the first sensations I felt as I came back were of patches of skin rubbed raw where I'd been dragged along the ground, and localized pains that would later blossom into purple bruises the size of my hand.

My return to consciousness was gradual. My mind sputtered like an engine that was having trouble turning over. Thoughts flashed one after the other, none of them connecting.

The Technicolor field of wildflowers in the summer sunlight.

The overhead rustling of pigeons in their dirty nests.

The intense focus in Casey's brown eyes as she aimed the capsaicin at me.

The expulsion of air from my lungs as my rib cage compacted against the ground.

And then—

My throat was still raw, and my face felt as if I had suffered the worst sunburn of my life. My eyelids were swollen shut, but no amount of effort could push them open. That was when it came to me that I was blindfolded.

I seemed to be sitting with my back against a pole of some sort with my arms behind me. I tried to move them, but I was unable to separate my wrists. I was handcuffed, I realized. Probably with my own cuffs.

Casey Donaldson was Martha Tarbox.

Four nights earlier, I had thought she wanted me to rescue her. But she and someone else, probably the other woman, Becky, had lured me to the abandoned house to ambush and abduct me. It had never occurred to me that Casey might have been brainwashed during her long imprisonment and was suffering from Stockholm syndrome: the psychological disorder in which a captive begins to feel trust and affection toward her kidnapper. I hadn't thought it possible.

What had Menario said to me the night before? What were the words he'd used? "You make a lot of assumptions, you little punk. Someday they're going to catch up with you."

The detective had been right. Not since my first months on the job had I felt such a sense of mortification and failure. I had been a fool, an utter fool. Now it was likely that I would pay for my carelessness with my life.

But I couldn't give up. I needed to gather my resources—I needed to "secure my shit," as

Tommy Volk would say—and take action. Self-pity was a luxury I couldn't afford.

The room I was in felt cool, as if I were underground. My nose searched for odors in the air, but the pepper spray had damaged the receptors in my sinuses and mouth. So I was deprived of my sense of taste and smell, as well as sight.

What did that leave me with? My head ached so hard I had trouble focusing.

Remember Charley's checklist, said a voice in my head.

What do I hear?

A mechanical humming overhead. Not a furnace. Not an air-conditioning system. Maybe a big blower fan, like the kind used in construction projects? If I called out, I would never be heard above the machine.

What do I feel?

My fingers felt for the ground and encountered a smooth, hard surface. Poured concrete. The pole against my back had a coating of paint. I was in a basement.

I brought my hands close to my back and discovered that my gun belt had been removed. No surprise there.

They'd taken off my ballistic vest, too.

I pushed my spine against the pole and brought my knees up. The muscles in my calves and quads were sore from the Taser. But I pressed hard and found that I could slide against the pillar until I was on my feet. Standing, I felt suddenly queasy. The blow (or blows) to the head had brought on vertigo.

I gave myself a few minutes for the nausea and unsteadiness to pass. Then I made a circle around the pillar. I braced myself against the steel column and extended a leg as far as I could, trying to see if it would make contact with anything. But no, I seemed to be in the center of a room.

At the academy, we'd received a few minutes' training in what to do if we were ever taken hostage—communicate, have faith, keep up your morale, cooperate until you find an avenue of escape—but the lecture had been perfunctory and was of no help in my current situation.

I hadn't told anyone about the call I'd gotten from "Martha Tarbox."

Or that I was heading to a remote location down the rarely traveled Horseshoe Pond Road.

My captors would have known enough to destroy the GPS in my cell phone. Or, better yet, throw it in the back of a pickup headed somewhere far from where they were taking me.

No one knew where I was.

Including me.

My breath began to come quicker and quicker. I could hear my staccato heartbeat inside my aching skull. There was no denying the truth: I was terrified.

As far as I know, I didn't make a noise. I didn't let out a sob. I didn't begin to shiver or shake.

But I must have given myself away somehow because a woman's voice said, "What's a matter? Are you scared?"

Then she began to laugh.

It was Becky. She had been in the room with me the whole time.

40

Even blindfolded, I knew where she was sitting. Her voice had given her location away. She was twenty feet or so directly in front of me, which told me that this basement was big. I hadn't heard her moving or breathing. That told me she was careful and dangerous.

Now I heard a chair scrape along the floor as she pushed it away. Heard her voice grow louder as she advanced on me. "You *should* be scared," she said in that unmistakably shrill voice. "You're going to die today. It's going to hurt, too."

My bee-stung tongue had a hard time forming even a single word. "Becky?"

"That's my name. Don't wear it out."

"You don't want to do this."

"No, I kind of do."

"Killing a cop—they'll execute you for that." This was no lie. Maine didn't have the death penalty, but the feds still did, and the US attorney would crucify anyone who assassinated a police officer—even a game warden.

Her laugh was a series of rasps. "I'm not the one who's going to kill you, douche bag."

I waited for her to explain what she meant, but she didn't. She was standing just out of reach of my legs. Maybe nine feet away?

One of the imperatives we'd been given at the academy, if we ever found ourselves in a hostage situation, was to humanize yourself. "My name is Mike Bowditch. I have a wife and—"

"Bullshit." She called me out on my lie. "You have a girlfriend named Stacey. You don't have any kids. You don't even own a dog."

"How do you know that?"

"Because he is smarter than you. The big guy is a genius."

"Who are you talking about?"

"You'll find out soon enough. Or maybe you won't? I'm kind of hoping you don't. It's sadder to die without any answers. My pop died of lung cancer and he never knew how he got it. Never smoked a day in his life. At the end it made him insane, dying for no reason he could understand."

The more I talked, the better I seemed to smell, the more I seemed to taste. "I'm sorry about your father."

She burst into a coughing fit of laughter again. "That is *so* lame! You're not sorry about anything—except getting caught like this. You should be sorry. We thought we might have trouble catching you. We were wrong about that, I guess."

"You got me there," I said, hoping the admission might throw her off-balance. "You fooled me pretty good."

"Keep trying, Warden. It ain't going to get you nowhere."

The woman was smart or, at least, smart enough. She had recognized every stratagem for what it was.

"You don't have to kill me." I tried not to make it sound like a plea. I wasn't going to beg for my life. "You have other options."

"Oh, yeah?"

"Just take off again. It's obvious that the state police can't keep up with you. You've outwitted—"

"Do you know how tempted I am to shoot you right now?"

I heard the click of the hammer being pulled back on a semiautomatic pistol.

"I got your gun pointed at your chest, just so you know. SIG Sauer P226! And, yeah, I've fired one of these before. I'm a crack shot, the big guy says. Jesus knows we practiced enough. See, what you don't understand is how pissed we are. We had a good deal going. What's the expression you people use up here? A 'wicked good' deal? You ruined that for us. And now you have to pay."

"Where's Casey?"

"Who?"

"Casey Donaldson."

"Oh, you mean Kendall. She's upstairs. Don't worry, though. She'll be down soon enough.

You're even going to see her! We'll take off your blindfold so you can gaze into her pretty, pretty eyes."

The message couldn't have been clearer: they were going to execute me soon.

The only comfort I could take was that, so far, they hadn't removed my blindfold. As long as there was something they didn't want me to see, I had a chance. It meant that my death wasn't entirely preordained. The moment to panic would be when they no longer cared what I saw.

"I called in my location when I arrived at that abandoned barn."

"No, you didn't."

"Are you willing to bet your life on that?"

"It's not my life that's forfeit. You're the one who fucked it up for us. The big guy is merciful. But he ain't going to forgive you that. You've made things too difficult, you stupid man."

"Becky—"

"Save it," she snapped. "There ain't a single thing you can say now that'll stop you from getting what you deserve. It's all foretold at this juncture. It was foretold the moment you knocked on our door that night. You've been dead this whole time and not even known it. I'd feel sorry for you if I wasn't so fucking pissed about having to move again. I hate moving!"

Just then an electronic noise echoed through the basement: chirping electronic crickets.

I heard Becky take a step away from me. "Hi, baby."

The cell phone speaker wasn't loud enough for me to hear the other side of her conversation, but I could recognize that it was a man's voice on the other end.

"Yeah, I've got him handcuffed to one of the poles in the basement. He's awake now." She paused. "I didn't know where else to take him. I understand that it creates problems for you. I'm sorry, baby."

More male mumbling.

"We left his truck in the barn and closed the door as much as we could. You can't see it from the road now. And I threw his cell phone into a pickup headed south, like you said I should. There ain't no way now they can track us here. Even if they find the truck, they won't know which way he might've went. He's one hundred percent off the radar."

The man on the other side raised his voice in reply, but I still couldn't make out more than garbled words.

"Well, we had to do something!" Becky pleaded. "He was the only other one that saw me. So what if they got that sketch? I can change my face. I done it before."

I heard the man on the other end raise his voice even louder.

"I was trying to protect you, baby. I just figured

it was her turn now. She needs to do it. It's her initiation. We can't trust her until she does one."

Her answer didn't seem to placate the man on the other end.

"I shouldn't have brought them here." She sounded genuinely contrite. "I'm sorry. I am very sorry. . . . Yes, baby, I'll take my punishment. I'll take it and like it."

She paused a long time while I heard indecipherable ranting on the other end of the line.

"I won't do nothing until you get here, baby. I promise." She paused. "Can I take his mask off? I want to see the look in his eyes. You know that's my favorite part. I want her to see it, too. . . . Thank you, baby."

Her next words were directed at me. "I gotta go upstairs for a minute." The tone of her voice rose in amusement. "Don't go nowhere while I'm gone."

I listened as she ran up the basement stairs, her steps as light as a child's.

My head ached and my insides burned, but I knew I had only a few minutes to deconstruct the phone call I'd overheard.

Becky had seemingly gone rogue. I wasn't sure if the plan to kidnap me had been her idea or that of her master, the "big guy," but he clearly disapproved of her having brought me to this house. In his mind, my being here had created a problem—perhaps because he had no desire to burn the place to the ground, as he had done with the others, to destroy DNA traces that proved I'd been here.

As I'd feared, they had seemingly done an expert job at hiding my truck and disposing of the cell phone the Warden Service would use to locate me.

I smacked my lips and drew in a deep breath through my nose. The faintest of smells registered in my brain. Basement-floor sealant?

What had Becky said? "I figured it was her turn now. She needs to do it. We can't trust her until she does it."

They had killed someone before, and I had a strong feeling it wasn't the baby Stacey and I had found.

Their plan was for Casey to kill me. I was to be the final rite of initiation into the gang or the cult or whatever it was.

Just then I remembered the hidden dagger in my boot. I squatted down and brought my feet to the sides of the pole. I stuck my index finger into the top of the boot, hoping to snag the ring at the top of the skeletonized steel blade. Where was it?

Two sets of footsteps on the stairs now.

The first, staccato, had to be Becky's.

The second, slower, tentative, almost shambling, must have been Casey's.

Through my blindfold I became aware of an overhead light coming on. The utterly black fabric became an espresso-colored brown.

Frantically, I tried my left boot, thinking that maybe I had concealed the dagger in that one instead. I clearly remembered picking it up that morning.

"Looking for this?" Becky said.

I heard something metal hit the floor off to my left.

"We found your hidden knife. We searched you from head to toe. Kendall did, I should say. Too bad you were out cold. You would've enjoyed getting felt up by such a pretty girl."

"Casey?" I said, pushing myself back up to a standing position.

Becky's response was sharp and immediate. "Shut up! Don't listen to him, Kendall! Remember what I told you? This douche bag wants to break up our family. He pretends like he gives a shit, but he doesn't. This douche bag wants to kill our husband! He wants to kill all of us."

"That's not true, Casey."

"Stop calling her that! Think about it, Kendall. If something happens to the big guy, who's going to give you your medicine? How did you feel that time we couldn't get your medicine for you?"

"Sick."

"You thought you were going to die. You

probably would have died! This douche bag doesn't give a shit about you."

"Casey—"

"What do you want to do to him, Kendall?"

"Hurt him."

"So do it!"

"I don't know—"

"Like this!"

In that instant I felt a boot crushing down on the slender bones on the top of my left foot. My knee buckled and then I felt a second kick glance off my left kneecap. If it had hit directly, the joint would have sprained backward and torn one of the ligaments.

Reflexively, I dropped to my knees. Another kick landed on my thigh. If I survived the day, I would have some pretty bruises to mark the occasion.

"Do it, Kendall! Come on, bitch! Do it!"

I felt another kick—much softer—to the meat of my quad. It had to have come from Casey.

"Harder!" screamed Becky. "Don't be a pussy, Kendall. Hurt him! Hurt him or I'll hurt you!"

I should have known to press my thighs together. The next kick hit me in the scrotum and sent my balls halfway up into my abdomen. Just as I had nearly retched when I'd been sprayed with capsaicin, I nearly retched again. I toppled forward and was only stopped from hitting the floor by the handcuffs holding my arms behind the pillar.

I was panting, cantilevered above the concrete, not strong enough to pull myself up, when Becky yanked the blindfold from my eyes.

The fluorescent brightness caused my tender eyes to blink and water again. Two human shapes loomed before me. The nearer one, with her taut, wiry body, must have been Becky. Casey held back, her arms sort of floating at her sides as if she wasn't sure what to do next.

"Hey, douche bag!" Becky screamed. "What did I tell you?"

Saliva bubbled from my lips. "I don't—"

"You're going to die today. Maybe you don't believe me? Hold his head up, Kendall. Don't be a pussy, bitch, do it!"

Through my smeared vision I saw Casey step to one side of me, almost as if she were afraid I would whip my head around and attach my teeth to her wrist. She pinched my ear and used it to swing my entire head around to the right. My tear ducts were still trickling from the pepper spray. It took me a long time to focus my acid-burned pupils and even longer to recognize the vague shape in the corner for what it was—for what *he* had been.

They had tied Steve Nason to another pillar. Like me, he was seated on the floor with his arms secured behind him. Unlike me, he had been tied with rope. Unlike me, he had his pants and boxer shorts down around his ankles. His limp, hairy penis was on full display as if mockery had been part of his torture. His genitals were wet as if he'd urinated all over himself. Unlike me, he had a plastic bag pulled like a hood over his head. I couldn't see his face through the fogged plastic, but there was no question he was dead. Murder by suffocation: the preferred method of execution used by the Khmer Rouge.

Casey released my earlobe and my head lolled forward on my neck. I lifted my face in time to see the blurred shape of Becky advancing on me. She'd tossed aside the blindfold and was holding something shapeless and opaque in her hand. The next thing I knew she had pulled the plastic bag down over my chin. I breathed in, but no air would come.

41

I began to struggle, tried using my whole body to free myself. Fog clouded the interior of the bag. I attempted to suck in air but only succeeded in pulling the plastic taut across my gaping mouth. I hadn't even prepared myself by filling my lungs first. My human brain—the product of millions of years of evolution, capable of foresight and logic and self-consciousness—was reduced in an instant to a primordial mass of simple cells at the base of its stem. The lizard brain, scientists called it.

I had become nothing more than a dying animal.

Suffocating, I banged the back of my skull against the steel post for no reason. Felt intense pain in my thumbs as I pulled them hard against the handcuffs, willing to sacrifice my hands to save my life. Sucked the plastic into my mouth again with one deep inhale, then bit down hard with my canines. I chewed down and thrashed my head with the bag mashed between my teeth.

Somehow I tore a hole. A trickle of air entered. I gasped at it, the ripped plastic still in my mouth. Inhaled hard through my nostrils.

Not enough. Not enough.

I tried biting again but couldn't reach the torn

edge of the plastic rubbing against my upper lip.

I felt myself beginning to slip away—the adrenaline in my blood insufficient to the task of keeping me conscious.

Then suddenly the bag was gone.

"Weird," I heard Becky say. I blinked my burning eyes, but the room seemed off-kilter. Everything was tilted. She had poked a finger through the hole I'd chewed through the plastic. "Guess we need a thicker bag, Kendall."

I was hyperventilating. I still couldn't get enough oxygen no matter how hard I gasped.

But the neurons in my cerebral cortex had begun to spark again.

Remember your first-aid training. What is the treatment for a hyperventilating individual? Tell them to breathe from their diaphragm.

I squeezed my eyes shut and focused on my abdomen below my rib cage. Pulled with my stomach muscles upward. Felt them ripple as they pushed the breath from my lungs, then forced myself to suck air through my pursed lips. My heart was a metronome set at the highest setting.

"That was just a test run, anyway," Becky said to me. "So you know what's going to happen. The next time it's for real."

Other sensations began to return as I regained control of my breathing. My wrists were bleeding from where I had cut them on the edge of the cuffs. I had worsened my probable concussion when I'd slammed my head against the pole.

"The worst thing is having time to think about it," Becky continued. "Knowing what's coming and there's nothing you can do to stop it."

The room had seemed angled because I was leaning. I fought to right myself.

Both of the women had removed their ridiculous wigs. That's all they'd done, and yet they seemed utterly transformed.

Becky had dirty-blond hair, longer on top than in the back or on the sides. I hadn't expected her to be a blonde. Her eyes still had the same squinty meanness, her lips were just as flaky and raw, and the V-shape of her chin gave her an overall resemblance to some sort of goblin. She wore a man's T-shirt commemorating a past Fryeburg Fair, cutoff denim shorts, and boots appropriate for thru-hiking the Appalachian Trail. Her bare arms and legs were thin, but I could see muscles shift beneath the pale skin when she moved.

Casey looked even worse than when I'd glimpsed her in the house. Her hair hung in tendrils around her face. Her skin had a waxy pallor. A cold sore had erupted on her lip. She, too, wore an oversize man's shirt, a standard white T, and those boxy shorts worn by high-school girls who play team sports. She was barefoot, I noticed. Her toenails were painted pink.

When she'd kicked me before, it had probably hurt her more than it had hurt me.

I noticed one last thing, the most important thing, the detail that explained so much.

Casey Donaldson, unlike Becky Cobb, had needle tracks on the insides of both of her arms.

So that was how they were controlling her.

That was why she hadn't tried to escape.

"Casey, my name is Mike Bowditch." My voice was hoarse from the pepper spray and the minutes I'd spent suffocating. "I'm the one who found your baby girl."

"Oh, shut up." Becky studied me with undisguised disdain.

"Your baby was being eaten by a pig."

"I said, 'Shut up.'"

"They buried her there so that would happen, so that the pigs would eat her flesh and bones and there would be no evidence."

Before I could say another word Becky kicked me in the crotch again.

I doubled over, my arms outstretched behind me around the pillar, and sank down to my knees.

"I knew I should've brought duct tape. We'll just have to use a rag. Go find something to gag him with, Kendall."

The command took a while to register in Casey's drugged mind. Slowly she made her way back up the basement stairs.

"This is all your fault, you know. What's happened to you. What's about to happen. See that sad sack of shit over there." Becky pointed at

Nason, with the clouded bag around his head and his pants down around his ankles. "He wouldn't be dead if not for you. Think about that."

I became aware of a sudden change in the house. The blower upstairs had stopped. Now I could hear footsteps overhead, two sets, heavy ones and softer ones. A man was up there. I could hear him speaking but couldn't make out his words through the ceiling joists.

Becky's head whipped around. "Oh, shit," she muttered to herself. "Oh, damn."

For the first time, I saw her stiffen with nervousness. Like a girl whose prom date has just arrived.

She began glancing around the floor until she located the blindfold where she'd tossed it. Quickly she tied the cloth back around my head and knotted it hard. Once more I found myself in darkness.

I heard Becky start up on the stairs, then a door opened at the top and she said, "I was just coming up."

There was no answer.

The door closed. Then slowly a man began to descend the steps with her. I could tell from the way the boards creaked.

Casey must have remained upstairs. Clearly, they had no fear of her running off or calling for help.

I listened carefully as the two of them paused at

the base of the stairs. Instead of approaching me, they went first to the opposite corner, where their former accomplice Steve Nason sat dead.

The words spilled out of Becky's mouth at a torrential rate. "I know I shouldn't have done it, baby, but I didn't know where else to bring them. Maybe we can spray the place down with some bleach or something. Would that work? We don't have to burn your house down. There's got to be another way. I'll find a way to erase all the traces of us. You can trust me. You know you can trust me."

The man whispered something harsh into her ear.

"I don't know why I pulled his pants down. I thought it would be funny, I guess. After having to suck his itty-bitty prick all those times. That's why I sprayed him with the pepper. You should have seen him thrash, though. He was so scared. I know you would have liked watching him plead and cry. You told me you always hated him. I didn't think you'd mind. Do you mind? You can punish me for that, too. I deserve to be punished."

The man let out a sigh.

I heard them coming in my direction. As they drew near, I became aware of a new smell in the room. Cinnamon chewing gum.

"Hello, Nisbet," I said.

But it was Becky who replied. "Shut up!"

For half a minute the room was utterly silent. Then came clapping. Slow, sharp, mocking clapping.

"Take off his blindfold," Nisbet said. "He never needed it, anyway. It wasn't like he was ever going to leave this room."

I felt Becky's strong little fingers around my ears.

Before me stood the overweight reserve police officer I had derisively nicknamed Fat Elvis. He was dressed the same as he'd been at the Swan's Falls boat landing in Fryeburg. Dressed all in blue with a sliver of white belly peeking out above his gun belt.

"Becky, go upstairs and keep Kendall occupied. I don't want her thinking too much about what's going on down here." His tone was different from what I remembered, more confident, more educated sounding. "The warden and I need to have a talk."

42

After Becky had left us, Nisbet dragged a sawhorse from the corner of the room and set it in front of me. If it had been made of wood, it probably would have snapped when he sat down on it, but this adjustable steel model merely squeaked. He crossed his hands in his lap and smiled. He had a handsome face under the layers of fat. He actually bore a slight resemblance to Elvis Presley.

"My girls really did a job on you, didn't they?"

"I don't suppose your department ever sent you to the police academy?" I rasped.

"They don't bother sending reserve officers. We're just summer help."

"Then you don't know what it's like to be pepper-sprayed or tased."

"No, I don't."

"It's not so bad."

"It must have been bad enough for you to have ended up here." He pressed the pads of his fingertips together. "What about putting a plastic bag over your head? Did they do that to you at the academy, too?"

My nose was still running from the capsaicin. I licked the mucus from my upper lip and spat it on the floor.

"How much do you weigh?" he asked, seemingly out of nowhere.

"One ninety."

"The last time I weighed one ninety I was a freshman in high school. These days I yo-yo between two fifty and two eighty. Right now I'm at two fifty-six because of the heat. I always find it easier to lose in the summer."

"Congratulations."

"The reason I ask is that there's an advantage to being fat. Really only one advantage, and I bet you don't know what it is because you've never been overweight in your life. I can tell that by looking at you. The advantage is that people assume you're dumb. They conclude that you're fat because you don't know enough to eat healthy. Or that you're weak willed. When you're a tub like me, you go through life being underestimated."

Nisbet was correct in one regard. I hadn't given him enough credit. I should have noted his inquisitiveness that day Charley and I met him at Swan's Falls.

"I didn't underestimate you," I lied. "I figured out it was you."

"Yeah, but too late. I mean, look at where we are at the moment." He pushed his black pompadour back with one big hand. "What gave me away, though? I need to make a note for future reference."

405

"You mentioned you had a 'cousin' who rented from the Nasons. You went out of your way to make me suspicious of them." I nodded at the dead man in the corner. "Steve was always going to be your fall guy, wasn't he? He was easy to manipulate. You had Becky treat him to blow jobs in exchange for keeping quiet. What did he think you were really doing in his rentals?"

"Selling drugs—which I do. Nothing big-time. Just some heroin and pills for a little extra income. Easy enough to do when I'm working the river."

"I saw the needle tracks on Casey's arms."

"Keeping a woman in line is hard work. You gotta do what you gotta do."

"Especially when it comes to sex slaves."

The smile never left his handsome face, but his eyes narrowed. "I researched you after we met on the river. I read up on your past cases. You've had quite a colorful career! I've never had a real adversary, someone with enough smarts to catch me. Do you know why ninety-nine percent of cops are so dumb? Because ninety-nine percent of criminals are so dumb. There's no incentive for departments to hire people with superior intelligence. I had high hopes for you, Mike, based on what I found online. You seemed like someone who could keep me on my toes and help me improve my game. But you've turned into such a disappointment."

"Instead of insulting me you could just kill me and get it over with."

"Oh, I'm not going to kill you."

This time, I was the one who laughed.

He slid off the sawhorse. He took a step toward me, and I could smell his halitosis now that the gum in his mouth had lost its flavor. "In fact, I've never killed anyone in my life."

"What about Nason over there?"

"That was Becky. That girl is a stone-cold killer. I saw it in her the first time I picked her up on the side of the road. She was a runaway. Her brothers were sexually abusing her until she cracked one of them over the head with a hammer. She might have killed him, but she didn't stick around Jersey long enough to find out. Becky has always been willing to do whatever I ask."

"Including killing Connie Fales. She's leaving quite a body count."

His teeth gleamed when he smiled. "Yes, she is."

"Did you kill Martha Tarbox, too?"

"Martha? No, she's away in Texas for the time being with her family. One of the advantages to being a cop is that I know which homes are occupied and which aren't. Martha is such an odd duck, I knew you couldn't help but show up at her property with your guard down."

He was right, and I had to admit his craftiness before I could respond. "Maybe you're unfamiliar with the legal concept of conspiracy to commit murder—never having graduated from the police academy."

The capillaries in his cheeks flushed with blood as he scowled. For the first time I seemed to have found a soft spot where I could stick in the shiv.

"I know what you're trying to do now. You're trying to provoke me. But it won't work. I have too much self-control. As I said, people assume that obese individuals are lacking in willpower. But I have more willpower than anyone you have ever met."

"So that's what this is about? Secretly exerting your godlike power over women? While everyone who thinks they know you assumes you're a stupid, harmless oaf?"

"There are two types of people in the world. Those who bend to reality and those who bend reality to suit their desires."

"Who said that?"

"I did."

"You're a regular Benjamin Franklin, Nisbet."

The jab at his intelligence caused his face to darken again. "I'm surprised you're not asking me questions about what happened with Casey."

"What would be the point? I'm going to be dead soon. Knowing your master plan doesn't really interest me."

He leaned his fat ass against the sawhorse once more. "You're such a liar."

Of course I was lying. I wanted to stall him and keep him talking—anything to give someone an opportunity to find me. But clearly the one thing Nisbet craved above all was respect for his towering intellect and awe at his personal power. Denying his superiority, mocking his pretentious self-regard, was a risky gambit, but what other hand did I have to play?

I straightened my spine. "You abducted a teenage girl, caged her up, and shot her full of heroin for four years. That doesn't make you a superman. It makes you a pathetic creep."

He brought his hands together again, but this time he began kneading his palms, almost as if contemplating the satisfaction of throttling me. "Let me ask you something. The night you first came to my house. The night you saw Casey. Did she say anything to you? Did she cry for help?"

"No."

"What was stopping her?"

"She was afraid of Becky."

"Bullshit. She didn't cry for help because I trained her to do whatever I tell her to do. I have totally erased her previous identity. She doesn't remember who she used to be. That's why I call her Kendall. Casey Donaldson is dead."

I couldn't stop myself from saying, "So what's your long-term goal? You have a secret harem of brainwashed women living in ratty shacks across greater Fryeburg?"

He bounced up and down on the sawhorse. He clapped his hands together with delight. He had found the chink in my own suit of armor. "I knew you were lying! You want to know what happened the night Casey disappeared. You think it has something to do with John Blood's old cabin, but you're not sure of the connection. Why have I spread the word that homeless people are free to camp in those woods?"

"I know why."

"Oh?"

"Because you're always on the lookout for the next vulnerable girl. It's why you work the night shift on the Saco. It's why you pick up hitchhikers and give runaways and drifters a place to hide from the world. You're looking for the next Casey. You're looking for girl number three."

"Who said there haven't been others, Mike?"

Nisbet had been leading me to this place from the start, the way you lead mice to a trap with cracker crumbs. The sense of failure and humiliation I had felt before rushed back like a rising tide. I pulled with all my strength against my handcuffs, causing the stanched blood to flow freely.

"You son of a bitch."

"There we go." He laughed. "That's what I wanted to hear."

"Who's Frank Cobb?"

"Just a name I got off a tombstone."

"What happened to Casey's baby? Was she born alive? Did you make Becky kill her? Whose idea was it to leave her to the pigs?"

"And now I believe my work here is done." He dragged the sawhorse loudly back into the corner. "I'm going to tell Becky to give you some time—I won't say how much—for those questions to eat a hole in your heart. I want your last hours to be a period of reflection in which you contemplate your utter stupidity and defeat. And of course, I need to have an unshakable alibi for your time of death, not that anyone is ever going to find your body."

With that, the monster I'd insultingly called Fat Elvis popped a fresh stick of gum in his mouth and plodded heavily back up the stairs.

43

I knew why Nisbet had given me this stay of execution. He wanted to get as far away as possible from the house in the event my corpse was ever discovered. Medical examiners always say that time of death is never conclusive. All sorts of biological and environmental factors can conspire to confuse the issue. But it wouldn't hurt Nisbet to have an unquestionable alibi for the span of hours when my heart ceased pumping oxygen to my brain.

This was the house I'd seen under construction on the road into the homeless camp. I was sure of that much. Nisbet had bought a piece of John Blood's land at the edge of the dying man's property to build his custom torture chamber.

There were no windows, of course. And the insulation above me was thick. Eventually Nisbet would decide he needed to soundproof it as well.

For now I could hear voices. Nisbet's and, I was guessing, Becky's. The words were just vague sounds. But I had to assume they were making a plan on what to do with both me and the lifeless body of Steve Nason.

They'd taken everything from me: my gun belt, my bulletproof vest, my dagger.

Or had they? Had they found the secret pocket where I kept my spare handcuff key?

For the first time in a long time, I felt a surge of hope. I tried bringing my chained hands around the pole to my front pocket. But I couldn't get them that far.

Damn it! Is the key still there or not?

The door opened at the top of the stairs. Light from above spilled down the steps. I heard floorboards creak at the top.

I pulled as hard as I could against one of the steel bracelets. I was willing to sacrifice a thumb if it meant my life. But all I did was succeed at opening another vein.

I watched as Casey Donaldson descended the stairs. She had a canister of pepper spray in one hand: my canister of pepper spray this time, the one from my gun belt. In her other hand she carried another plastic bag.

She seemed to need to rebalance with every step, the way a drunk does when taking a roadside test for driving under the influence. Her shoulders slumped. Her pupils were as small as birdshot.

But she was still pretty, still (barely) recognizable as the vital young woman I had seen in the YouTube videos.

She was still Casey. Even if she no longer believed it, I had to convince her of the truth.

"Hi, Casey," I said hoarsely.

She hesitated on the very last stair. "He told me not to talk with you."

"Who did?"

"My husband."

"Jeff Nisbet isn't your husband, Casey."

She refused to come any closer. "That's not my name."

"I met a man this morning who said it was. He was very nice. His name is Tom Donaldson. He's lost his stepdaughter and doesn't know where she is."

They must have injected her again before sending her down, because she was a sleepy, slobbering mess, barely capable of forming a sentence. "I'm not supposed to listen to you."

"Then why are you here?"

"To watch you."

"You don't have to be afraid of me. I'm handcuffed to this post and I can barely see. You sprayed me pretty good before."

She didn't respond, but she did step off the bottom step.

"You can sit down if you want. Don't worry, I'm not going to do anything. I can't do anything. I'm all tied up."

She refused to look me in the face. They must have warned her that I would try to persuade her to let me go. Was this some sort of initiation test? Becky had argued to Nisbet that Casey would

414

need to kill me before they could ever fully trust her.

"You're over there, and I'm over here. You can sit down if you're tired. There's nothing I can do to you."

She scanned the floor around her, then lowered herself awkwardly onto the sealed concrete. She sat with her knees raised and pulled up close. She wrapped both arms around her calves but kept the canister pointed, more or less, in my direction.

"My name is Mike Bowditch, Casey. I'm a Maine game warden."

"My name is Kendall."

"That's strange, because you look just like the stepdaughter of the man I met this morning, Tom Donaldson. He lives in Westbrook. His daughter Casey was a student at the University of New Hampshire."

She sank her head against her knees.

Christ. She's going to pass out on me. "Casey."

Her head bobbed up.

I made my voice soft again. "I was saying that I'm a game warden. Do you know what game wardens do? We protect fish and wildlife in the state of Maine. That means we're out in the woods a lot. I found something horrible in the woods the other day. I was up on the Knife Creek Trail, not too far from here. It was the worst thing I have ever seen. I think you know what it was."

She made a gurgling noise in her throat.

"It was a dead baby, Casey. A baby girl."

She slurred, "My name's not Casey. It's Kendall."

"Someone had buried this baby in a pool of mud and pig shit. They couldn't even be bothered to dig a real grave. They just left that precious baby to rot. Who would do something like that?"

She lifted her head, the dark strands of hair hung down, but I could see tears shining in her eyes now.

"Do you know what the worst part was?"

She paused, then shook her head no.

"When I found the baby, she was being eaten by pigs. Whoever buried her there had done it on purpose. They wanted that little girl to be eaten up, so there would be no evidence that she ever existed."

Casey began to sniff because her nose was running.

"But that little girl had a name, didn't she? What was her name?"

Her face wrinkled and turned red as she started to sob. "Kylie."

"Kylie Cobb?"

She nodded.

"She was your baby girl. She was your baby girl who died and you wanted someone to remember that she'd been alive. That's why you scratched her initials on the tree."

Just then, at the top of the stairs, I heard clapping.

It was the same slow, perfectly rhythmic, mocking applause I had heard earlier. I saw a big shadow on the staircase.

Nisbet descended into his do-it-yourself dungeon. "That was a nice try. I was curious to see how you would go at it. I assumed it would be the baby angle. But I didn't figure you'd bring up her stepdad."

"I thought you were leaving to establish an alibi."

"I've never understood why people are so willing to believe whatever you tell them."

I tilted my chin in the direction of the sobbing young woman on the floor. "So did she pass her test or not?"

"Who said it was *her* test?"

I closed my swollen eyes and tried to focus on my breath. I listened to my heart beating—the echo percussive inside my aching head—and willed it to slow down. I did everything I could to gather myself.

I opened my eyes and smiled. "You should have given her the key to the handcuffs."

He made a piggish noise through his nose. "Really? Why would I do that?"

"Because I knew she couldn't save me. I understand that I'm already dead. It would have been a real test if you'd given me some incentive.

I knew that all I could do was to stall her. You didn't get my best effort."

"I think I did. It doesn't matter at this point, anyway. Besides, Becky has your gun belt. I think she wants to keep it as a souvenir. She's going to be mad at me when I tell her we have to dump it."

Casey hugged her knees as she cried. I wondered if, in her grief, she might still be listening to us. I hoped she was because I needed her to hear what I said next.

"You might consider getting a vasectomy, Nisbet. If you're going to keep raping young women like Casey here. How many other babies have you had to kill?"

He glanced at the girl on the floor and raised one of those soft hands to his double chin, as if contemplating how I might be trying to outmaneuver him. "I told you I have never killed anyone. In retrospect I should have buried the child somewhere else. But when I saw those wild boars come through the yard, I thought . . . Clearly, it was a mistake, or you wouldn't be here now. But I pride myself on never making the same mistake twice."

Suddenly Becky shrieked from the top of the stairs, "Baby!"

"What?" he bellowed.

Her voice echoed down the staircase. "There's a police car out front. It just turned down the drive."

He raised his head to the ceiling beams. "Son of a . . ."

I tried not to grin. I didn't want to goad him now. If anything, I wanted Nisbet to forget about me.

"Is it a deputy or a trooper?" he yelled.

"A trooper. A woman."

Dani.

It had to be. Why was she here? And did she have any clue of the danger waiting for her?

Nisbet removed the .45-caliber semiautomatic from the holster on his belt and tucked it in the back of his pants. He unfastened the buckle on his gun belt and dropped it to the floor. He was going to go out to meet Tate looking as if he were unarmed.

He glared at me, unsure of how I'd managed to effect this unexpected visit. But he didn't have time to quiz me now.

He reached down and pinched Casey's neck so hard she screamed. "If he moves, put the bag over his head. You do it, you stupid bitch, or I'm going to take away your medicine."

She made blubbering noises to signal her surrender.

The last thing he did was to bend down and remove his handcuffs and handcuff key from the pouch on his holster. He stuffed them in the front pocket of his baggy blue pants. He gave me a final, gloating smile. "Wouldn't want to forget these."

For a heavy man, Nisbet stepped quickly up the stairs. A moment later the blower started up overhead, drowning out all sound from above, along with any cries for help I might possibly give.

Casey and I were alone again.

44

I couldn't hear a thing from upstairs, and that worried me to death. I had come to terms with the idea of dying myself, but the thought that Dani Tate might now be walking into a lethal trap—*How the hell had she found us, anyway?*—raised goose bumps along my neck and arms. I had believed my adrenal glands to be spent, but they sent one last burst of energy into my bloodstream.

This was, quite literally, my final chance.

"Casey?" I said softly. When she didn't respond, I tried again, "Casey?"

She raised her red-streaked eyes. This time there was no bullshit about her name being Kendall.

Mentioning her dead baby had broken through the wall, but how could I widen the gap? Maybe if I kept repeating her real name. Nisbet had spent years breaking this poor girl's spirit, with the goal of making her his personal slave.

But what about Becky? What were Casey's loyalties to that cruel and unstable woman?

"You need to listen to me. You need to watch out for Becky. She's not your friend."

Casey made no answer. Her numbed brain cells

were struggling to make sense of what I was saying and why I was saying it.

"She's jealous of you because he wants you more than he wants her."

I had no idea if what I was saying was true, but Casey didn't refute me.

"She's going to kill you someday. In your heart of hearts you know she will."

"I can't think right now. Please leave me alone."

I needed to try another tack. "Tell me about your mom, Casey. Her name was Claire, right? I saw a picture of her. She was beautiful. You must miss her so much."

Casey's eyelids fluttered. "My mom?"

"We found your mom's ring, Casey. Her diamond ring. You thought it was lost forever, but we found it."

"Where?"

"It had fallen out in Noah's canoe. Remember Noah? Remember Angie? Your friends miss you so much, Casey. They want you back. Don't you miss them, too? You can see them again if you help me."

She focused her small pupils on me. "There's nothing . . ."

"When you searched my clothes before, did you find a key in my front pocket?"

"Car keys?"

"No. A little key. It would have been inside

a small pocket in my front right pocket."

Her blank expression suggested that she hadn't.

"I need you to do something now. I need you to reach into that pocket and feel for it."

Her hands were shaking.

"I'm not going to hurt you. Please, Casey." I swung my body around so that my right side was facing her. "Help me get out of here, and I'll take you to see your friends."

She pushed herself to her feet and wobbled in place a moment. Then she took a tentative step in my direction.

"You can do it. You're a brave person. You've had to be brave to survive what's happened to you."

Another step closer.

"My right front pocket."

She stretched out a hand. With the other she pointed the canister of pepper spray at my face. She stood as far away from me as possible as she slid two fingers into my pocket.

At that moment, the basement door banged open and someone began to descend the steps in a hurry.

Before I could speak again, Casey dropped my second handcuff key to the floor. It bounced behind me, out of view.

Becky leaped down the last stairs. Her face was ugly as a war mask. She waved my SIG Sauer in the air. The heavy gun looked huge in her small hand.

"Put the bag on him," she hissed at Casey. "Do it now!"

When the younger woman didn't move, Becky slapped her in the back of the head. "Do it!"

"No, Casey," I said. "Please."

Her face was contorted with fear again. Whatever courage she had rediscovered had deserted her. Becky, her tormenter, was simply too terrifying.

I leaned back against the pillar as Casey picked up the bag. She advanced on me again, her mouth tight, tears streaming once more down her pasty cheeks.

"Please, don't do it," I said.

She mouthed the words, "I'm sorry," as she pulled the suffocating hood down over my head.

This bag, unlike the other, had a drawstring, and she pulled it tight. It was also larger and heavier—too thick for me to bite through.

Once again I found myself desperate for oxygen, but this time I'd been prepared enough to fill my lungs before my air supply was cut off. I figured that I had, at most, two minutes.

Instead of struggling, I dropped to the floor. I focused all of my energy on my hands. I needed to find the key. I felt my way along the smooth concrete, hoping that Becky would be distracted enough by Dani's presence outside not to notice what I was doing. An ache was growing in my skull, as if a clamp were closing around my temples.

My little finger touched something. But the force of the touch pushed the object away.

My blind fingers scrambled to recover it.

I could feel the last of the oxygen bleeding through the walls of my lungs into my bloodstream as I closed my hand around the metal ring at the top of the handcuff key.

I dug the key into the lock and turned it clockwise.

Nothing happened. Of course they had double-locked the cuffs.

Suddenly, I heard a shriek. "What's that? What's he doing?"

The walls of my lungs—all those air-sucking alveoli—seemed suddenly aflame. I reversed the key and used the nub at the top to push the pin in the keyway. Then I tried the lock again. I never heard a click, but the spring opened, and suddenly my left hand was free.

"You bitch!" Becky said. "What did you do?"

As I tore the plastic bag off my head, I heard another scream—but this one was different, higher pitched.

Before me, Casey was directing a mist of pepper spray directly into Becky's eyes. The older woman tried to block the stream with her left forearm, but she still had hold of my gun. She swung her right arm around in Casey's direction to fire it at her.

As she did, I pressed my feet against the floor and pushed off. The handcuffs were still attached to my right hand. I used them now as a weapon. I brought the metal bracelet down like a nunchaku on Becky's gun hand. The force must have shattered half the bones because she couldn't keep her grip on the pistol. The SIG dropped to the concrete and spun away.

I stepped forward and whipped the handcuffs across Becky's face. Blood drops splattered from her nostrils as her nose shattered. She collapsed to the ground, sniffing, groaning, clawing at her injuries—not unconscious, but incapacitated by the acid burning her eyes and the fragments of cartilage stopping the air from entering her sinuses.

I scarcely felt much better. Still gasping, I gathered up my .357 from the floor and spun around on Casey.

She stood behind me, hunched over, crying again, with the empty can of pepper spray still clutched in her quivering hand.

"Stay here! If she moves—"

I was at a loss what to say. For Casey's sake, I prayed that Becky would remain down for the count until I could return from saving Dani.

45

The blows to my body had robbed me of all grace. I lurched more than I walked. My dripping wrists left a trail of blood on the stairs.

I paused at the top to ready myself for what I might encounter beyond the door.

First choice: I could move quickly to maximize the element of surprise.

Second choice: I could take a quiet peek.

I had never been one to choose the cautious option.

I bulled my way through the door and found myself on the first story of a house under construction. The air was still and dusty and hot. The floors were plywood with nails scattered about. The windows were opaque sheets of plastic the color of a blind man's eyes. There were no walls yet between the support beams. I could see from one end of the building to the other. Leave it to Nisbet to finish his dungeon before he tackled the rest of the house.

The blower was on merely to create noise. The big machine sat in the middle of what might eventually be a living room, whipping up siroccos of sawdust and causing the plastic nailed to the windows to ripple and snap. Tracks were all over the dusty floor: from Casey's bare feet, Becky's hiking boots, Nisbet's tactical footwear, even drag marks that must have been my own trailing toes as the two women had pulled me through the house and down the stairs into the torture chamber.

I used the key to remove the handcuff from my other wrist and let the manacles drop to the floor.

The sawdust told me where to go. A set of Nisbet's prints led to the front door. They were the steps of a man proceeding confidently, a man who knew exactly where he was going and what he intended to do.

I followed the tracks into the future foyer. The front door was large, windowless, and made of steel. I stepped to the nearest plastic-sealed window and cocked my head to listen. The blower behind me was so damn loud. But not so loud I couldn't hear them shouting at each other outside.

Dani: "Drop the gun! I said, 'Do it now!' "

Nisbet: "If you shoot me, my girls are going to kill the warden."

Dani: "Drop the gun and get down on the ground!"

Nisbet: "It's your choice whether he lives or dies. Because I'm not dropping the gun."

Dani: "I will shoot you!"

Nisbet: "And I will shoot you. And they will shoot the warden. That's how this is going to go if you don't do what I say, Trooper. Now put down your gun."

I pulled at the edges of the plastic over the window, trying to pry it up enough to get my bearings. But the sheet was nailed fast to the casement. I was as senseless to what was happening—where they were standing and how far apart—as if my eyes were still blindfolded.

Dani would have taken cover the moment Nisbet stepped through the door. If she had found her way to his house, she would have known he was suspect, if not dangerous. Nor would she drop her firearm now. Every police officer is taught the same lesson: "You lose your gun, you lose your life." Besides, how could she be sure I was even inside the house?

I tried the next window. Also firmly fastened. Blood dripped down my forearm as I reached up, looking for a loose corner.

Through the backlit plastic I heard Dani repeat her command with the same fierceness: "I said, 'Drop the gun, Nisbet.' "

"Sorry, Trooper. Not going to do it."

"Last chance."

"Kill me and you'll never find the others."

For the first time, there was hesitation in Dani's voice. "What others?"

"Eileen Lafferty for one."

I recognized the name. Years earlier, a young woman had vanished from the side of a road

429

during a rainstorm when her car had hydroplaned into a swale of phragmites. I remembered because I was at the academy at the time, and it happened in the town of Scarborough, where I had gone to high school. Eileen Lafferty still hadn't been found.

I didn't hear any response now from Dani.

"Throw your gun out," said Nisbet. "Toss it onto the dirt."

Don't do it, Tate.

Then came the first gunshot.

As soon as I heard it, I threw my weight against the plastic sheet and fell forward into space. I heard the answering shot before I hit the ground. I landed hard on my left shoulder. The impact was as excruciating as every other injury I had suffered that day. The window was more than six feet above ground level. I was lucky I hadn't landed on my head and snapped my neck.

The brightness of the full sunlight blinded me a moment. Then I felt a puff of dirt in my face. Followed by the sound of a gunshot.

Have I been hit?

Even as my brain was answering the question in the negative, my body was responding. I rolled away from where I'd felt the bullet strike the dirt and kept rolling. I heard multiple shots from what must have been Dani's gun. Suddenly, I collided with a heavy object. It was a wheelbarrow. My sun-dazed eyes recognized the shape. With all my strength, I reached up, grabbed the nearest handle, and pulled. The weight of the steel barrow fought me for what seemed like seconds, then the cart toppled over my prone body.

Nisbet's next shot struck the metal and ricocheted into space.

I had cover now. Most of my body was still exposed, but my vision was clearing. And Nisbet, wherever he was, was returning fire against two opponents. If he'd had a moment to take aim, there was no way he would have missed hitting my legs at least.

"Mike?" I heard Dani shout.

"I'm all right."

Another shot caromed off the wheelbarrow. I curled up in a ball behind it. At the same time, I tried to triangulate Nisbet's location. Somewhere behind me and to my right. He had taken cover against the stairs leading up to the front door.

I peered around the edge of the wheelbarrow and saw him there, crouched against the concrete stoop. In that position he was protected from Dani for the moment, which was why he had been firing at me. A bright red splotch had appeared below his right collarbone where she had shot him. He had emptied his spent magazine and was fumbling as he tried to reload another.

"You're not getting out of this, Nisbet," I shouted.

He glanced up at me, his hair powdered gray

431

with sawdust, his face sweaty and flushed with panic. He said nothing as he hammered the base of the magazine hard into the grip of his gun.

I steadied my right hand and squeezed the trigger of my SIG.

The shot struck him in the meat of his thigh. He fell back against the landing and began to writhe on the ground.

Dani came sprinting up on my left, shouting at him. "Show me your hands!"

I used the handle of the wheelbarrow to get myself up onto my knees—and nearly pulled it over again.

"Just shoot him!" I shouted.

"Both hands, Nisbet!"

Dani was standing with her legs apart and both arms outstretched, aiming her .45 at Nisbet. He was now sitting against the basement cinder blocks. He had his dirty left hand in the air but, despite the wound to his shoulder, was somehow supporting his considerable weight with his right.

I climbed to my feet and began to stagger toward them, my own pistol aimed at his center mass now. "Where's his gun? Can you see it?"

"Both hands!" Dani said again. "Let me see them."

His response was the last thing I expected. He flashed us a smile. "I wasn't lying about Eileen. Ask Becky."

"Bullshit," I said. "You're bluffing. You lost, you son of a bitch."

"No," he said with surprising calmness, "I won."

"What?" Dani said.

"It was my choice. Remember that. I made you do this. You did what I wanted you to do."

With his hidden right hand, he lifted the pistol from the ground.

Dani fired three shots before I could fire one. If she had been shooting at a paper bullseye, she couldn't have hoped for a tighter pattern.

Dani found no trace of a pulse in Nisbet's carotid artery. I watched her with one hand clasped around the bloodiest of my wrists.

She'd shot a man to death, and she was struggling to pretend the experience had left her unaffected. I felt sorry for her because I knew what a pernicious lie it was: the widely held belief among cops that you could just tough out these moments, and everything would return to normal. From my own experience I knew that the ghost of Jeff Nisbet would be making unscheduled visits to Dani's dreams for the rest of her life.

"How did you find us?" I asked, still out of breath.

She raised her head from the lifeless corpse at her feet. "The Smiths."

"Who?"

"You told me to stop a blue T100 with Pennsylvania plates if I saw it." She finally, belatedly, reholstered her weapon. "They passed me out on 302 this morning, so I pulled them over. I asked them about 'John Blood.' The wife is a piece of work. But I kept pushing. The man they described sounded a lot like the Fryeburg cop who showed up at Fales Variety after I found Connie dead."

"Nisbet was there?"

"He must have thought he could get away with seeing Becky's handiwork for himself, being a cop. I called the Fryeburg PD, and asked about him. I got the sense he wasn't very popular in the department. His sergeant told me he was building a house down here. I thought the location was interesting, being so near the cabin you said burned down. I decided to drive out to see for myself."

If only I'd had the same insight—to ask Prudence and Jackson for a physical description of the man who claimed to own the land— what other calamities might have been averted? Not that it mattered. I hadn't asked them, and now Nisbet was dead. Unless Becky talked, the family of Eileen Lafferty would never know had happened to their daughter.

"When he was taunting me downstairs," I said, "I finally realized how Casey met Nisbet in the first place. *He was actively looking for her.*

When the search started, the Fryeburg police sent out every officer to comb the riverbanks. But Nisbet knew the side roads better than just about anyone."

I could see the horror dawning on her. "When she saw his police car, she must have been so happy. She thought she'd been rescued."

"Nisbet understood that no one knew where she was. He could do whatever he wanted with the girl. He could take her back to John Blood's old cabin, where he'd stashed Becky, and no one would ever know. And that was what he did."

"He was supposed to be her savior," said Dani. "I wish I could kill the son of a bitch again."

I limped my way back up the concrete steps and through the front door. I had only glimpsed the half-built house through the eyes of someone eager to escape it, but now I had a moment to take in the entire scene: the stuffy, overheated interior; the electrical wires dangling from the unfinished ceiling; the sweet smell of recently sawn pinewood; the dull roar of the construction blower. I dragged myself over to the electrical outlet and jerked the cord of the fan from the wall. The blades slowed—*whup, whup, whup*—then came to a stop.

The bloody handcuffs lay where I had dropped them. I picked them up.

I made my way to the basement door. With my index finger I ejected the magazine of my sidearm to see how many bullets I had left. There were ten, not counting the one in the chamber. Then I slammed the magazine back into the grip with the heel of my hand. I tucked the gun into the front of my pants and took a breath, preparing myself to descend back into the torture chamber.

I opened the door and found myself gazing down an unremarkable set of wooden stairs no different from those I'd seen in dozens of other family playrooms. Fluorescent lights glowed dull white below. I saw the sealed concrete flooring at the base, streaked crimson where I had come through and speckled elsewhere with spots of blood.

"Casey?" I removed my SIG from my waistband and took a step onto the first stair. "Casey, where are you?"

No answer.

Had I screwed up leaving her here with Becky? Self-doubt was as heavy as a stone in my belly.

Step by step, I made my way down into the brightly lit basement. I ducked my head and focused on the pole to which I had been chained. The scuffs on the floor from my heels around it, the crazy marks in the sawdust, all that blood.

But no plastic bag. I expected to see it where I'd dropped it: a washed-up jellyfish.

"Casey?"

As I descended below the level of the joists, I peeked to my left and saw Becky's feet, then her legs. She lay prone on the floor exactly where I had last seen her. She lay motionless on her chest, her arms at her sides. She lay with the plastic bag pulled tight around her head.

I bounded down the last few stairs until I stood over the lifeless woman.

I could see Becky's eyes open through the smothering plastic. All the capillaries in them had burst. She looked finally, in death, like the demon she had been in life.

Casey was a huddled ball in the corner of the room, clutching my forgotten dagger lest Becky arise from the dead. She was shaking silently, like an injured animal. I wanted to say something to her; I wanted to gather her up in my arms. But I recognized that it would take more than soft words and human touch to bring her back from the hell that had been her home for so long.

46

Stacey was waiting for me at the hospital in Portland. She met me outside the emergency room when the cruiser pulled up to the door. Pomerleau had arranged for a trooper to take me down to the city after I refused to go in an ambulance. I would have preferred to have driven myself but for the inconvenient facts that my patrol truck was hidden in the barn of an abandoned farmstead, miles from the crime scene, and my eyes kept zooming in and out of focus.

"You stupid asshole" were Stacey's first words to me. Then she hugged me so hard I thought I would lose consciousness again. She stepped back, eyes glistening, and touched one of my still-swollen eyelids. "Oh, baby, what did those monsters do to you?"

"Trust me. You don't want to hear it." I sounded like someone whose lungs had been scorched by volcanic ash. "Where were you? I was worried that something had happened to you?"

"*You* were worried about *me?*"

She had merely decided to run on a different path, she said. She'd run up the Knife Creek Trail to the Burnt Meadows highland and found a barren overlook where she could sit

438

and contemplate her life and the choices before her.

She pressed her hand to my cheek again. "Your face looks like you were attacked by killer bees."

I walked myself into the emergency room after refusing help from the hospital staff. Under no circumstances did I want to be pushed around in a wheelchair or, worse, strapped to a gurney. My resistance wasn't macho bluster. It was just that I had been beaten up enough in my job—shot, stabbed, and clobbered—to know that I was in no danger of dropping dead, despite how ghastly I might have appeared.

I didn't need a doctor, either, to tell me that I had a concussion, but there was no getting out of the tests. Was my vision blurred? No. Was I suffering from mental fog? That depended. Did a light mist count?

I was told to avoid physical exertion and any activity that might involve thinking and mental concentration.

"Why are you laughing?" the ER doctor asked me.

Miraculously, I had no broken bones. The lacerations and contusions left by the handcuffs did not require stitches, but I ended up wearing a pair of white bandages around my wrists that made me look as if I were a tennis player from the sweatband era of John McEnroe.

Two hours after being admitted to the Maine Medical Center, I was released into the custodial care of my girlfriend.

Stacey insisted I wear sunglasses even though it was past dark as we drove home.

"Did you talk with her afterward?" she asked.

"Casey? No."

"They brought her in to the hospital in an ambulance before you arrived. I only got a glimpse of her. She looked wretched."

"Nisbet had been injecting her with heroin for years to keep her docile. It's probably what killed her baby. But it's not like the medical examiner could have picked up traces of heroin from the infant's bones and half-eaten flesh. The poor woman is going to be in detox for a long time. She's going to be an addict for the rest of her life."

Stacey's face was lit by the dashboard. "In the waiting room I heard a cop say she killed that Becky woman."

"There's no way the prosecutors are going to press charges. The details might not even make it into the news."

"The radio is crediting Dani Tate with rescuing her. They never even mentioned you."

"In a way, she did rescue her."

"I hate it when you don't get the praise you deserve, Mike."

"They ambushed me and took me hostage. I

don't deserve any praise. I failed, Stacey. I let myself get cocky and overconfident."

She reached over to squeeze my hand, then remembered how tender it was. "Nisbet is dead. How is that a failure?"

In my memory I heard him crowing in those last seconds about how he'd won because he was still controlling us. From the moment Dani had first driven into his dooryard, he'd known he had only one final power play. He had forced us to kill him. Our distress would be his postmortem triumph.

The last remaining question was whether he'd been lying about Eileen Lafferty. With Nisbet and Becky both dead, we might never know. I thought of that woman's poor family. There might have been a chance for them to receive closure, but Tate and I had robbed them of the opportunity.

At last we pulled into the driveway of our home. Outwardly, it looked the same as always. My Scout was in the garage. Lights were on in the upstairs windows. But somehow it seemed like a memory from the distant past; like a place where I had lived once and was visiting again after an interval of many years. I felt nostalgic for a moment that hadn't even passed.

Or maybe this strange line of thought was the effect of having been beaten senseless.

"This is your second concussion, right?" Stacey guided me into the living room and my favorite chair. "If you keep this up, you're going to end up like one of those boxers with Parkinson's."

"You have a lousy bedside manner, Stevens. Has anyone ever told you that?"

"Do you want a glass of water?"

"I'd prefer a glass of whiskey, but I suppose that's out of the question."

She returned from the kitchen with a tall glass of water from the tap. She pulled an ottoman over to the foot of my chair and perched on it. Her skin was even more tanned from her day of exercise on the Burnt Meadows highland. She looked vital and clear-eyed and beautiful.

"The doctor said you shouldn't go to sleep for a while."

"So you want me to tell you everything that happened?"

"Only if you feel up to it."

"All right," I said. "But I have a question for you first. What did you decide today up on your mountain?"

"About my future?"

"Yes."

"I won't leave Maine if you won't come with me. I don't think I could bear it, Mike."

"Well, here's a complication, Stace. Before any of the shit happened today, I got a call from DeFord. He and the colonel had wanted me to come into the headquarters tomorrow. But I suppose our appointment will be rescheduled.

They're offering me the investigator's job. And I'm pretty sure I am going to take it."

She leaned away from me on the ottoman. Then a tear slid down her cheek. "I'm really proud of you, Mike."

The next day, Pomerleau and Finch drove out to the house to take my official statement. We sat at the picnic table in the backyard listening to the cicadas droning in the trees. Stacey brought us some lemonade, which in turn attracted yellow jackets eager to sip sugar from the lips of our glasses. The stubborn presence of the stinging insects seemed to disturb Finch, who kept waving at them to the point where he ceased to hear anything I said.

"How's Menario doing?" I asked.

"Physically or otherwise?" said Pomerleau.

I adjusted my sunglasses; wearing them constantly, I had begun to feel as if I should audition for a blues band. "So he's going to pull through?"

"He'll recover."

"What about the legal ramifications?"

Pomerleau applied a fresh coat of zinc sunscreen to her lips. "Let's just say that I'm glad that I'm not the one investigating his case."

"And Dakota Rowe turned himself in?"

"Accompanied by two criminal defense attorneys from Portland. His lawyers negotiated the surrender. They didn't even throw him in jail for a few hours. The judge released him on bail on his own recognizance. It's good to be rich."

"My sense is that none of us is going to come out of this smelling like a rose," I said.

"Except Tate," said Pomerleau.

"It's a good story. Young female trooper rescues young female sex slave."

"You don't mind not getting any credit?"

"If I'm going into the investigation division, it's probably better for me to stay out of the news."

"Son of a bitch!" Finch cried. The yellow jacket, at the limits of its own patience, had stung him on the fleshy part of his hand between his thumb and forefinger.

47

Six weeks later, Stacey and I sat side by side on the couch in our living room and watched the only interview Casey Donaldson had granted to an American television network. It aired in prime time, on a Sunday evening, so that the whole nation would be watching.

The interviewer, an attractive middle-aged woman, had real journalistic credentials; she'd filed reports from Baghdad's Green Zone before being "promoted" to the network's morning show to chat with TV stars about their diets and sip mimosas with her vapid co-host. She seemed visibly excited to be an actual reporter again with a bonafide exclusive.

Right off, I was struck by the change in Casey's appearance. Her face was less bloated, leaner, and she had a glowing complexion. Her stylists had pulled her glossy black hair away from her heart-shaped face and fastened it in the back to suggest the workaday look of a pretty administrative assistant or a paralegal: a woman seeking to minimize her sexual appeal while still appearing attractive. She was meant to look like anyone's daughter.

Tom Donaldson sat beside her, wearing a spiffy blazer and a tie. Someone had cut and styled his thinning hair. He clutched his stepdaughter's hand the whole time as if terrified of ever letting go again.

The interviewer in her introduction retold Casey's story as if anyone in the country was unaware of the sordid details. The loss of her mother at a young age. The self-discovery that came with making new friends at the University of New Hampshire. Then the fateful rafting trip down the Saco. The interviewer closed with a promise: "Tonight you will hear Casey Donaldson describe her four-year nightmare in her own words."

"This is so exploitive," said Stacey. "I feel dirty watching it."

I put my arm around her shoulder.

The first words Casey spoke were "Sheer terror doesn't even begin to describe how I felt."

It struck me, as she began with the night of her abduction, that there was no mention of Dakota Rowe. His family's lawyers must have succeeded in persuading the network that any mention of their client would constitute slander. I remembered Pomerleau's words: "It's good to be rich."

Casey described her fright during the lightning storm, trying to find her way out of the swamp to safety in the dark. As Charley had surmised, she left the boat as soon as she found what looked like solid ground. But as she sank to her hips in the muck and the canoe floated away, she had already begun to doubt her judgment.

She said she eventually found trees where she could take cover. To me it sounded as if she might have taken a different path from the one Charley and I had used, because she'd intersected the dirt road well south of John Blood's cabin. It was sobering to realize that not all of our suppositions had been correct.

"That was when I saw the police car," Casey said. "He flashed his lights when he saw me so I would know who he was. All I can remember was how happy I was."

Nisbet was nice at first; he was Officer Friendly who had come to take her to safety. But she found it strange that he asked her to sit in the cage in the back of the cruiser where the inside doors had no handles. And instead of taking her toward civilization, they seemed to be going deeper into the woods.

The screen showed a portrait of the dead policeman in his powder-blue uniform, his pompadour hidden beneath his trooper-style campaign hat.

Casey described her arrival at John Blood's cabin as a moment of utter confusion. She wanted to know where they were. Nisbet answered, "Your new home."

He was too strong for her to fight him. He dragged her to the cabin. A woman was waiting in the doorway. She was wearing a platinum wig.

"I know it sounds weird, but the woman scared me more than the man. She gave me a hug. It was a hug that was strong and domineering. It was saying, 'Don't you dare do anything I don't tell you to do.' That was Becky."

The screen showed the medical examiner's photograph of Becky's face as she lay on his steel table, about to be bisected. Her skin was as gray as meat gone bad, and she looked halfway to becoming a skeleton. Mercifully, her exploded eyes were closed.

"It seems like they should have warned people they were going to show that," Stacey said. "What if kids are watching?"

"This kind of stuff is family viewing now."

The scene returned to the studio. Casey said that when they were all inside the cabin, Nisbet told her, "I will kill you if you try to escape. I will kill you if you make a noise. I will kill whoever comes here to find you."

His breath was foul, she said, and twitched her nose as if she could still smell it. He chewed gum all the time. He said cinnamon was good for covering all sorts of odors. But it never made a difference. The disgusting odor seemed to be coming from his insides.

"I said, 'If you're going to kill me, please leave my body where it can be found. I want my dad to know that he can stop worrying about me.' "

Her voice was steady, but Tom Donaldson was blinking back tears.

Becky helped Nisbet take his clothes off, like a servant helping a king disrobe. When Casey screamed, Becky said they would duct-tape her mouth shut if she didn't stop.

Nisbet said he had a better idea. He injected her with heroin. The drug, unfortunately, didn't render her unconscious. She remembered Becky stripping her naked and then standing by while Nisbet raped her.

"After he was done, I closed my eyes and curled up into a tight ball. I felt broken beyond all repair. The first thing I felt, when I awoke, was the needle in my arm again—and then there was this warm wave that washed through me, as if nothing mattered."

Whenever the drugs began to wear off, she would begin to sweat and shiver and feel sick. It sounded as if they were detoxing her deliberately—forcing her to go cold turkey—to demonstrate their control.

"Every time I thought this cannot get worse, but it always did. At a certain point, I stopped even feeling human."

Casey described the endless blur of days that followed. Nisbet would leave her alone with Becky, whose job it was to train her to be his chosen wife. Becky told Casey that she had a new married name: Kendall Cobb. They would watch DVDs. Becky loved horror movies. They would cook elaborate meals for Nisbet, who always returned with loads of groceries. After dinner, he would have sex with them both or watch them have sex together. Sleep became Casey's only oasis. Sleep and heroin. Whenever she began to feel a sensation, the next shot would dull it.

"I don't know when I stopped thinking of myself as Casey and started thinking of myself as Kendall."

The interviewer wanted to know how it was possible that they were never found out.

"They moved me around a few times," Casey explained. "It was always a different rental house—but always the same house, if that makes any sense. I knew I couldn't escape because I was afraid of becoming sick. I'd feel so awful when I didn't get the injections. Eventually, Becky let me wander free inside the house because she knew I was their slave."

The interviewer said she needed to turn to a painful subject: the birth and death of Casey's daughter.

"He never used birth control because Becky couldn't have kids," Casey said. "But I got pregnant."

Her daughter—whom Casey had decided to name Kylie—wasn't stillborn. "I heard her cry when Becky took her out of me," Casey said.

450

"It was only later that she told me Kylie had strangled on the umbilical cord. I knew it was a lie because I'd heard her crying."

Going up the mountain later was a test. They had seen the feral pigs go by from the window, and Nisbet had followed them, and that's when he must have gotten the idea to bury the infant in the wallow. Becky had watched a movie once about killers disposing of corpses by feeding them to pigs. They wanted Casey to dig the grave, but she was too wasted to hold the shovel. Eventually Becky took over.

"That was when I scratched the initials in the tree," Casey said, "because there was no tombstone. I was afraid I would forget she'd even existed if I didn't make a mark."

Casey had no memory of my coming to the door. But she did recall Nisbet arriving in his pickup and telling them to gather everything up. He drove them to the house he was building at the edge of John Blood's property.

"He hated us being there. He preferred us being in rental homes not linked to him. He never wanted us to stay any place that could be connected to him."

The next day, the two of them sat her down and explained the plan. The first stage was getting Steve Nason to come to the house. Becky had been providing him with oral sex in exchange for his silence, so that was easy.

451

"I had no idea they were planning to kill him," Casey said.

The second stage of the plan was to lure a game warden to an abandoned farm. Casey was supposed to call him and pretend to be someone named Martha Tarbox and tell him she'd seen feral pigs. When he came into the barn, she needed to spray him in the eyes with pepper spray and keep spraying until the can was empty.

Casey looked directly into the camera, and I felt a chill. "I want to apologize, now, to the warden for what I did."

I forgive you, I wanted to tell her.

I remembered the rest. I was there.

After they'd finished discussing my session in the torture chamber, the interviewer asked how Casey had felt when she learned Nisbet was dead.

"How do you think she felt, bitch?" Stacey said.

But Casey said she preferred not to discuss that subject.

Frustrated, the interviewer became pushier. She asked if Casey had signed a book or movie deal yet.

Tom Donaldson responded with real anger, "We don't want money. We want Casey to lead a normal life again."

The interviewer asked if that would ever be possible.

"No," Casey admitted. "I will always be the girl who vanished."

The interviewer then wanted to know why, if their only desire was to return to normalcy, they had agreed to come on television.

Stacey was fuming. "Because your damn producers spent weeks badgering them!"

Once again, Casey faced the camera. "I want other young women to know what happened to me and to answer those people who are criticizing me for not trying to escape. I don't expect what I have to say will stop that because they weren't there. People want to think that they'll be heroes in bad situations, but they're just fooling themselves."

48

The next morning, Stacey lay in bed watching me get dressed for my new job. As a warden investigator, I would no longer wear a uniform. I was the equivalent of a plainclothes detective now. On the prior Saturday, I'd had to drive down to the Maine Mall to buy button-down oxford-cloth shirts and dress pants because I'd never worn a business-casual outfit to an office in my life.

I barely recognized myself in the full-length mirror attached to the bathroom door. DeFord had advised me to grow out my hair a little. He said a crew cut, let alone a buzz cut, could come off as too hard-core when I wanted to persuade a civilian to open up to me.

Only after I'd clipped my badge to my belt and attached the holster, holding my SIG .357, did I begin to come to terms with my new self.

I finished adjusting my knit tie and turned so that she could see me in my spiffy new clothes and I could see her half-naked on the bed. "What do you think?"

"You look handsome." She pushed the sheets down on the bed. August had arrived, just as hot as July. Her dark hair was spread out upon the pillow; her neck was beaded with perspiration.

"What are you up to today?"

"My friends and I are doing a three-mile swim out on Sebago. I told you I'm doing a triathlon in Camden in September."

"When I tried out for the Warden Service, they made me tread water for fifteen minutes fully clothed and then swim one hundred yards. It wasn't hard, but it wasn't fun, either."

"We don't have to like all the same things, Mike."

"We like most of the same things."

She studied me with concern. "Are you feeling up to this? Starting a new job?"

"The doctor said I'm cleared for duty."

"That's what the NFL doctors always say, too. How many of the ex-players end up as the walking dead?" She rose up from the bed to kiss me good-bye. "Go to work, Mike. I don't want you to be late on your first day because of my worrying."

The training for becoming a warden investigator was like a tutorial in the dark arts. I was acquiring the power of second sight. Where a regular patrol warden might see an "accidental" shooting, I could now detect the bloodred aura of murder. I was being instructed in how to read the thoughts of a guilty person in the smallest of gestures.

This new knowledge came with a price. When I left the office that evening, my brain felt as sore as it had during the worst days of my concussion. I drove on autopilot until I hit the Cumberland County line in Casco. I was busting along at seventy miles per hour when I passed Dani Tate's cruiser, parked in a turnaround with her radar detector pointed in the direction from which I'd come.

She recognized my champagne-bronze Sierra as an unmarked warden vehicle. But that didn't stop her from pulling me over.

Instead of stopping behind me, she swung her cruiser around in the opposite direction so that we could talk through our driver's side windows.

"Nice truck. That classy color must have been extra."

"Come on, Dani."

She flashed me a smile that showed off her dimples. "Mike, I'm really happy for you. You're the best person I know for that job, but you might not want to hear the reason why I think that."

"Why?"

"Because you're a jerk. You're not afraid of asking insulting questions even if they make you look dumb. You use bluntness as a weapon."

I couldn't help but laugh. "I guess there's a compliment buried in there somewhere. In that case, let me ask you a blunt question. Why did you leave the Warden Service?"

She rolled her eyes. "Why are you preoccupied with this?"

"You owe me an answer because I saved your life."

"You didn't save my life. I saved your life!"

"Then we're bound together in a fateful incident."

"Whatever you say, Shakespeare." She shrugged. "I left because I looked around and realized I wasn't going anywhere as a game warden. That's all. No big secret."

"I always thought you were a rising star."

"Me? No way. You might not have noticed, but the Warden Service has never promoted a woman to a senior position."

"Kathy was a sergeant, before she was forced to retire."

"Meanwhile women in the state police are becoming lieutenants and captains. Look at Pomerleau. Kathy was opposed to me quitting. She hated to think that some of the same chauvinistic bullshit was going on as when she started. She understands my choice, but I think she's still kind of mad at me for not sticking it out."

That explained Kathy's refusal to answer my questions. "I guess I should have figured you were ambitious."

"Says the new warden investigator! I think ambition is something you and I have in common. One of a number of things."

The softness in her voice as she spoke those words caused a flutter in my chest. The reaction startled me and made me suddenly self-conscious as I had never been with her before.

"I should be getting home."

"And I should be getting back to work. I'll see you around, Mike Bowditch."

"Same here, Dani Tate."

It was dark when I arrived at the house. It had rained briefly during the afternoon, and the puddles in the driveway reflected the motion-sensitive lights mounted above the garage. I climbed out of my new, unmarked truck and took a deep breath. The heat and humidity had finally broken as the front had moved out to sea. I paused a moment and watched a firefly bounce along in flight across the lawn. Another appeared a moment later, heading for the backyard. I decided to follow the glowing insects around the corner of the garage.

To one side of our property was a mound of earth that the builder had cleared when he'd dug out the basement. Not knowing what to do with the spare dirt, he'd left the pile for later and had then forgotten all about it. Over the years, the hillock had been reclaimed by weeds and wildflowers: goldenrod, purple asters, and Queen Anne's lace.

Among those renegade flowers were hundreds of tiny flickering lights.

Never had I seen so many fireflies at once.

Some were green, others yellow, a few even orange. They flittered and bobbed about the weeds like tiny fairies holding court. I felt awed, as if I were witnessing some magical apparition, as if this gathering of lights were not meant to be seen by a mortal man.

My mother had been a devout Catholic; my father just as devout a nihilist, although he would not have recognized the word. To her, this life was just a proving ground for the next. To him, the present moment was both alpha and omega. My own religious journey had taken me from the faith of childhood, through skepticism, and then into the darkness my father had inhabited. But lately—

To spend as much time in nature as I did was to be confronted constantly with mysteries. Sights and sounds that defy easy explanation. The animism of ancient peoples—who saw demons in forest fires, gods in thunderbolts, and avatars in the wizened faces of trees—had become increasingly relatable to me. The natural world had so humbled me that it had reawakened some of the eagerness I had felt as a boy to believe in a universe of greater meaning.

I unlocked the kitchen door and called, "Stacey, come quick."

A minute later, she appeared, dressed in her workout clothes, T-shirt and running tights. "What is it?"

"Look!"

I pulled on her wrist and led her around the garage to the flickering wall.

"Have you ever seen anything like this? So many fireflies at once?"

"It's beautiful," she admitted. "They must have been waiting for the rain to stop before they came out."

I stepped behind her. She smelled sweaty, but not unpleasant, from her exercise. I wrapped my arms around her waist. But she didn't relax at all into my embrace.

She turned her head toward me. "You're never going to leave Maine, are you, Mike?"

There was no answer I could give that would satisfy her, and we both knew it. After a while, she tapped me on the hand I'd pressed to her abdomen. It was, unmistakably, a sign to let her go.

Author's Note

I must begin with a confession. Feral swine are not invading Maine. Not yet, anyway, although there is an honest-to-goodness breeding population of wild pigs in central New Hampshire, as Mike Bowditch notes, and some intrepid stragglers may yet wander across our man-made border.

Beyond introducing rampaging boars to Maine, I may or may not have exaggerated some of the excesses that occur on the Saco during the height of summer, but the river's regular paddlers will recognize that I have altered its environs and current course for my own purposes. There is, for instance, no Oxbow Island. Nor does the town of Birnam exist.

Patrolling the Saco is as demanding a job as exists in Maine law enforcement, and the presence of certain unsavory characters in this novel should not be viewed as disparagements of any real-life police officers. By almost all accounts, the Saco offers a safer, better-managed recreational experience than it did in decades past, and credit should be given to the Fryeburg PD.

I have fully exercised my artistic license

elsewhere in *Knife Creek*, but I will leave it to readers to identify those occasions.

As always, I have many people to thank for having made the writing and publication of this book possible.

I am grateful to Corporal John MacDonald of the Maine Warden Service for fielding my many, often ridiculously nit-picky, questions about the job he and his colleagues do.

Thank you to Sgt. Scott Gosselin of the Maine State Crime Laboratory for giving me an extensive behind-the-scenes look into Maine's state-of-the-art forensics resources.

Judy Camuso, Wildlife Division Director of the Maine Department of Inland Fisheries and Wildlife, helped me speculate how Maine might deal with a feral swine apocalypse.

To my friend and police consultant, Bruce Coffin, retired Portland Police Detective and accomplished author of the John Byron crime novels: I owe you a breakfast.

At Minotaur Books, I am grateful to Charles Spicer, April Osborn, Sarah Melnyk, Hector DeJean, Paul Hochman, and Andrew Martin for having stuck with me from the beginning. Thank you to the incredibly supportive crew at Macmillan Audio, not to mention my unsung series narrator, Henry Levya.

Agent Ann Rittenberg, I couldn't do this without you.

To my first readers—Kristen Lindquist, and David and Vicki Henderson—I appreciate your helping me work out the knots and kinks.

Bless my family.

And Kristen, this one again is for you.

Books are produced in the United States using U.S.-based materials

Books are printed using a revolutionary new process called THINKtech™ that lowers energy usage by 70% and increases overall quality

Books are durable and flexible because of smythe-sewing

Paper is sourced using environmentally responsible foresting methods and the paper is acid-free

Center Point Large Print
600 Brooks Road / PO Box 1
Thorndike, ME 04986-0001 USA

(207) 568-3717

US & Canada:
1 800 929-9108
www.centerpointlargeprint.com